Health Policy

Health Policy

The Decade Ahead

James M. Brasfield

LYNNE
RIENNER
PUBLISHERS

BOULDER
LONDON

Published in the United States of America in 2011 by
Lynne Rienner Publishers, Inc.
1800 30th Street, Boulder, Colorado 80301
www.rienner.com

and in the United Kingdom by
Lynne Rienner Publishers, Inc.
3 Henrietta Street, Covent Garden, London WC2E 8LU

Library of Congress Cataloging-in-Publication Data
Brasfield, James M., 1942–
  Health policy : the decade ahead / by James M. Brasfield.
    p. ; cm.
  Includes bibliographical references and index.
  ISBN 978-1-58826-772-6 (hc : alk. paper)
  ISBN 978-1-58826-797-9 (pb : alk. paper)
  1. Medical policy—United States. I. Title.
  [DNLM: 1. Health Policy—trends—United States. WA 540 AA1]
  RA395.A3B698 2011
  362.1—dc22

                                                    2011009471

British Cataloguing in Publication Data
A Cataloguing in Publication record for this book
is available from the British Library.

Printed and bound in the United States of America

       The paper used in this publication meets the requirements
  ∞   of the American National Standard for Permanence of
       Paper for Printed Library Materials Z39.48-1992.

   5 4 3 2 1

To Judy—
Her taskmaster tenaciousness, editorial touch, and
loving encouragement were essential for completing the book

To Maureen—
My daughter, who has been a solid rock of support
through all the difficult years.
Without all she has done, this book would never have been possible

To Conner, Emma, Carson, and Haley—
My grandchildren will all come of age in the next decade.
I hope the world they inherit includes a comprehensive, fair, and
effective health care system as a result of wise choices made by
policymakers in the decade ahead

Contents

Illustrations

Tables

Figures

Health Policy

1

The Political Economy
of Health Care

For most of us, the idea of a trillion dollars is just a number on a page and not something tangible. As a nation, we spent $2.5 trillion on health care in 2009.[1] It is difficult to grasp the significance of this number. But this amounts to $8,086 for each person, including children.

Throughout this book, I scrutinize the intersection of politics and economics in the health care system. In this chapter, I use summary statistics to describe the economic contours of that system and historical narrative to chronicle its development, especially in the past half-century. This intersection of the worlds of politics and economics in health care is not episodic, but a fundamental hallmark of this large and complex subsystem of our nation.

Economists and political scientists individually study the world from the point of view of their disciplinary paradigms. This book is an account of health policy from my view as a political scientist. After this descriptive introduction to the political economy of health care, I offer a useful conceptual model of the political process to serve as a blueprint for understanding how decisions made in the political arena transform the economic underpinnings of the health care system.

In the chapters that follow, I examine major public programs such as Medicare and Medicaid, assess the recent health reform endeavor, review attempts to control costs, and compare the US health care system with that of other nations. Health policy is path dependent. Current policy is in large part a function of historical developments and past decisions. I give consideration to the antecedents of current policy, but my primary focus is on the future. I devote special interest and attention to both anticipated future problems and feasible policy options for confronting these issues.

The Health Care System in
Political and Economic Terms

Advanced study in a discipline tends to influence the way we think about the world. After listening only a few minutes to a discussion, one can probably identify the discipline of the speakers by their vocabulary and perspective. In the health policy arena, participants are lawyers, academics, legislative staff, bureaucrats, and lobbyists. Each brings to the discussion a conceptual framework about the health care system and the delivery of services that was probably molded in their college classrooms years earlier. As the various disciplines become more isolated, dialogue is challenging because the vocabulary is distinctive. In these opening pages, I attempt to return to the older idea of political economy with a condensed description of the health care system in both political and economic terms.

The provision of health care services is one of the largest economic segments in the country. About one out of every six dollars of economic activity each year involves health care services. The delivery of these services is a huge industry and the livelihood for millions of Americans. Just over half of these dollars is raised and spent in the private sector. The rest passes through the national and state governments in the form of taxes collected and money spent to purchase or provide health care services.

Decisions made by the national and state governments determine which service providers receive payments, the size of the reimbursements, eligibility for services, and what types of services are offered. Almost half of all money spent in the health care system was originally collected as a tax, and legislatively established rules control many of the elements of service delivery.

A century ago a country doctor might have accepted a chicken in exchange for services from a farmer with little cash, and an urban hospital owned and operated by a religious denomination might not have expected more than a token payment from a poor patient. But today health care workers are well-paid professionals who expect and deserve a fair payment for their time and expertise.

Conceptualizing the health care service delivery system as a large business within a market economy is an authentic way to view it. Yet it is also valid to view it as an essential community service regulated and significantly financed by public funds. It is both a business and an essential public service. Often the health policy debate begins with participants' disagreements based on the view of health care as either a business or a public service. In fact, it is both.

Basic Measures of Health Care Spending

As we explore the political economy of health care, it is useful to look at some of the basic numbers to help us understand this huge segment of the economy. It is possible to find literally thousands of explanatory numbers in tables and charts. The five basic measures below are similarly formatted each year. There is a complex reality behind them, but they portray an easily comprehendible picture of the political economy of health care.

Percentage of Gross Domestic Product Spent on Health Care

As mentioned above, according to the most recent statistics on national health spending, the United States spent $2.5 trillion on health care in 2009. This was 17.6% of the US total gross domestic product (GDP) of $14.1 trillion.[2] Figure 1.1 traces how, as a society, the United States has steadily increased the share of GDP spent on health care over the past forty years, and allows us to project what future health care expenditures will consume. In 1960, the United States spent $27.5 billion, which was only 5.2% of GDP. Percentage of GDP is one of the most common comparative measures used in the health policy literature. Is the chart in Figure 1.1 a sign that health care expenditures are out of control, or does it reflect on a national preference and concern about individual health versus other individual spending?

Annual Rate of Increase in Health Care Spending

There has been a consistent pattern over the past fifty years: health care expenses rise faster than general inflation. From 2008 to 2009, health care expenses rose 4.0% (the lowest single increment in forty-eight years) while inflation was 2.7%. Figure 1.2 shows the differential between the annual increase in health care spending and the Consumer Price Index (CPI) over the past decade. This pattern has

Figure 1.1
National Health Care Expenditures
as Percentage of Gross Domestic Product (1960–2009)

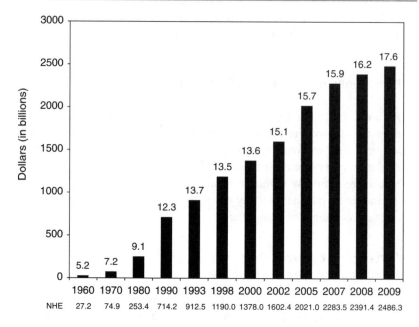

	1960	1970	1980	1990	1993	1998	2000	2002	2005	2007	2008	2009
NHE	27.2	74.9	253.4	714.2	912.5	1190.0	1378.0	1602.4	2021.0	2283.5	2391.4	2486.3

Source: Centers for Medicare and Medicaid Services, National Health Expenditure Data, www.cms.gov/NationalHealthExpendData/downloads/tables.pdf.
Note: NHE = national health care expenditures in billions of dollars.

persisted for more than thirty years. If the increase were equal to the general rate of inflation, the health care expense trajectory would flatten. Cost control victory will be achieved when health care expenditures rise at the same rate as other segments of the economy.

Percentage of Total Health Care Spending Raised by Taxation

Americans do not like to pay taxes, and some perceive any spending of government appropriations for health care services as socialism. In 2009, $1.08 trillion (or 44%) of $2.5 trillion spent on health care was public spending. In 1970, public funds accounted for 38% of total spending. In 2009, public sector spending increased 10% over the previous year.

Figure 1.2
Annual Increase in National Health Care Expenditures
and Consumer Price Index (2000–2009)

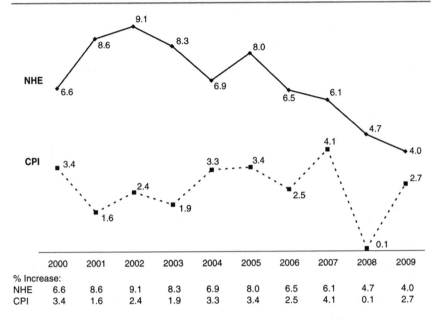

% Increase:	2000	2001	2002	2003	2004	2005	2006	2007	2008	2009
NHE	6.6	8.6	9.1	8.3	6.9	8.0	6.5	6.1	4.7	4.0
CPI	3.4	1.6	2.4	1.9	3.3	3.4	2.5	4.1	0.1	2.7

Source: Centers for Medicare and Medicaid Services, National Health Expenditure Data, www.cms.gov/NationalHealthExpendData/downloads/tables.pdf; US Department of Labor, Bureau of Labor Statistics, Consumer Price Index, www.bls.gov/cpi/tables.htm.
   Notes: NHE = national health care expenditures in billions of dollars. CPI = Consumer Price Index.

Governments paid more than half of the costs for hospitals and nursing homes. Depending on one's political perspective, when public spending for health care passes 50%, it will be an occasion for joy or alarm.[3]

The Share of Health Care Dollars
Spent for Hospital Services

The rate of growth and the ultimate percentage of dollars spent for hospital services is a key system measure. Hospital care accounted for 31% of all health care expenditures in 2009, down from 38% in 1970. Tests and even some surgeries may be conducted at outpatient centers, but the greatest expenses per person are still incurred during hospital stays. This is the largest category of health care expenses and, therefore, it is a critical element.

Private Insurance Premiums as a Share of Total Health Care Spending

Since 1990, private health insurance premiums have consistently been about one-third of total health care spending. In 2009, private insurance premiums represented 32% of all health care expenses and increased 1% over the previous year. In 1970, private insurance was only 21% of health care expenses, Movement up or down from this number in subsequent years will signal a shift in the way that the health care system is financed.

Basic Ideas Offering Insights into a Complex System

These five measures do not tell the whole story, but over time they provide a quick snapshot for understanding the basic political economy of health care. When attempting to understand a large and complex system, it helps to focus on a few major concepts to understand how the system is organized and how it functions.

Next I propose five big ideas in the political economy of the health care system and show how each individually contributes to our understanding. Taken together, the five offer insights into the complex health care system.

A Few Individuals Account for a High Share of Total Health Care Expenses in a Given Year

Becoming very ill and thus incurring high health care costs in a given year is similar to winning the lottery; many people pay into the system, but there are only a few big beneficiaries. Patients with cancer or patients who have had a heart attack are not likely to see themselves as "winners," but the cost of their care is very large compared to the average person's yearly health care expenses. A huge health care bill would bankrupt a typical family without the protection of health insurance. The same principle applies to homeowners' insurance in the case of a fire, but that seems to be less abstract than health insurance.

In a classic 1992 article, M. L. Berk and A. C. Monheit document the concentration of health care expenditures. In a given year, a high share of total expenditures is spent providing care for a few individuals. Subsequent examinations find this continuing to occur in general as well as in particular programs such as Medicare.[4] Figure 1.3 is based on a Kaiser Foundation analysis with 2004 as the base year. It reflects all health care expenses in that year.

The explanation of Figure 1.3 is simple. In a given year, 50% of the population incurs 97% of the total health care expenses. The other 50% of the population generates 3% of the total costs. At the other end of the illustration, 1% of the population accounts for 23% of the total health care expenses in that year. Assume that you are an insurance company executive. Which of these groups would you prefer to be in the pool of people you insure? If you opted for the 50% who will incur only 3% of the costs, you pass the basic insurance executive test.

Let us do a quick math exercise. Remember that in 2009 total health care spending in the United States was $2.5 trillion. If we count only the money actually spent on personal health care services excluding such items as research, the figure is "merely" $2.3 trillion. If we divide this latter number evenly among the population of 312

Figure 1.3
Concentration of Health Care Expenditures in the United States (2004)

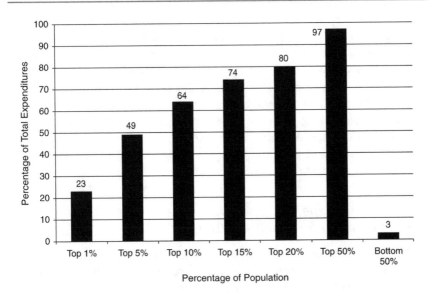

Source: Kaiser Family Foundation, Data Spotlight, www.kff.org/charts/112706.htm.

million, the average expenditure per person is $7,371. Yet the health care expense lottery allocates high costs to only a few individuals.

One percent of the population is 3 million people, and 30% of the expenses is $690 billion or $187,000 per person. Thus, the most expensive 1% of the population generates an average cost of $221,000 each. The least expensive 50% of the population spends $56.3 billion at an average cost of $442 per person.

Neither individuals nor health insurance companies know for sure who is going to win this lottery each year, but demographics and past history may offer clues. The older a person is, the greater are his or her chances of having a serious health problem, and if he or she has a history of heart disease or cancer, the future risk is even larger. If the insurance risk pool has 100,000 people, there are going to be a few with large expenses, but most with minimal costs in a year. If there are ten people in the risk pool, one person with large expenses will consume the entire premium collected from the group plus substantially more. Small risk pools are much less attractive to insurance companies.

Studies of subgroups such as Medicare and Medicaid recipients show similar patterns, even among older people. The top 5% of the Medicare population generated 43% of the total costs, and the bottom 50% incurred 4% of the total. For Medicaid, the top 1% of enrollees accounted for 26% of all expenditures.[5]

All insurance is based on the principle that, in a given year, most of those who pay premiums will collect little or nothing in benefits. Our houses do not burn down, our cars are not totaled, and we live through the year. We purchase insurance to protect ourselves against unexpected high losses. We are part of a health insurance system out of fear that we may be the unlucky lottery winner this time. For those in between the top 1% and the bottom 50%, health insurance also helps pay routine health care expenses and covers the costs of serious, but less than catastrophic, expenses. As I discuss the various facets of health policy in the pages ahead, keep in mind the yearly concentration of expenses. It is an idea important to most of the policy discussions.

Health Care Expenses Have Grown Faster Than Inflation for a Half-Century

The Committee on the Cost of Medical Care (CCMC) carried out the first national calculation of health care expenses in 1929. It found a total of $3.6 billion, which was 3.5% of the gross national product

(GNP). Seventy-eight years later, we spent $2.5 trillion or 17.6% of (GDP). There were enormous changes in the health care system and its technology in these decades. Since 1961, national health expenditures have grown faster each year than inflation in the Consumer Price Index (CPI), which grew between 1.5% and 4% most years. Health expenses grew 1.5 to 3.0 times the CPI in most years. General inflation and population increases account for part of the annual growth, but intensity of medical services provided and price of those services are clearly important contributors to health care cost inflation.[6]

In 1960, health expenses were 5.2% of GDP. Five dollars of every $100.00 of economic activity was spent for health care. Today $17.60 of each $100.00 is spent on health care. A Congressional Budget Office study projected health care spending to be 50% of GDP in 2082.[7] This seems fanciful, but it would have seemed impossible to think in 1929 that the 3.5% would grow to 16% in less than eighty years.

As long as health expenses grow faster than inflation, people will continue to spend a higher percentage of their total wealth for health services. They may prefer to spend money for physicians, hospitals, and other health care services rather than on consumer goods, education, or alternative uses of their resources—this is a choice. At some point, however, society will become dissatisfied with the share of individual income that is directed to health care. Already public opinion polls show growing dissatisfaction with rising health care costs.[8] It is impossible to have a policy discussion about health care without the subject of cost increases quickly becoming a point of debate. Rising health care costs permeate the following pages of this book.

If Public Spending Equals Socialism, Are We Almost There?

In the recent health reform debate, critics often alleged that new government initiatives would lead to "socialized medicine." For close to a century, this has been the effective cry of those who prefer the status quo. Responding with a dictionary definition of "socialism" is not an appropriate rejoinder. Over the years, public spending for health care services has risen both absolutely and relatively. In 2009, spending by all US government entities for health care was 44% of the total.

Part of the public funds spent for health care is clearly socialized medicine by any definition. The Veterans Administration spent $33 billion providing health services to veterans. This is about 5% of the total public funds. The Defense Department spent a similar amount for military health care. In 2009 Medicare accounted for $502 billion, which is about 40% of public expenditures, and Medicaid was smaller at $374 billion, including both federal and state funds. In 1960, 25% of health spending was from the public sector. That quickly jumped to 40% after the enactment of Medicare and Medicaid in the mid-1960s. By the mid-1990s, public spending had increased to 45% of total spending. The recent health reform legislation will add new public expenditures in a few years; at that point, the government share will creep past 50%. Whether this constitutes socialized medicine depends on political philosophy, not policy analysis.[9]

Most of the public funds used for health care are paid to those who provide services and goods, not public agencies or employees. A physician in private practice with Medicare patients, a community hospital receiving Medicaid reimbursement for services to a poor person, and a privately owned pharmacy dispensing drugs for Medicare recipients are all paid with funds collected through the tax system. Typically, this is not defined as socialism. But with greater public funding comes pressure on public agencies to limit total spending. Fraud or the appearance of fraud in public programs inevitably leads to bureaucratic rules that often have unintended consequences and diminish administrative flexibility.

Public tax dollars also come with legal constraints requiring fairness and equal treatment. Greater public sector participation in the funding and delivery of health care services carries both positive and negative consequences. A vigilant press enforces impartial policy rules benefiting the disadvantaged. Americans have tended to prefer a mixture of public and private institutions to deliver social services such as education. The evolution of the health care system reflects this penchant for the mixture of both public and private institutions for the delivery of services.

There are many ways to slice the total health care spending pie. Figure 1.4 breaks down expenses by sector showing the public and private pieces. The household component is composed of out-of-pocket costs, premium cost sharing, and Medicare premiums paid by recipients. Private businesses pay a significant share of employee premiums as well as Medicare tax. This slice includes only actual services and supplies, excluding such items as medical research. The government share is 40%.

Figure 1.4
Health Care Expenditures by Source of Funds (2009)

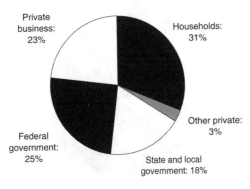

Source: Centers for Medicare and Medicaid Services, National Health Expenditure Data, www.cms.gov/NationalHealthExpendData/downloads/tables.pdf.

Employment-based Health Insurance Declines

Employment-based health insurance began in the 1930s. Today, as Figure 1.5 illustrates, 60% of the working-age population obtains health insurance through the workplace. This includes workers and their dependents in approximately equal numbers. In 2008, 160 million people had employment-based insurance. Another 16 million purchased individual policies, and 40 million had coverage through Medicaid. Medicare was the source of insurance for 7 million, and an equal number were part of the military health care system.

Employment-based health insurance is declining. The recent high point was 2000, when 68.4% of the population had employment-based insurance. This percentage has dwindled to 59% in 2009. Individually purchased insurance has also declined from 7.5% to 5.2% since 1994; this represents an absolute decline in the number of people who were covered by individual policies from 17.3 million to 13.8 million. During the same period, the number of people covered by Medicaid increased from 29.1 million to 37.6 million, which represents 14% of the non-elderly population. Various studies have identified reasons for the employment-based insurance decline, which include decline in the number of companies offering insurance, growth in part-time positions, and increased employee cost sharing with more employees declining coverage.[10]

Figure 1.5
Sources of Health Insurance Coverage

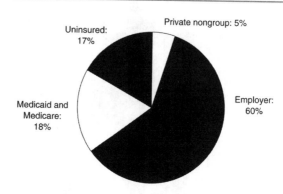

Source: US Census Bureau, Current Population Reports, "Income, Poverty, and Health Insurance Coverage in the United States: 2009," www.census.gov/prod /2010pubs/p60-238.pdf.

There are two slightly different measures used to generate conclusions about private health insurance coverage. One relies on surveys that ask participants about the source of their health insurance coverage. The other asks companies about whether or not they offer coverage and how many employees decline coverage that is offered. Depending on which measure is used, the results differ slightly.

Figure 1.5 is based on survey research. It shows that 60% of the non-elderly population (almost all older Americans are covered by Medicare) are workers with employment-based health insurance or the dependents of workers. Public programs cover 18%, with 5% purchasing individual policies. This leaves 17% uninsured. These are 2008 statistics, but the numbers do not shift radically from year to year.

Individually purchased policies declined from 7.5% in 1994 to 5.0% in 2008. Public coverage, especially Medicaid, increased to 18% after a low of 10.5% in 1999. The uninsured climbed from a low point of 15.6% in 2000 to 17.4% in 2008.[11]

In 2000, health insurance was offered by 69% of all companies. This dropped to 60% by 2008. Large companies (those with more than 200 workers) almost always offer health benefits, with 98% doing so in 2008. This has not changed over the past decade. Today, only 46% of small firms (three to nine workers) offer coverage. This dropped from 58% of small firms in 1999.[12]

The larger the firm, the more likely it is to offer health insurance. In 2008 78% of firms with ten to twenty-four workers offered coverage as did more than 90% of those with more than twenty-five workers. Workers at small firms are those least likely to have employer-offered health insurance. Firms with a higher proportion of low-wage or part-time workers are less likely to offer insurance. Less than one-third of workers are part time, but only 30% of firms offer health benefits to part-time workers. Those not offered coverage tend to work for small firms, work part time, or work for low wages. There are industry variations, and those employed in manufacturing are much more likely to be offered health insurance than those in retail. About 80% of all workers offered insurance by their employer actually take the coverage; this is consistent across all firm sizes.[13]

From the two types of data about employment-based health insurance, we can draw a few conclusions about the political economy of health care. First, the major decline in employer-offered health insurance is found in small businesses. Large employers have been offering and continue to offer health insurance to full-time workers. When the economy declines, small firms are less likely to offer health insurance.[14] As structural changes occur in the economy, they contribute to a decline in the offering of health insurance. Fewer workers are employed as a consequence of the global financial crisis of 2009–2010, fewer high-wage manufacturing jobs exist, and more people are forced to work part time out of necessity rather than choice. In some families, one spouse works at a job with health insurance and covers the rest of the family as dependents. For one-worker households, the risk is greater. The decline in coverage by employer-sponsored insurance is real, but unlikely to plummet in the decade ahead because the decline is concentrated among low-wage and part-time workers in small firms. Employment-based coverage is in danger for a growing segment of US workers and their families.

Those Outside the Financial System Are Sicker

Since half the population spends relatively little on medical care, does it really matter whether or not one has health insurance? A variety of evidence suggests that it does. The Institute of Medicine recently published a report drawn from a large number of studies. It concluded that, "in sum, despite the availability of some safety net services, there is a chasm between the health care needs of people *without* health insurance and access to effective health care services. This gap results in needless illness, suffering, and even death."[15] The report analyzed dozens of individual studies, and found significant evidence to support the contention that individuals without health insurance have less access to care and, consequently, are less healthy. Most of the studies focused either on children or adults. The health consequences differed for each category.

Uninsured children are less likely to have a usual source of care than those whose families have private insurance or public coverage. A usual source of care is associated with immunizations and well-child care in addition to the monitoring of developmental milestones and asthma care. Children with a usual source of care also receive more timely diagnosis of serious problems. Children with special needs who have health insurance are more likely to see specialists.[16]

A 2009 study at Johns Hopkins Children's Center examined data from 1988 to 2005 covering hospitalizations of over 20 million children. It found that uninsured children experienced a 60% increased risk of dying. The authors concluded that this was not the result of differential treatment once in the hospital, but a result of delayed entry into the medical system despite a life-threatening condition.[17] In a review of studies of adults without health insurance, the Institute of Medicine found they were:

- Less likely to receive preventive services
- More likely to forgo visits with physicians or delay effective therapies despite chronic conditions
- More likely to be diagnosed with late-stage cancer, to be undergoing treatment for hypertension, and to have worse glycemic control of diabetes
- More likely to have poorer health outcomes[18]

In their analysis of access to health care services, the Kaiser Commission on Medicaid and the Uninsured found that the uninsured were five times less likely to have a usual source of care, seven times more unlikely to have preventive care, and twice as likely to go without care or prescription drugs because of cost.[19]

The relationship among disease, health insurance coverage, and economic status is complex. Some have argued that these studies do not prove that lack of insurance is the direct cause of serious illness or death.[20] This is technically correct, but the association between lack of health insurance and less access to care is clear. The studies demonstrate that, when access to routine care is constrained by financial limits, more serious conditions go undetected and untreated for a longer time.

The Evolving Practice, Delivery, and Economics of Medicine

> Those who cannot remember the past are condemned to repeat it. —*George Santayana*

The next few pages provide a sprint through a century of history that traces the evolution of the organization, delivery, and economics of medicine in the United States. If we jump into a time machine and travel back to the dawn of the twentieth century, many things are familiar. Trains are running, houses are being built, and even baseball games are being played much as they are today. But the practice and organization of medicine in 1900 would be almost unrecognizable.

The beginning of the twentieth century marked the culmination of significant changes in American life. The practice and economics of medicine would never be the same again. The Civil War was both a demarcation and a contributory cause. The material demands of war propelled the nascent Industrial Revolution forward, especially in the north. The US economic engine steamed ahead into the twentieth century, and with it came the economic base for medical revolution. The establishment of land grant colleges and the expansion of science education at major private institutions created the scientific base on which twentieth-century medicine was built. The forty-year span from the Civil War to the turn of the century saw a prodigious change in the understanding of biology and physiology first in Europe, and then in North America. The rapid advance of transportation and communication technology enabled people and ideas to move across national borders and vast land expanses faster than at any time in history. The convergence of these economic and technology developments propelled the rapid advance of the scientific foundation of medicine, and the diffusion of new insights and applications across the country.

To make this historical summary less complex, the story unfolds in five eras:

- The era of the general practitioner: 1900–1920
- The era of the community hospital: 1920–1950
- The era of the medical center: 1960–1980

- The era of the health maintenance organization (HMO) and managed care: 1980–2000
- The era of market redux: 2000 to the present

Of course, real life does not offer sharply distinctive timelines; no newspaper headline on January 1, 1920, hailed the beginning of a new era. But retrospectively, this helps us to understand the critical intersection of major events as they lead to system changes.

The Era of the General Practitioner: 1900–1920

In 1912, Harvard professor Lawrence Henderson asserted, "for the first time in human history, a random patient with a random disease consulting a doctor chosen at random stands a better than 50/50 chance of benefitting from the encounter."[21]

These first two decades of the twentieth century encompassed the revolutionary developments in medicine that had taken place over the previous four decades. A middle-aged practicing physician in 1900 would have been perhaps forty-five years old, born five years before the beginning of the Civil War, and received his medical education in about 1880. This education typically consisted of an apprenticeship with an experienced physician, and a short time spent at a small pro-prietary medical school. The physician's office, not the hospital, was the nucleus of a general medical practice in a small town.

After the birth of that average 1900 physician, medicine under-went a meteoric transformation. The era of the general practitioner was in essence the end of the predominant place of this role in US medicine. The surgeon was about to replace the general practitioner as the central player. These first two decades of the century were essentially the transition from the general practitioner to the surgeon as the embodiment of medicine.

In the middle years of the nineteenth century, the use of ether, nitrous oxide, and finally chloroform allowed the surgeon to conduct operations of greater duration and complexity without the patient undergoing excruciating pain. English surgeon Joseph Lister in 1867 pioneered antiseptic techniques and the subsequent broad acceptance of aseptic (sterile operating field) approaches that drastically reduced fatal infections associated with surgery. Finally, German physician Wilhelm Roentgen discovered the principle of the X-ray in 1895, which allowed physicians to peer into the thoracic cavity without an incision. Together, these techniques rendered all types of surgery safer and more feasible, especially abdominal intervention. The Mayo brothers performed 54 abdominal surgeries between 1889 and 1892, but 612 in 1900. By 1905, the number had risen to over 2,000.[22] However, in this first decade of the twentieth century, the average physician was not a surgeon, did not live in a major urban area, and was not wealthy. Health insurance did not exist. Despite the growing urban middle class, the typical family income did not provide enough of a surplus to afford high physician fees.

Organizationally, physicians were separating into specialists and general practitioners. Despite the prominence of the Mayo Clinic group model, the typical physician was a solo practitioner dependent on individual fees. The new surgery specialists were likely to have had at least part of their education in Europe, and were exposed to a more science-based approach to medicine.

The Carnegie Foundation–sponsored Flexner Report of 1910 was a devastating critique of US medical education, especially the proprietary schools. Most quickly closed their doors. The Johns Hopkins Medical School with its European-style scientific approach to education became the national model. Across the country, physicians educated after 1915 experienced a more rigorous and scientific medical school education. The best of these graduates were more likely to gravitate toward surgery and other emerging specialties.

The average small-town general practitioner in 1900 probably did most of his work in the office or at in-home visits called "house calls." His community was likely in the process of raising money to build a local hospital. In 1904, there were 1,500 hospitals in the nation.[23] A century earlier, there had been two hospitals in the United States.[24] Most were established after 1880. Prior to the growth of surgery, the typical hospital was an asylum maintained by local governments or religious denominations for sick people who were poor or without families to provide care. The emerging new surgical techniques required an institution capable of achieving the necessary sterile environment and providing X-ray machines and recuperative nursing care essential for successful operations. The professionalization of nursing, which began in the latter part of the nineteenth century, also advanced exponentially. Without the emergence of this group of health professionals, the emerging hospital would not have been possible.

Individual physicians developed about half of these proprietary institutions. This form predominated in the South and West. In the

Northeast, religious groups, private philanthropy, and local government were the most likely sponsors. Before the twentieth century, hospitals were often free because their sponsors perceived them as charities and their "customers" were unable to pay for services. At the turn of the century, as middle- and upper-middle-income Americans began to routinely have more surgery, hospitals became commonplace. With expanded use, capital and operating costs escalated. Fees were charged. Surgery patients became the mainstay of the typical hospital with an average length of stay around three weeks.[25]

World War I hastened the further development of hospitals as major medical schools sent physicians to Europe with the expeditionary force, and field hospitals were established to treat the wounded. After the war, the lessons learned from this experience contributed to the continued expansion of the role of hospitals in the practice of US medicine. By the end of the second decade of the twentieth century, the era of the general practitioner was drawing to a close. The physician continued to be the dominant figure in the practice of medicine, but surgery was emerging as the preeminent focal point of medicine. The use of hospitals in the decades to follow had profound implications for the organization and financing of medical care.

The Era of the Community Hospital: 1920–1950

The 1920s was a decade of prosperity and modernization in America. One of the prominent features of urban middle-class prosperity in the 1920s was the emergence of the community hospital as a symbol of modern health care delivery. New hospital construction occurred everywhere at a scale that would not be seen again until the 1950s. The glittering new community hospitals moved away from the older ward layout to private and semiprivate rooms. Special facilities for operations, X-ray, and physical therapy were essential parts of the modern hospital. By the 1930s, most births were taking place in hospitals. Obstetrical services represented about one-fifth of the patients, and tonsillectomies about one-third. Appendicitis cases and accidents were also major causes of admission with about 10% each. These four areas represented about 60% of all admissions.[26]

Although many hospitals made lines of credit available to patients, daily hospital costs nearly doubled in the decade of the 1920s. Middle-class Americans consumed higher levels of hospital service, and even they were beginning to feel a financial pinch when hospitalization was necessary. Insurance companies adopted the premise that the decision to enter a hospital represented "moral hazard" and, thus, was uninsurable. Insurers had no method to assess risk and, therefore, had no basis for establishing a premium.

In the years leading up to World War I, some labor leaders and advocates of the progressive political agenda began to argue for a social insurance idea similar to what had been established by Otto von Bismarck in Germany in the 1880s. The cash payments for sick workers were closer to what we today call disability insurance. The onset of World War I ended the discussion without any legislation being enacted. By the mid-1920s, the rapidly rising cost of hospital care created discussions about some type of a financing system to help cover hospital costs. As mentioned above, costs were rapidly becoming a concern for middle-class clients of private hospitals. Many urban areas had established free public hospitals for the poor and working class, but these were not seen as attractive options for the growing middle class.

In 1926, a group of American Medical Association (AMA) leaders from academic medicine established a committee, which led to the ultimate creation in the following year of the Committee on the Cost of Medical Care. The purpose of the CCMC was defined as providing a solution to the problem of the middle class being unable to afford modern scientific medicine.[27] Its mission was to study the subject and make recommendations. Under the leadership of its associate director, I. S. Falk, twenty-three major reports were issued over the next five years.

By the end of the 1920s, the stock market had crashed and the economy had tumbled into the Great Depression lasting more than a decade. But regardless of the economy, the cost of health care services continued to rise. In many urban communities, publicly funded hospitals were the only point of access for care. Financially strapped local governments were unlikely to be able to transform these institutions into facilities comparable to the private or nonprofit community hospitals.

In a federal political system, national policy sometimes emerges from local experimentation. The development of a health care financing system for the middle class was a noteworthy example. In 1929, a financially strapped Dallas private hospital and teachers in the local school district joined in an experiment in which the teachers paid fifty cents a month into a hospital fund. In return, they were entitled to a maximum of twenty-one days a year of care in the hospital at no cost. This arrangement soon spread to other employee groups in Dallas.

The success of the Dallas experiment led to similar arrangements in other communities. In a few years, the individual hospital plans were replaced with an association of multiple hospitals that had similar agreements with multiple employee groups. By the end of the 1930s, these Blue Cross plans had spread across the country. Meanwhile the commercial insurance industry, which had not regarded protection against hospitalization as an insurance risk, began to rethink the viability of hospitalization insurance. By 1940, these companies were seeking to gain a foothold in the group health insurance market.

Political progressives in the 1930s viewed the changing economics of health care services as a basis for again trying to place national public financing on the agenda. In 1935, a task force of the Franklin D. Roosevelt administration recommended health insurance as one of the elements of a proposed new Social Security system that also included a public pension system, unemployment insurance, and a set of welfare payments for people with disabilities and mothers with dependent children. Opposition from physicians led President Roosevelt to exclude health coverage from the Social Security legislation. This absence of a public program opened the door for expansion of group insurance through the workplace.

The key element for financing the growing expense of providing a bundle of hospital-based services was to find a mechanism for pooling large numbers of people who would pay relatively small amounts of money into a common fund. Concentration of health expenses was just as present seventy-five years ago as today. Since the government was not willing to organize this pool, the emerging Blue Cross system and commercial insurance companies began to do so with employment groups as the basis for the risk pool.

During World War II, wage controls were used to keep wartime scarcity from driving high inflation. With young men in the military and out of the workforce, employers needed to find a viable incentive to attract and keep good workers. Wage increases were severely limited, but adding or expanding health insurance for employees was not considered wages under government regulations. This became a recruitment and retention tool for wartime employers. In 1935, the National Labor Relations Act (Wagner Act) provided a statutory legal position for labor unions, especially industrial unions. The continuing Depression and then World War II kept the unions from leveraging their new legal status. By the end of the 1940s, unions were aggressively pursuing a new postwar social order in which generous wages and benefits were obtained for workers through collective bargaining. Hospitalization insurance was one of those benefits.

In 1948, the Harry S. Truman administration revived the Roosevelt task force plan for a national health insurance plan through Social Security. The AMA vociferously opposed this effort, and the legislation never emerged from the committee stage in Congress. Physicians had also initially objected to the emerging Blue Cross service guarantee system for hospitals. Yet by the end of the 1930s, physicians had begun to establish a similar but separate system for physician payment. Soon these systems were joined for marketing and administrative purposes, and called Blue Cross and Blue Shield. For decades, the two components remained under separate internal governance despite consumers perceiving it as a single insurance system.

In the mid-1950s, the Internal Revenue Service issued new rules that treated the employer contributions for employee health insurance as taxable income. Congress reacted to the public outcry by amending the law to exclude this as income subject to tax. In the meantime, both Blue Cross and commercial insurance companies continued to thrive and expand their health insurance businesses. Both entities did sell policies to individuals, but the employer group market was the core of the business and the way that most families arranged for health insurance coverage.

By the end of the 1950s, the community hospital had become the centerpiece of US medicine. With the help of federal grants under the Hospital Survey and Construction Act (Hill-Burton) and the ability to borrow capital because of steady patient revenues from health insurance, community hospitals grew and modernized across the country. New technology and patient amenities that were inconceivable a few decades earlier had become commonplace.

Rosemary Stevens states the following about emerging technology in community hospitals in the 1950s:

> The most pervasive image of hospital technology in the 1950s was the hospital intensive care unit. Except for the smallest hospitals the great majority of American hospitals established intensive care units between 1950 and 1960. By 1960 virtually all short-term hospitals had clinical laboratories, diagnostic X-ray, and electrocardiography; over half had a postoperative recovery room and a blood bank; over one-third provided X-ray therapy; and one-fifth had a radioisotope facility.[28]

With two glaring exceptions—the elderly and poor people—the previous two decades had seen the development of a financial mechanism capable of providing medical care to the population without significant use of tax revenue for this purpose. Health insurance pools organized around the workplace provided a way to both collect money and spread risk even as the total cost of providing health care had grown exponentially.

The Era of the Medical Center: 1960–1980

In the previous era, the hospital became the central institution in the US health care system. The technology for treating illnesses and our understanding of disease and treatment advanced at an astonishing pace. By the middle of the twentieth century, life expectancy in the United States had increased significantly. In the early 1960s, most medical innovations were pioneered at major medical centers. These hospitals usually were located in major cities and affiliated with a university medical school. Their mission was to both treat complex disease and train the next generation of physicians.

Medical progress was not cheap. By the early 1960s, the percentage of GDP spent on medical care had doubled from the 3% found by the CCMC in 1929. Each year, more US workers and their families were offered health insurance and received it as an employment benefit. While this often did not cover all costs for extended treatment, it relieved fear that even routine hospital treatment would devastate the average family budget. For the poor and uninsured, public hospitals still offered an alternative, although they were increasingly perceived as inferior institutions.

Because employment-based insurance expanded exponentially in the 1950s, the most obvious group not included in the emerging system of health finance was older people. By the late 1950s, reformers narrowed their focus for a public program to older Americans. In the early 1960s during the John F. Kennedy administration, one of the highest legislative priorities was Medicare, the proposed public health insurance plan to cover hospitalization costs for older people. Finally, after President Lyndon B. Johnson's decisive election victory in 1964, Congress passed Medicare in early 1965. Included in the legislation was a program of federal grants to the states for medical payments for the poor covered by the existing welfare program. This later came to be called Medicaid.

By the late 1960s as these two new public programs were fully implemented, both community hospitals and the increasingly important (and expensive) medical centers were receiving substantial reimbursement to cover the high costs of treatment for serious illness. The government and private insurance company reimbursements were typically made on a cost basis. It is oversimplifying to say that the hospitals sent the bill and the government or insurance company paid it, but this is an apt generalization of the process. In such a system, rising costs led to higher reimbursements. Until the end of the decade, general inflation was low, but health costs tended to rise much faster. By 1970, the United States was spending 7.2% of GDP for health care, up from 5.2% in 1960.[29]

The higher costs associated with medical centers were easily passed on to insurers and the government. Treatment based on advanced technology also became routine in the community hospitals, as recently trained physicians demanded support from hospitals for the latest technology.

By the early 1970s, federal government officials voiced concern about Medicare and Medicaid cost increases, and private insurance companies began to experience resistance to rising premiums from employers. The 1970s were characterized by oil price–driven inflation, and medical cost inflation exceeded general inflation. By 1980, health care spending was 9.1% of GDP.[30] Despite congressional attempts to contain health care inflation, no effective approach was found.

The Era of the HMO and Managed Care: 1980–2000

By the early 1980s, many community hospitals began to routinely use technology that was not available even in medical centers twenty years earlier. In 1983, Congress passed the first major reimbursement reform for Medicare, which was a prospective payment system using Diagnostic Related Groups. Congress adopted a new Medicare physician fee schedule system later in the decade.

The escalating cost of group health premiums led to new experiments with cost control measures, especially managed care. During the early 1970s, there was, for a time, the sense that integrated delivery systems featuring prepaid group practice (such as Kaiser Permanente in California) were a hopeful approach to cost control. By the 1980s, it was clear that this type of system change would be difficult to implement. Managed care was a less comprehensive reform. It featured limits on the choice of physician and hospital based on reimbursement negotiations between the provider and insurance company. It also included tighter utilization control featuring preapproval for many types of procedures. Many insurance companies and state Medicaid programs implemented the managed care approach. Some of these efforts were successful, but a backlash also developed because of the insensitivity and heavy-handed application of utilization review. Employers faced with unremitting premium increases shifted more of the cost to the employee.

In the early 1990s, the William J. Clinton administration proposed comprehensive reform of the health care financing system, but there was no congressional majority for the plan. The measure died in the fall of 1994 and, in the November elections, the Democrats lost control of Congress. The window of opportunity for major reform closed.

In the boom times of the late 1990s, the number of uninsured Americans declined marginally. Jobs were more plentiful than at the beginning of the decade. Also, passage of the State Children's Health Insurance Program (SCHIP) brought working-class children and families into Medicaid despite levels of income above previous eligibility levels.

The Era of Market Redux: 2000 to the Present

As the first decade of the twenty-first century began, there was an economic downturn. The global financial crisis brought a recession bordering on depression at the end of the decade. Even during better times, the persistent rise in health care costs and insurance premiums led to calls for reform of the health care financing system. The ideological belief in the power of market reforms to solve both cost and financial access issues waned. In many metropolitan areas, hospitals became more integrated into large systems as the recent consolidation trend continued. Larger insurance companies expanded their market share as the once independent local Blue Cross companies were acquired by private companies.[31]

In any generic discussion of the health care system, there has always been a view of a single government system versus a lively marketplace of both insurers and providers. To some extent, this has always been myth. In 2010, almost one-half of all health care system revenue was raised by federal and state government taxes. The marketplace has contracted as both insurance and hospital industries have consolidated. This oligopoly confers potential bargaining power to both hospitals and insurance companies since leading firms possess a high market share. But since both industries are consolidating, the power to negotiate favorable prices may be limited. Neither is in a position to press an absolute advantage because each ultimately needs the other.[32]

The health reform debate of 2009–2010 attempted to find the proper roles for government, employers, consumers, and insurance companies as congressional legislation sought a balance between cost control and expanded financial access for the uninsured.

This has been a quick sprint through 100 years of health care finance to provide a historical overview as preview for the chapters to follow. There has been a steady development and diffusion of medical technology. With each new breakthrough, medical science is able to work additional "miracles" to preserve, extend, and add to the quality of life. The cost of these miracles continues to strain governments, employers, and households.

Scenarios for the Future

In this first chapter, much of the narrative has outlined the historical development of the US health system. This is an important preface for the next chapters because, as we examine programs and policy issues, they need to fit into a common context. To organize this effort, I conceptualized the past century as consisting of five eras of roughly two decades each. In the three brief scenarios below, I try to anticipate possible major developments in the next decade or two. These scenarios set the stage for the coming discussions of Medicare, Medicaid, reform, and cost containment.

The scenario technique allows us to view alternative paths into an uncertain future. "Scenarios make sense of future events in the same way as historical accounts make sense of the past."[33]

Employment-based Insurance Rapidly Declines

Two out of three non-older Americans receive health insurance through group policies arranged for and mostly paid by employers as part of a benefit package. Employment-based insurance has been the key element of risk pooling since the late 1930s. There has been a decline in the past decade as union manufacturing jobs diminished, and more adults worked part time or as contract workers without benefits.

In the first scenario, employment-based insurance steadily declines over the next decade or so. It declined from a 2000 high of 68% to 56% in 2009. Let's assume a drop of 10 percentage points over the next decade. The same percentage decline over the next two decades means that, by 2030, only 40% of Americans will have employment-based health insurance.

This will result from fewer jobs that offer full benefits, coupled with employers discontinuing health insurance coverage because of escalating premium costs. Workers and their families will need to purchase individual policies, participate in public plans (if they have moderate income), or go without health insurance.

Under this scenario at some point, perhaps as the number reaches 50%, there will be political pressure on the government to take action. Since administrative and marketing costs of individual policies tend to be two to three times higher than group policies, the premium cost for the same coverage will escalate, rendering it even more expensive in the future.

If the government seeks to respond, either a broad public program (like Medicare) can be created to serve those without employment-based insurance or the government can provide expanded subsidies for the purchase of private health insurance as planned under recent health reform legislation. The existence of this type of alternative to employment-based insurance will probably lead many employers to drop their coverage and allow their workers to participate in a government plan.

Whatever the outcome that this scenario envisions, the current employment-based system significantly deteriorates because of a changing job structure and escalating employer benefit costs. The latter particularly impacts low- to middle-wage employees.

Inflation Causes Rationing

We currently spend 17% of GDP on health care, higher than any other major industrialized country. This is an increase from 13.6% in 2000. The Center for Medicare and Medicaid Services projects this number to rise to 19.3% by 2019, if no actions are taken to restrain growth in costs.[34] This scenario assumes that no effective short-term action is taken to constrain costs. As a result businesses, households, and the government all find health care in its current form to be unaffordable.

New forms of subsidies for households or businesses will not be a practical solution because the existing tax system will not support a sufficiently high level of revenue generation for subsidies. Increases in the out-of-pocket costs borne by households will also be unsustainable. Thus, a public rationing scheme is the logical policy choice.

This new policy could take many forms. Perhaps the most likely form is a combination of government limits on new capital expenditures (thus constraining the high capital and operating costs of new technology) along with a public reimbursement system that has utilization restrictions as well as waiting lists for services because of restrictions on providers. In this scenario, the current service-on-demand model will be replaced by one that is far less desirable.

Tinkering and Adjustment Keeps the Current System in Place

In the current mixed private-public health care system, we are currently struggling to find a set of public policies that will enable us to simultaneously expand financial protection against health care expenses and control system costs. At previous junctures in the past, the system has been tinkered with to forestall rapid cost increases and the decline of the dependence on employment-based insurance.

In the 1980s, Medicare moved its reimbursement systems away from those based on costs to prospective payment. At the same time, private insurers and Medicaid adopted managed care systems to control utilization. SCHIP was adopted by Congress in the late 1990s to address part of the problem of the uninsured with greater coverage for children, but this was not comprehensive reform. Incremental revenue and payment adjustments have been utilized by Medicare to postpone a time when revenue and reserves do not equal annual outlays in the Part A Medicare Hospital Insurance Trust Fund. Similar incremental adjustments might be made by both public and private insurance entities to stave off the worst-case problems without ever adopting comprehensive reform measures.

How we approach policy in next decade depends on how we view these scenarios. Each scenario is both feasible and plausible. As I examine the various policy issues in the chapters of this book, keep in mind these three possible scenarios.

Notes

1. Anne Martin et al., "Recession Contributes to Slowest Annual Rate of Increase in Health Spending in Five Decades," *Health Affairs* 30, no. 1 (2011): 11.

28   *Health Policy*

2. Ibid.

3. "National Health Expenditures Accounts: Definitions, Sources, and Methods" (Washington, DC: Centers for Medicare and Medicaid Services, Office of the Actuary, 2009).

4. M. L. Berk and A. C. Monheit, "The Concentration of Health Expenditures: An Update," *Health Affairs* 11, no. 4 (1992): 145–149. See also Anna Sommers and Mindy Cohen, "Medicaid's High Cost Enrollees: How Much Do They Drive Program Spending?" (Washington, DC: Kaiser Commission on Medicaid and the Uninsured, March 2006); Congressional Budget Office, *Medicare High Cost Beneficiaries* (Washington, DC: CBO Publications Office, May 2005); "Concentration of Health Care Spending in the US Population" (Washington, DC: Kaiser Commission on Medicaid and the Uninsured, February 3, 2011), http://facts.kff.org/chart.aspx?ch=1344.

5. Lisa Potetz and Juliette Cubanski, *A Primer on Medicare Financing* (Washington, DC: Kaiser Family Foundation, July 2009), p. 8; "Medicaid: A Primer" (Washington, DC: Kaiser Commission on Medicaid and the Uninsured, June 2010), pp. 23–25.

6. Martin et al., "Recession Contributes to Slowest Annual Rate of Increase in Health Spending in Five Decades."

7. Congressional Budget Office, "Technological Change and the Growth of Health Care Spending" (Washington, DC: CBO Publications Office, January 2008), p. 7.

8. "Gloomy Americans Bash Congress, Are Divided on Obama," Section 3: "View of Health Care Legislation" (Washington, DC: Pew Research Center for the People and the Press, March 18, 2010), http://people-press.org.

9. Martin et al., "Recession Contributes to Slowest Annual Rate of Increase in Health Spending in Five Decades."

10. John Holahan, "The 2007–09 Recession and Health Insurance Coverage," *Health Affairs* 30, no. 1 (2011): 4.

11. Paul Fronstin, "Sources of Health Insurance and Characteristics of the Uninsured: Analysis of the March 2009 Current Population Survey," Issue Brief No. 334 (Washington, DC: Employee Benefit Research Institute, September 2009), p. 5.

12. *Employer Health Benefits: 2010 Annual Survey* (Washington, DC: Kaiser Family Foundation and Health and Research Educational Trust, Publication 8085, September 2010).

13. Gary Claxton et al., *Employer Health Benefits: 2009 Annual Survey* (Washington, DC: Kaiser Family Foundation and Health Research and Educational Trust, 2009), p. 200.

14. Gary Claxton et al., "Job-Based Health Insurance: Costs Climb at a Moderate Pace," *Health Affairs* 28, no. 6 (2009): 1002–1012.

15. "America's Uninsured Crisis: Consequences for Health and Health Care," Institute of Medicine of the National Academies (Washington, DC: National Academies Press, 2009), p. 83.

16. "America's Uninsured Crisis: Consequences for Health and Health Care," Report Brief (Washington, DC: Institute of Medicine of the National Academies, February 2009).

17. Michelle Andrews, "Deaths Rising for Lack of Insurance, Study Finds," *New York Times,* Prescriptions Blog, February 26, 2010, http://prescriptions.blogs.nytimes.com/2010/02/26/deaths-rising-due-to-lack-of-insurance-study-finds.

18. "America's Uninsured Crisis," pp. 72–81.

19. "The Uninsured: A Primer" (Washington, DC: Kaiser Commission on Medicaid and the Uninsured, October 2009), pp. 7–8.

20. Megan McArdle, "Myth Diagnosis," *The Atlantic,* March 2010, www.theatlantic.com/magazine/archive/2010/03/myth-diagnosis/7905.

21. Theodore Marmor, *The Politics of Medicare,* 2nd ed. (New York: Aldine de Gruyter, 1970), p. 3.

22. Paul Starr, *The Social Transformation of American Medicine* (New York: Basic Books, 1982), p. 157.

23. Rosemary Stevens, *American Medicine and the Public Interest* (New Haven: Yale University Press, 1971).

24. Charles Rosenberg, *The Care of Strangers: The Rise of America's Hospital System* (New York: Basic Books, 1987), p. 337.

25. Stevens, *American Medicine and the Public Interest,* p. 24.

26. Ibid., p. 114.

27. Joseph Ross, "The Committee on the Costs of Medical Care and the History of Health Insurance in the United States," *Einstein Quarterly Journal of Biology and Medicine* 19, no. 3 (2002): 129–134.

28. Stevens, *American Medicine and the Public Interest,* p. 231.

29. Centers for Medicare and Medicaid Services, "National Health Expenditure Data," www.cms.gov/NationalHealthExpendData/downloads/tables.pdf (accessed May 7, 2011).

30. Ibid.

31. Jonathan Cohn, "How Blue Cross Became Part of a Dysfunctional Health Care System" (Washington, DC: Kaiser Commission on Medicaid and the Uninsured, March 8, 2010), www.kaiserhealthnews.org/Columns/2010/March/030810Cohn.aspx.

32. William B. Vogt, "Hospital Market Consolidation: Trends and Consequences" (Washington, DC: National Institute for Health Care Management, November 2009); James Robinson, "Consolidation and the Transformation of Competition in Health Insurance," *Health Affairs* 23, no. 6 (2004): 11–24.

33. Kees Van Der Heijden, *Scenarios: The Art of Strategic Conversation,* 2nd ed. (Hoboken, NJ: Wiley, 2005), p. 134.

34. Centers for Medicare and Medicaid Services, "National Health Expenditure Data."

2

The Health Policy System

I want the government to keep their hands off my
Medicare.
—a citizen at a health reform forum in summer 2009

Antireform activists saw this comment as symbolic of public anger at
the prospect of a larger role for government in the organization and
operation of health care service delivery. Others laughed at the incon-
gruity of the statement. Medicare is a government program financed
by the tax system, and has been since 1965. About half of all money
spent on health care in the United States is raised by taxes and spent
as public funds. There has always been an intersection of the health
care and political systems with government policy having a significant influence on health care. In this chapter, I examine the basic
institutions and processes of government, especially Congress. It is
through these governmental structures that policies critical to the
health care system are developed.

Many readers may not have explored the world of government
structure and process since sixth-grade civics. Others may be familiar
with the basics and wish to skip parts of this chapter. Because major
policy is created by legislation, I start with the fundamentals of the
legislative process and congressional decisionmaking. I also examine
a conceptual model or way of thinking about policy, the role of interest groups, and health program bureaucracy in a federal system.

The Legislative Process

The Senate and House of Representatives are very different institutions.
The Senate has 100 members, the House has 435. Senators represent

31

entire states and most House members only a part of the state. Each body jealously guards its prerogatives and independence and has its own history and traditions. The legislative process and its rules are often Byzantine in their application, but the basic steps are as described below.[1]

Introducing the Bill

No matter who actually drafts the legislative language of the bill, it can be introduced only by a member of Congress. Executive branch experts, congressional staff, or interest groups may actually take policy ideas and put them into formal legislative language. Thousands of bills are introduced during each legislative session, which is the almost two-year period between the January in odd-numbered years after an election and early October of the following year just prior to the next election. Most never see the light of day because they are referred to committee and either die or become merged with another bill. A bill introduced on the first day of the legislation session must either become law by the end or begin anew in the next session.

Subcommittee and Committee

After introduction, a bill is referred to committee. There is relatively little discretion in the bill assignment. The twenty committees of the House and sixteen committees of the Senate each have established jurisdiction to review various types of bills. Thus, the House Ways and Means Committee is the body to which tax bills are referred. The Senate Committee on Health, Education, Labor, and Pensions (HELP Committee) has jurisdiction over health legislation, but when taxes are also involved it shares review authority with the Finance Committee.

Each committee has subcommittees, and that is where detailed consideration of bills occurs. First, the subcommittee, and then the full committee, may hold hearings on proposed legislation to provide a public opportunity for supporters and opponents to make a record of their stance as well as suggest language changes. Once the bill has been "marked up" in the subcommittee, it is sent to the full committee. Again, it may be modified by the committee before vote, and sent to the floor for a vote of the entire membership.

The membership of each committee is based on the partisan division in the body. If one party has a total 60% majority, each committee will approximate that division. Democrats and Republicans in each house have a process for assigning members to committees. Once on a committee, a member typically remains and develops seniority, which is a major, but not the only, factor in subcommittee or committee chairmanship.

Each committee has professional staff who assist members in drafting and amending bills as well as preparing for hearings. The staff are both subject experts in the topics considered by the committee and knowledgeable about the legislative processes. Staff play a key role at every phase of the process.

The Path to the Floor

In the House, the path to the floor is through the Rules Committee. This formal body determines a "rule" or set of stipulations under which a bill will be considered by the full House membership. This includes such items as the length of time for debate and the number and type of amendments to be offered. Years ago, the Rules Committee was autonomous and often held up bills that its members did not support. In the past fifty years, the Rules Committee has become a reflection of the Speaker and House majority party leadership. When the Rules Committee holds a piece of legislation, it is more than likely because the leadership does not have the votes for passage and is therefore reluctant to bring the bill to the floor.

Because of its size, the House requires that the largely formal process be controlled by the leadership of the majority party. The larger and more cohesive the majority, the less likely that the minority will be able to exercise influence in the process. Assembling enough votes to pass legislation is a key focus, and recently this has been almost exclusively within the purview of the majority party.

Typically, Democrats and Republicans have both bitterly complained about this lack of participation when they were in the minority in the House. The Speaker and majority leader control when a bill will come to the floor and the conditions for consideration, such as length of debate and amendments allowed.

In the Senate, with its smaller membership and tradition of a more leisurely and less formal process, the majority and minority party leaders negotiate the timing for bringing bills to the floor. The unanimous consent agreement is the key element in this negotiation. The leaders bring their agreement for Senate approval, and it tends to function much like the House rule. The agreement sets the terms of debate, may limit or restrict amendments, and sets out the time deadlines for bringing the bill for a vote. The threat of filibuster, one element in the negotiation of the unanimous consent agreement, basically suspends the rules during the debate and vote. Senate rules have always been less formal than those in the House. Senate rules exist in a culture of accommodation of individual members. Without suspension of the rules under unanimous consent, a single senator could delay any deliberation for an extended period.

Floor Debate and Vote

Depending on the significance and controversy surrounding a bill, it may be debated in both the House and Senate for multiple legislative days before final passage or rejection. In recent years, there has been an increasing use or threatened use of the filibuster on significant or controversial legislation. This means in the Senate there needs to be sixty, not fifty-one, votes for passage. To preclude a threatened filibuster in the House, the debate and the vote are more formal, and the majority can stop debate and bring the bill to a vote.

In the House, amendments are typically restricted by the rule under which the bill is considered. Amendments must be germane to the bill. A health care–related amendment cannot be offered to a farm bill. The Senate does not restrict amendments or require they be related to the bill. In the Senate, a wholly different bill could be added to a piece of legislation as an amendment as long as it is supported by a majority.

Procedures are important to legislative bodies. They are both the link to the past and the common ground allowing the 435 representatives and the 100 senators to make critical policy decisions.

Conference Committee

To become law, a bill must be approved by a majority in both the House and the Senate. Either body could accept the bill passed by the other in the same exact form. This rarely occurs. But in the case of the 2010 health reform legislation, the House accepted the Senate version. When similar but not identical bills pass both bodies, a conference committee composed of members from each house is established to resolve the differences. No new items should be inserted in the conference committee report, but in fact this can happen. A new provision may be necessary to arrange the compromises required to assemble a single bill from the two passed by each house. The conference committee report, with the single melded bill, is returned to the House and Senate for a final vote.

Presidential Signature or Veto

Once a bill has been passed by both houses, it is sent to the president for signature. Once signed, it immediately becomes law. If the president vetoes the bill, it is returned to Congress and requires a two-thirds vote in each house to override the veto. Bills are not vetoed often and are rarely overturned when they are.

The basic structure of Congress and legislative processes described in this review are not enough to answer questions such as: Why do some bills pass and others not? How are the views of the public taken into account? What is the role of interest groups? Is the president a critical actor in the process or just a final step? What are the factors that contribute to the decisionmaking on the part of individual members of the House or Senate? In subsequent pages, some of these more complex questions will be addressed.

The Kingdon Model of Policymaking

When trying to make sense of the complex world around us, we tend to fall back on mental models. These conceptual frameworks organize the way that we think about and interpret the millions of bits of information that bombard us every day. There are a number of such frameworks developed by political scientists, but one of the most compelling and widely employed is John Kingdon's model.[2]

Many policy process conceptual frameworks are linear, and they identify steps and stages. Kingdon views the development of policy taking place simultaneously in three streams: a problem stream, a political stream, and a policy stream. When these three streams come together at a critical time, a window of opportunity is created and new policy is more likely to be adopted.

The Problem Stream

In the problem stream, conditions come to be seen as problems. Problems are brought to the political agenda by external events, bureaucratic routines, or the elevation of the problem by key actors in the political system. Kingdon distinguishes between the government agenda and the decision agenda. The former occurs when a condition becomes a problem under discussion. An item is placed on the agenda when there is the prospect of a decision.

The Political Stream

The political stream is composed of factors such as swings of national mood, election results, changes of administration, changes of ideological or partisan distributions in Congress, and interest group pressure campaigns. It is in the political stream that majority coalitions become available to enact policy change.

The Policy Stream

In the policy stream, ideas are explored, debated, and either advanced or rejected. These ideas are analyzed within policy communities as proposals are subjected to scrutiny based on technical feasibility, acceptability of values, and costs. Political entrepreneurs work among groups within the policy community to fashion and design policy proposals that will ultimately be capable of acceptance by a coalition in the political stream large enough to gain passage of policy in the political arena.

The Window of Opportunity

Windows are opened by problems that are thrust forward or changes in the array of forces in the political stream. There is a coupling that joins solutions to problems and links both to the potential majority coalitions in the political stream.

Kingdon's model helps us understand the dynamics of the policy process by highlighting these three activity streams. Figure 2.1 illustrates the Kingdon model. As with individuals, Congress as an institution typically has more to do than time available.

The problem stream is the set of activities that determines which issues in a given year or session receive primary attention. Placement on the agenda means some participants in the policy process believe this issue is important enough to justify effort spent to enact policy change. Unless an issue has a place on the agenda, it will languish in the process.

**Figure 2.1
The Kingdon Model of Policymaking**

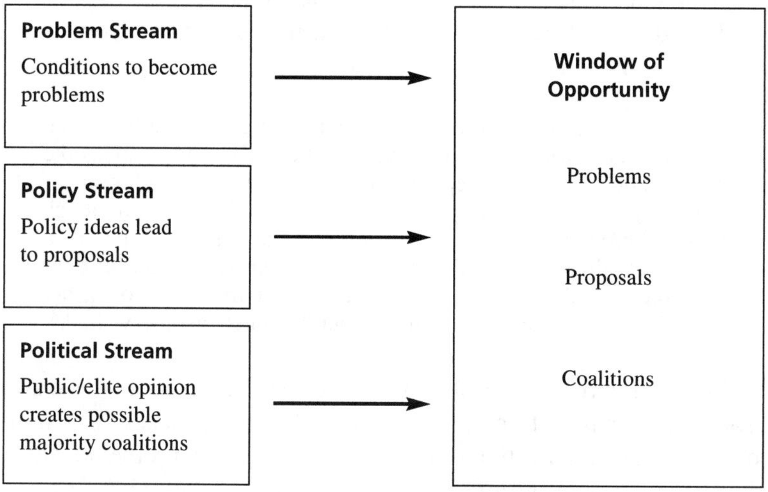

In a democratic political system, majority coalitions must be built at each stage of the policy process. In the legislative arena, this first means having an available coalition. There needs to be the possibility of a majority. In recent years, there has been a sharp partisan division in both the House and the Senate. Republicans and Democrats clearly have different views on policy issues. If Democrats are in the majority, there is not likely to be an available coalition for Republican policy ideas. It is in the political stream that the media build support or opposition by the stories they feature, and interest groups try to sway the public on the issue.

The policy stream is the incubator for new ideas. Policy communities are the driving force of the policy stream in Kingdon's model. Composed of specialists in a policy field (e.g., health), these communities cut across branches of government and include individuals outside of government such as consultants, academics, and interest group specialists. Elected or appointed officials may be part of a policy community, but usually the government participants are in staff roles.

People in the policy communities are not as driven by variations in the agenda cycle or election calendar as are elected officials. Some policy communities are more fragmented than others, but there is a tendency for participants to know each other and interact regularly at conferences and other gatherings. Kingdon classifies the health policy community as less fragmented than many others.[3]

Kingdon captures the essence of a process that is sometimes almost random and haphazard with the following:

> One key coupling is that of a policy alternative to something else. Entrepreneurs who advocate their pet alternatives are responsible for this coupling. They keep their proposal ready, waiting for one of two things: a problem that might float by to which they can attach their solution, or a development in the political stream, such as a change of administration that provides a receptive climate for their proposal. . . . A window closes quickly. Opportunities come, but they also pass. If a chance is missed, another one must be awaited.[4]

"Solutions looking for problems" captures the essence of parallel streams rather than finding a logical and linear process. The more common conceptualization of policymaking is that a problem leads to identification and adoption of a solution by a legislative body. Kingdon finds a more complex dynamic. Solutions exist in the policy stream without necessarily being tied to any particular problem. Policy windows open when there is a temporary coupling between a policy and a problem, and an available coalition in the political stream. The open window is a short-term opportunity. If a policy is not enacted, the window may slam shut for a long time. When one examines the history of health reform, as I do in Chapter 7, there is a history of open windows, but failure to take advantage. Often the next opportunity may not come for a decade or more.

Conceptual models are useful when they help. If Kingdon's way of looking at the policy world assists in simplifying what is otherwise a jumble of bits and pieces of information, then it is a useful model.

Interest Groups

> Among the numerous advantages promised by a well-constructed Union, none deserves to be more accurately developed than its tendency to break and control the violence of faction. —*James Madison, Federalist No. 10*

Thus began one of the most well-known of the *Federalist Papers*. Madison's definition of "faction" encompasses what we today call interest groups. Economic, cultural, and social interests differ in any society. Individuals sharing common interests tend to band together to pursue common goals. Madison saw democratic government as balancing the single-minded pursuit of self-interest with a commonly perceived need or goal of a group. A Madisonian view of government sees the balancing of these factional interests as a critical part of the policy process. In contrast, the public interest perspective identifies an abstract "best" policy position as the ideal. From this frame of reference, the public policy process is flawed to the extent that interest groups intrude by pushing for policies intended to favor their interests over others.

How does one define the public interest? Is it the greatest benefit for the most individuals? Does it take into account future generations? Is it a policy without clear winners and losers? This has been a long-standing unresolved debate within political science. Public opinion matters in the political stream. In the construction of legislative majorities, it helps to have public support for a policy idea. In the policy process, advocates for a particular approach often frame their ideas as promoting current and long-term public interest. If a policy proposal can be framed as in the public interest, its chance of success is enhanced. Some policy ideas so clearly benefit one faction over all others that it is easy to portray them as favoring special interests. Generally, it is less clear what the best policy is from the public interest perspective. Partisans of a particular policy idea tend to believe their approach is in the public interest and others are factional preferences.

This little diversion into political philosophy sets the stage for a brief discussion of health care–related interest groups in the policy arena. The health care system is a large and diverse segment of the economy. There is a multitude of factions within it. In some policy discussions, there may be health care interests united against a perceived threat from other interests. But more often, there are sharp divisions within the myriad of its own groups.

Two generations ago, the American Medical Association (AMA) symbolized health care interests. It has been credited with almost single-handedly derailing early attempts to enact national health insurance. Today, the group is just one of hundreds of health care–related interest groups, and probably not the most influential. In general, there are umbrella groups that span broad segments of the health care industry, and other groups that represent a narrower slice of the health care economy. Most groups are propelled by economic interests, but some represent employees rather than economic institutions. There are also public interest groups whose goal is to promote a particular policy perspective rather than an economic interest.

The *National Journal* recently listed major trade associations in its annual review. Over 100 health groups were listed, but only 14 energy, 8 food and beverage, and 12 construction groups.[5] Clearly, there are fragmented interests within the health care system. Several categories with examples of groups are:

- Professional worker associations: AMA, American Nurses Association
- Health insurance: America's Health Insurance Plans, Blue Cross and Blue Shield Association
- Disease advocacy: National Multiple Sclerosis Society, American Cancer Society
- Health products: Pharmaceutical Research and Manufacturers of America, Consumer Healthcare Products Association
- Institutions: American Hospital Association, National Association of Community Health Centers
- Education: Association of American Medical Colleges, Association of Schools of Public Health
- Public interest advocacy: Families USA, National Council on Aging

Depending on the issue, many of these groups may act in concert or they may seek to protect the particular interests of their group in the legislative process. Obviously, some groups are more influential than others. Factors associated with influence include money available for campaign contributions, lobbying skills of association leaders, group membership across congressional districts, and willingness of the membership to actively support positions. A broad group like the well-funded AMA has the ability to argue its position on issues more readily than a narrower group such as the American Association of Neurological Surgeons.

Health care groups make their views known in a variety of ways, including testimony before congressional hearings as well as visits with legislators and, often more important, staff. The professional staff of an interest group seek to stimulate legislation and influence public opinion. They write position papers, pen op-ed pieces in newspapers, and try to generate understanding and favorable coverage in the media for their positions. Any legislation dealing with health care issues is likely to have complex and interrelated impacts among multiple groups. Legislators are interested in knowing how these various groups view the legislative language and impact of pending bills on their group.

Lobby groups are actively engaged in the political process. In the agenda-setting process, lobbyists seek to bring situations that they perceive to be problems to the attention of public officials and the media. They wish to see issues of importance to them on the agenda. The lobbyists may make reports, papers, and studies available to promote policy ideas favorable to their group. On the other hand, they may simply sponsor policy research in areas that seem likely to be beneficial. During a period of legislative activity they not only lobby members of Congress and their staff, but attempt to frame issues in the media, build grassroots support for their position, and work with other groups to build legislative coalitions. In short, interest groups are essential players in the policy process. Do these lobbyists sometimes cause narrow provisions that benefit their group to be inserted into legislation to the detriment of the general public? Certainly, that does occur. But practically speaking, most major bills usually contain provisions seeking to achieve broad policy goals and narrow provisions with a very limited impact.

The fundamental elements of a major policy change are contained in the relevant legislative language. The purpose and impact of these elements are publicly debated and reported in the press. Lobbyists are among the participants shaping these provisions. Criticism of interest groups comes more from the insertion of hidden provisions in any bill than from their role in promoting any major parts of a bill. These small pieces or "earmarks" are perhaps only a sentence in a long bill. They provide special advantages to the members of a particular faction. The earmarks are usually not covered by the media or debated on the floor, and the import of the small pieces may not even be visible to the average person reading a bill. These earmarks continue to be criticized as bad public policy and are a source of popular discontent with Congress.

Congressional Decisionmaking

The policy process represents a series of decisions at every stage. The committee and majority party leaders normally exercise control over the agenda, although strong rank-and-file interest in an issue may propel it forward for consideration. The House and Senate, as well as their committees, render collective decisions. The act of any decision by the Senate Finance Committee is a group decision made in a formal public session and governed by procedural rules. A quorum must be present, and the focus of the decision is a written motion that may be amended. A majority must vote in favor for it to be a formal decision of the group. Collective actions are an aggregation of a set of individual choices. Each member of the Finance Committee who votes for a bill may have made that decision for different reasons. The outcome is no different because each individual rationale was distinctive. Nevertheless, to understand the basis for the decision, we must look at why a member of Congress decides to vote yes or no on bills.

Members of Congress make thousands of voting decisions in a year. Some are in committee, some are on the floor. Sometimes members cannot even explain the critical elements in a decision. Is it as simple as "this is a good bill" or "not a good bill"? Clearly not. Any particular vote is more than that. The decisionmaking process is representative of multiple pressures surrounding the casting of a vote. With so many votes to make in a year and the complexity and volume of major legislation that often is thousands of pages in length, members of Congress look for decision shortcuts. They seek simple decisionmaking on how to cast votes. The following elements are the most prominent guides to their decisionmaking.

Constituent Preference

Legislators are elected to represent their constituents. The simple decisionmaking rule seems to be a vote to reflect the constituents' point of view. Apart from the old dichotomy about being a "delegate" or "trustee," there is the practical problem of the voters' preferences. What if most of those in the electorate are not familiar with an issue? How does one measure citizen preference? Constituent views are frequently cited as the basis for a vote, but probably they are not the major factor in many decisions. Obviously, legislators do have a sense that voting too frequently for bills opposed by constituents could spell defeat in the next election. Perceived future reaction to the current vote is a variation of the "good bill" factor.

Party Advocacy

Nearly all members of Congress belong to a political party. The members of each party in a legislature have a stake in maintaining cohesion.

If they are in the majority, they organize the body, including committees. If they are in the minority, they wish to gain enough new seats to be in the majority. Often legislative party leaders pressure members on key votes to stay with the party position. Today, there is greater party cohesion (most of the members of each party voting the same way) than in the past. In part, this reflects a more common party philosophy on basic issues. Members of Congress frequently vote the way that their party's leaders ask them, which usually agrees with their own views. Voting with the party leadership is an easy decision calculus.

Presidential Request

Presidents have legislative agendas and press members of their party to support those bills. A legislator who considers opposing the president on a major piece of legislation risks losing White House support on other matters of importance. Skillful presidents use the powers and trappings of office to win critical votes. Some of the last necessary votes on the Patient Protection and Affordable Care Act of 2010 were gained by presidential lobbying. A dramatic recent example is President Barack Obama's invitation to Representative Dennis Kucinich of Cleveland to join him on an Air Force One trip to the district. This resulted in gaining his support for the health reform legislation.

Colleague Influence

Lobbyists are not the only ones seeking votes. Colleagues in the state delegation, friends in legislature, or members who are respected by their colleagues for their grasp of an issue are sometimes a critical source of influence. Sometimes these influences cross party lines, but even within a party, quiet cloakroom conversations are often critical in securing votes. The State Children's Health Insurance Program (SCHIP) legislation in 1997 was in part the result of Senators Ted Kennedy and Orrin Hatch working together across party lines to produce a result that brought greater health insurance coverage for children of the working poor.

Lobbyist Pressure

Media accounts sometimes leave the impression that lobbyist pressure is the only important factor. On major votes, it is probably less important than many other elements. Lobbyist advocacy can be critical, on the small and discreet provisions, if the lobby group is a major contributor of money and votes. Lobbyist influence on major issues is more likely to occur in the shaping of the components in the original draft of a bill, and in framing the media and public perceptions of the bill. Lobbyist pressure in major legislation is not just one-on-one advocacy with an individual legislator.

Personal Commitment

There are times when legislators have personal interest in, expertise about, or commitment to an issue. Senator Pete Domenici from New Mexico developed a personal commitment to expansion of insurance benefit coverage for the mentally ill, and he championed parity legislation to achieve this objective. The origins of any legislator's personal commitment may be the result of personal or family experience. The personal commitment also includes the legislator's philosophic views on the policy ideas in the bill. On many legislative items, members of Congress may not have deep convictions about the merits of one policy idea over another. Occasionally, there may be a strong philosophic conviction about what is "best for the country," and this might be the critical decision factor. The abortion issue is an obvious example.

The Bureaucratic System

Large federal agencies, such as the Department of Health and Human Services (HHS), are responsible for several kinds of functions. One is rule making. Statutes passed by Congress rarely contain all the necessary details. The secretary is authorized in a law to write regulations describing how the statute will be applied. Administrators in the relevant agency draft regulations and post them in the *Federal Register* for a comment period. During that time, interest groups as well as any citizen can make written comments. When the comment period is over, the proposed regulations may be amended based on the comments and then are formally issued by the secretary. While the comment and review process is not as directly open to interest group lobbying as the legislative process, it often does offer groups an opportunity to soften or modify provisions in the statute. Once formally promulgated, regulations have the force of law. They can be challenged in court and overturned if found to be inconsistent with the provisions of the law.

Normally, the regulations define how the law is interpreted and applied. These regulations not only define the powers and limits on action by federal officials, but may constrain the freedom of action of states, individuals, corporate entities, and nonprofit organizations. More than the statute itself, these regulations are likely to proscribe and prohibit behavior and action.

Some federal bureaucracies directly provide services to citizens, but most oversee the process of distributing federal funds to states or private entities to carry out the purpose of the statute. In the federal budget process, agencies are authorized to spend money to maintain the organization, such as paying salaries, and to pass funds to others in the form of grants or payment for services rendered to others. The Centers for Medicare and Medicaid Services pay billions of dollars a year to states and health care providers as reimbursement for services rendered to Medicare and Medicaid recipients. The National Institutes of Health distribute federal money for medical research projects to over 300,000 research scientists as well as conduct some in-house research led by 6,000 scientists.

Agencies also collect data on conditions relevant to their mission. These data are used by the agency and others to identify problems and begin the process of placing problems on the decision agenda. Officials sometimes work with relevant interest groups, congressional staff, and others to develop ideas for congressional consideration. This new legislation might be a wholly new policy proposal or a modification of an existing law. If congressional hearings are held on the problem, agency experts are likely to testify on the matter.

The bureaucracy is permanent. Most officials work all or a substantial part of their career for the agency. Top officials are political appointees who come and go with each new administration. These high-level officials depend on the career employees to provide information and perspective. An important function of the top officials is to represent the agency to the White House and other parts of the government. Major legislative priorities for the administration are determined by the president and his staff, but an aggressive agency may try to make the case that their ideas should be high on the action list.

Political scientists point to the importance of implementation in the total policy process.[6] Problems may arise because of flaws in the policy design, lack of commitment on the part of administrative officials, or the sheer complexity of the task. Resources may also be an issue. Congress may not appropriate sufficient funds to fully implement the law, thus ensuring some level of failure. The skill and effort of officials at all levels of the bureaucracy are key to the implementation success.

Bureaucracy in a Federal System

Many federal health programs involve partnerships with the states. Even agencies with a clear responsibility for direct service, such as the Centers for Disease Control and Prevention, must work with state public health departments to fully achieve their mission. In the federal system, states are sovereign entities with independent powers under the US Constitution. State officials protect their autonomy and prerogatives.

Federalism can be viewed as a layer or marble cake.[7] The older conceptualization was one of separation, the layer cake. State and federal governments each have their responsibilities and act largely independent of each other. The current understanding emphasizes the marble cake, especially at the working level; the activities of state and federal bureaucracies are blended together. Boundary problems may exist and political conflicts at the policymaker level may render cooperation more difficult. Interest groups may try to exploit differences in perspective between the states and the federal government. Depending on the issue and the group, most prefer national action to state regulation. A business operating on a national scale would clearly prefer to deal with a single national bureaucracy rather than fifty different states.

Hierarchy and authority are the glue holding large bureaucracies together. Roles and responsibilities are defined by the hierarchical structure. Authority is the willingness of people within the hierarchy to accept the legitimacy of commands from others in certain roles within the bureaucracy.[8] The effectiveness of the bureaucratic structure begins to deteriorate if authority is only grudgingly accepted, or not at all. In a federal structure, the national bureaucracy does not have the same hierarchy or tradition of authority. A state health department is not part of the HHS structure. Officials who write the regulations in Washington may prescribe into law actions that a state government may or may not take. If those rules seem too onerous for many states, the states are likely to enlist the assistance of their congressional delegation for relief. Federal officials in the bureaucracy know they cannot rely exclusively on the authority or issuance of regulations to achieve desired actions by state governments. In the federal structure, negotiation, not demand, becomes the hallmark of these relationships.

Federal HHS officials responsible for the management of health programs probably see themselves at the center of intersecting circles rather than as part of a hierarchy. In making decisions about ongoing implementation, these officials must take into account the wishes of their superiors in the bureaucracy, the problems and issues raised by counterparts in the states, the arguments of relevant interest groups, and the concerns of political actors at the White House and in Congress. It is not enough to just believe a certain decision or action is the correct path—a decision must be effective and generate sufficient support among stakeholders to be sustained, even in the face of possible lawsuit challenges in court.

The Health Care Bureaucracy

Today, "bureaucracy" is a pejorative word. Referring to an organization as a bureaucracy is a harsh criticism. It was not always that way. Max Weber, an early twentieth-century German sociologist, coined the term to describe an ideal organization. He argued that modern societies need effective public and private bureaucracies to implement policy and deliver services in a complex society.[9] Today, HHS is the cabinet department responsible for the management of federal health programs. If it performs its bureaucratic functions well, health programs will be effective and efficient. Even bills that are thousands of pages in length cannot completely address all of the details essential to carry out the new policy.

In the early days of the republic, Congress established a network of hospitals to care for merchant seamen. This Marine Hospital Service, headed by the supervising surgeon, was later to become the Public Health Service. As Congress enacted additional health care–related programs in the late nineteenth and early twentieth centuries, a number of agencies were established. These were consolidated into the Department of Health, Education, and Welfare in 1953, including the Communicable Disease Center, which had been established in 1946. The Communicable Disease Center was later to be renamed the Centers for Disease Control and Prevention. In 1930, the National Institute of Health was created to foster research into basic biological and medical problems. In the late 1940s multiple institutes were created, with each specializing in a disease area, such as mental health or heart disease. The umbrella organization responsible for the individual institutes was named the National Institutes of Health. These bodies eventually became a dominant force in medical research though the extensive funding provided by Congress and administered by the National Institutes of Health.

The name "Department of Health, Education, and Welfare" was changed to "Department of Health and Human Services" with the creation of the Department of Education in 1979 and the transfer of education programs to the new department. The current lineup of major agencies within HHS is:

- Centers for Medicare and Medicaid Services
- Food and Drug Administration
- National Institutes of Health
- Centers for Disease Control and Prevention
- Administration on Aging
- Administration for Children and Families
- Agency for Healthcare Research and Quality
- Agency for Toxic Substances and Disease Registry
- Indian Health Service
- Substance Abuse and Mental Health Services Administration
- Health Resources and Services Administration

Political Decisions and the Health Care System

Americans like to think of the health care system as being completely independent of politics and the political system. But this has never been true. As the total public dollars spent on health care climb above 50% in the next few years, political decisions will continue to fundamentally shape the US health care system. In subsequent chapters, I will examine major public programs, assess the paths that have brought these policies to where they are today, and discuss the critical policy issues likely to dominate future debates. Major health reform legislation, the Patient Protection and Affordable Care Act, was enacted by Congress in 2010. As of this writing, which is before its full implementation, many are calling for repeal. The ultimate outcome will depend in part on what happens in the political stream. Public opinion and shifting congressional majority coalitions will define the future of that law. What is almost certain to happen before the end of this decade is additional political discourse on health policy and some legislative change as the issue returns to the agenda and policy ideas find their way into the political stream. If there is a coupling of ideas and a majority coalition, a window of opportunity may be opened for policy change—large or small.

Notes

1. Walter Oleszek, *Congressional Procedures and the Policy Process,* 6th ed. (Washington, DC: Congressional Quarterly Press, 2004), is an excellent source for details of the congressional process.
2. John Kingdon, *Agendas, Alternatives, and Public Policies,* 2nd ed. (New York: HarperCollins, 1995).
3. Ibid., pp. 194–195.
4. Ibid., p. 173.
5. Bara Vaida, "The Envy List," *National Journal,* April 3, 2010, pp. 32–43.
6. Paul Sabatier and Daniel Mazmanian, "The Implementation of Public Policy: A Framework of Analysis," *Policy Studies Journal* 8, no. 4 (1980): 538–560.
7. Daniel Elazar, *The American Partnership: Intergovernmental Cooperation in the Nineteenth-Century United States* (Chicago: University of Chicago Press, 1962).
8. Chester Barnard, *The Functions of the Executive* (Cambridge: Harvard University Press, 1938), p. 163.
9. Charles Camic, Philip S. Gorski, and David M Trubek, *Max Weber's Economy and Society: A Critical Companion* (Palo Alto, CA: Stanford University Press, 2005).

3

Medicare: National Health Insurance for Older Americans

"President Signs Medicare Bill; Praises Truman," read the front-page headline of the *New York Times* on July 31, 1965. The House had approved the Medicare bill on July 27, 1965, and the Senate followed the next day.[1] In his remarks, President Lyndon B. Johnson said, "No longer will older Americans be denied the healing miracle of modern medicine. No longer will illness crush and destroy the savings they have so carefully put away over a lifetime so that they might enjoy dignity in their later years." With former president Harry S. Truman beside him, Johnson signed the bill, which to this day is the most significant health legislation in US history. The bill was signed in Truman's hometown of Independence, Missouri, to underscore its long legislative history. In 1945, Truman had proposed national health insurance. Twenty years later, this bill signing ceremony marked the end of a long legislative effort.

Over the past forty-five years, Medicare has remained the centerpiece of US health policy, and those present at the signing ceremony would still immediately recognize the basic structure of Medicare.[2] It is a government health insurance program primarily for those aged sixty-five years and older, with 47 million participants in 2010. There are four parts to Medicare:

- Part A: Hospitalization and skilled nursing facility payments
- Part B: Physician and outpatient services

• Part C: Medicare Advantage—to private plans such as a health maintenance organization (HMO)
• Part D: Outpatient prescription drug coverage

Figure 3.1 portrays the distribution of Medicare benefit payments. Hospital and physician payments account for nearly one-half of the total, and Medicare Advantage payments to private insurance plans represent another one-quarter. The Medicare program is funded from general tax revenue (40%), payroll taxes (38%), and beneficiary premiums (12%), which account for over 90% of program revenue.

Older Americans constitute 83% of the total Medicare enrollment (46.6 million), with the balance eligible because of disability. Recipients of Social Security Disability payments as well as those with end-stage renal disease or Lou Gehrig's disease are included in the 7.7 million people with disabilities who are eligible for Medicare.[3] In 2010, Medicare will spend $521 billion, which is 15% of federal government outlays, and 3.6% of gross domestic product (GDP).

A Bill Becomes a Law

Sweeping social legislation does not appear overnight. The roots of Medicare are found in the Social Security Act of 1935. Early drafts included broad health insurance coverage for the entire population, which was removed to avoid opposition from physicians. Subsequent efforts to pass a comprehensive national health insurance failed in the late 1940s, and social insurance advocates in the Truman administration developed a more narrow approach. Oscar Ewing, head of the Federal Security Agency, announced a plan in 1951 to offer sixty days of hospitalization for Social Security beneficiaries.[4] For the rest of the decade, liberals in Congress regularly introduced bills to provide hospitalization insurance as part of Social Security. The Dwight D. Eisenhower administration and congressional Republicans were opposed; they offered instead a plan for federal grants to the states to assist with medical costs for older people.

As the 1960 election approached, Senator John F. Kennedy, the Democratic nominee, made this a major campaign issue. In June 1960, a congressional coalition of Republicans and conservative Democrats passed the Medical Assistance for the Aged Act (Kerr-Mills), which provided federal grants to the states to assist poor older

Figure 3.1
Medicare Benefit Payments by Type of Service (2009)

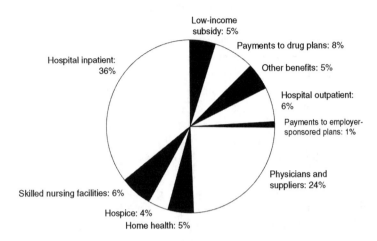

Source: "Medicaid: A Primer" (Washington, DC: Kaiser Commission on Medicaid and the Uninsured, June 2010).

people with medical bills. This set the stage for a philosophical clash in the early 1960s, with the Kennedy administration and liberal allies in Congress on one side advocating a broad social insurance approach for hospitalization insurance for older people (Medicare), and conservative Democrats and Republicans on the other side preferring grants to the states to aid older poor people. President Johnson won a landslide reelection victory in 1964 and carried on his coattails thirty-two new Democrats in the House, providing a 2–1 majority for the first time in thirty years. Passage of Medicare had been a major campaign issue for Johnson. With the expanded majority in the House, the ratio of Democrats to Republicans on the Ways and Means Committee increased. Medicare passage appeared certain.

In April 1965 during hearings before the Ways and Means Committee, Chairman Wilbur Mills shocked those testifying for the administration by proposing a bill to create a two-part Medicare system. There had been an apparent "Road to Damascus" conversion for Mills, who not only had switched from opposition to support for Medicare, but also had proposed an expansion of the bill to include physician fees. For decades, Mills had been given sole credit for the maneuver. Recently released White House telephone tapes reveal conversations between President Johnson and Mills a year earlier in which they negotiate this deal, with the president agreeing to let Mills take the credit.[5]

The large final vote margin in the House and Senate in favor of the expanded Medicare bill at the end of July 1965 obscured the legislative trench battles in the Senate Finance Committee and the final conference committee compromises. When President Johnson traveled to Independence, Missouri, a few days later for the bill signing ceremony, he brought a signup card that allowed President Truman to be the first Medicare recipient. The bill that he signed in the Truman Library created a health insurance program for people aged sixty-five years and older, which included both hospitalization and physician fee coverage. The two were financed by different revenue streams, with the physician coverage (Part B) technically voluntary, although few would fail to join. Almost unnoticed in the initial press coverage was the section (later called Medicaid) that provides comprehensive coverage for the welfare poor.

Implementation: 1966–1969

President Johnson had worked tirelessly for the passage of Medicare. After the early August 1965 signing, he told his aides he wanted any eligible beneficiary needing service to be welcomed at a local hospital on July 1, 1966, Medicare's first day in operation. Thus, a massive new federal health insurance program needed to be put in place in less than a year, and this was before the age of modern computer systems.

With any comprehensive statute, there are many details covered in the language of the bill, especially those subject to dispute during the legislative process. Other details are delegated for administrative rule making because of complexity, the absence of attention in the legislative process, or an inability to resolve conflicting views on technical issues. The politics of implementation can be just as intense as in the legislative process, but this phase is usually out of the public spotlight. Interest groups who are unhappy with a provision of a law may try to modify the impact during the drafting of administrative rules and procedures. In her comprehensive study of the Medicare implementation process, Judith Feder identifies two possible strategies for addressing implementation issues. With a balancing strategy, administrators seek to minimize political conflict by accommodating important interests. Alternatively, a cost-effectiveness strategy attempts to maximize value per dollar spent.[6]

The major administrative issues were hospital quality, reimbursement principles for hospitals and physicians, payment for capital investment, cost containment, and hospital desegregation in the South. Intrinsic to all of these issues was the question of the role of government and how aggressive the Social Security Administration (SSA) would be in their resolution, especially if a cost-effectiveness approach was adopted. Some physician groups were promoting a boycott of the program, and it seemed possible that pent-up demand would result in a throng of patients arriving at hospitals across the country on the first of July. The SSA officials, not health administrators, were part of a social insurance bureaucracy. It is not surprising that they choose to employ a balancing strategy.[7]

In the legislative process the American Medical Association was implacably opposed to public health insurance, but the hospitals represented by the American Hospital Association (AHA) and the closely tethered Blue Cross saw the potential benefit from an infusion of substantial new resources. Beginning in 1962, they were prepared to negotiate support for Medicare in exchange for a favorable reimbursement system. Cost-based reimbursement was becoming more common, and Medicare supporters included general statutory language establishing this approach to hospital payment in exchange for AHA support. The Kennedy administration also agreed to the use of insurance companies as fiscal intermediaries between the government and hospitals on payment questions. It was understood that Blue Cross would be the principal vehicle for payments.[8] When physician payments were included in the program, reasonable charges based on "customary" and "prevailing" fees were the standard in the statute.[9]

Medicare implementation occurred at the zenith of the civil rights movement, as the system of racial segregation in the South was about to crumble. Medicare administrators were committed to integration, but chose to work behind the scenes to achieve this goal rather than publicly confront recalcitrant hospitals.[10]

In 1969, Richard M. Nixon succeeded Johnson as president. Medicare's implementation period ended, and a period of political consensus supporting the program had begun that would last for more than two decades. The program administrators in the SSA had utilized a balancing strategy to successfully launch Medicare in a brief time, and ensured broad provider support by responding to major interest group concerns. The payment system was generous with Blue Cross, the fiscal intermediary, to avoid direct conflict; hospitals were able to borrow money for quality upgrades with the confidence that Medicare payments supported capital expenditures. Medicare had, in three years, been successful in its implementation. Despite the partisan shift in the White House, there was no move to repeal or diminish Medicare. The balancing strategy had successfully built broad support for Medicare.

Cost Trumps Expansion: 1970–1977

Expansion of Medicare beneficiaries to include those on disability began to be considered in Congress in 1967. People with disabilities had been covered under Social Security since 1956. The provision to extend Medicare coverage to them was included in the Social Security Amendments of 1972.[11] A two-year waiting period after the disability determination was included to make certain the status was permanent, and allow workplace coverage to expire first.[12] At the same time, Medicare coverage was also extended to patients with end-stage renal disease. Thus two small, but expensive, subsets of the non-older population were added to Medicare.

The original Medicare benefit structure tended to resemble a good Blue Cross–Blue Shield policy circa 1965. Private group insurance had improved coverage by the 1970s. Medicare recipients were subject to larger cost sharing than a typical working person. This provided an opportunity for private insurance companies to develop Medigap policies to supplement basic Medicare benefits. The growth of this supplementary coverage diminished the prospects for expansion of coverage within Medicare.[13]

Beginning in 1969, the most significant development in Medicare policy was the emergence of cost as the critical policy issue. Costs, especially for hospital care, led to the 1969 characterization of Medicare by Russell Long, Senate Finance Committee chairman, as a "run-away program."[14] In 1970, a book on budget priorities published by the Brookings Institution pointed to a 6% rise in health care costs per year and a rise in hospital charges of twice that rate as leading to a rapid cost escalation of government medical care programs.[15] Fiscal watchdogs in Congress and budget scholars were by then raising warning flags about Medicare expenditure trends.

Payment Reform: 1978–1991

The rate of increase, especially for hospital costs, was growing faster than health costs in general as well as other segments of the economy. During the 1976 presidential campaign, Jimmy Carter had promised to pursue the elusive national health insurance goal sought by liberal Democrats. Once in office, he found it essential to pursue cost control as a prerequisite for universal coverage. Medicare costs, especially for hospitalization, had to be a key part of restraining the growth of health care spending. Section 222 of the Social Security Amendments of 1972 differentiated between "routine" and "ancillary" Medicare hospital costs, and determined routine costs could be limited because they were not related to the severity of patient illness. Beginning in 1975, this led to some restraints on hospital costs.[16]

Twice during the Carter administration (in 1977 and 1979), Congress considered legislation to create a universal hospital payment system designed to limit the growth of hospital expenditures.[17] Neither of Carter's proposals was enacted, but the cost problem persisted into the first years of the Ronald Reagan administration. Former senator Richard Schweiker served as secretary of Health and Human Services (HHS) under conservative president Reagan. Hospital and Medicare costs were perceived as out of control, and Schweiker was responsible for finding a solution. He concluded that cost-based reimbursement must end. The first step was the inclusion of language in the Tax Equity and Fiscal Responsibility Act of 1982 (TEFRA), in which hospital payment limits were extended to include ancillary as well as routine costs, and a cap was placed on average payment per case.[18] The statute also instructed the secretary to propose to Congress a Medicare prospective payment system (PPS) by the end of the year.

Schweiker's department was able to quickly propose such a system because, since 1980, an experiment with this type of reimbursement reform had been ongoing in New Jersey. With some modifications, he proposed a New Jersey–type PPS using Diagnostic Related Groups. Under the plan, hospitals were to be paid a fixed amount for each admission as adjusted for the patient diagnosis and the characteristics of the hospital.[19]

Early in 1983, the largest item on the congressional agenda was an evolving compromise to rescue the Social Security program from an impending bankruptcy of the trust fund. At the suggestion of Ways and Means Committee chairman Dan Rostenkowski, the Medicare PPS plan was added to the Social Security rescue bill as a separate provision.[20] Unlike a few years earlier with the Carter cost-containment bill, the hospital industry sought limited concessions on details, but did not actively oppose the proposal. In part this reflected the pending draconian TEFRA reimbursement limits and a growing sense in Congress of the need for permanent change in the way hospitals were paid under Medicare. The PPS approach seemed better than likely alternatives, and clearly the cost-based reimbursement system used for almost two decades was dead. In late April 1983, the Social Security reform bill, including the Medicare hospital payment provision, was signed into law by President Reagan. Implementation was to begin in October and be phased in over a three-year period. A Prospective Payment Assessment Commission was established to review the payment system and make annual reports to Congress on modifications.[21]

Cost Containment for Physician Fees

Medicare physician reimbursement payments were not affected by the PPS legislation. The definitions were modified over the two decades since Medicare had been implemented. The payments were based on usual, customary, and prevailing charges. Physicians determined their own fees as long as they were typical of physician fees in the community. Medicare paid on the basis of the charges. After the enactment of the PPS legislation for hospitals, Congress addressed the issue of physician fees.

Congress first froze payment rates and then limited the amount of annual increase in fees. A Physician Payment Review Commission (PPRC) was created to recommend a new system for paying physicians. What it recommended was a sharp departure from existing practice. Based on the academic research of economist William Hsiao, the proposed new approach to Medicare physician payment was a fee schedule based on a resource-based relative value scale (RBRVS). The starting point for the fee determination was an estimate of the amount of work required to perform a given service and the related practice costs.[22] The PPRC recommended this new fee schedule, a volume control to discourage an increase in procedures, and restrictions on charging beneficiaries additional costs above standard copayments. Congress enacted the new fee schedule approach as part of the Omnibus Reconciliation Act of 1989, and it was phased in over the following decade.[23]

Thus, by the end of the 1980s, Congress had addressed the explosive growth of Medicare expenditures by ending the retrospective payment system established at the beginning of the program and replacing it with a system of administratively controlled prices for most hospitals and physicians. In the ensuing three decades, there have been annual updates to the payment formulas as well as inclusion of those not originally part of the new system.

The End of the Era of Consensus: 1992–2000

William J. Clinton was elected president at a time when health reform again appeared on the national agenda. During the 1980s, health policy had been dominated by congressional efforts to restructure Medicare reimbursement policy by moving away from the original cost-based system to an administered pricing system. This had succeeded in slowing the growth rate of Medicare costs, but the balance in the Part A Hospital Insurance Trust Fund continued to decline, and the 1993 report issued shortly after Clinton took office projected a single-digit lifetime (six years) until exhaustion in 1999.[24] Obviously, payment reform had not been sufficient to address long-term Medicare finances.

As Jonathan Oberlander has chronicled, from shortly after its inception to the middle of the 1990s, Medicare experienced a three-decade run of bipartisan consensus. There was broad public support and a philosophical agreement about Medicare. Policy changes tended to be supported by a bipartisan majority.[25] In retrospect, the last such effort was the Catastrophic Coverage Act of 1988. Otis Bowen, former governor of Indiana, became secretary of health and human services in 1985, and immediately began to lobby within the Reagan administration for an expansion of the Medicare benefit structure to include catastrophic coverage, which was not included in the original legislation. For many, supplemental insurance provided this protection. But it was expensive for near-poor older people.

By the end of Clinton's first term in office, his health reform proposal had failed in Congress, and the depletion of the Medicare Part A Trust Fund was projected in less than a decade. Republicans had gained control of Congress in 1994 by staking out a conservative reform agenda. Conservative-oriented think tanks and policy analysts had been arguing for more than a decade that long-range reform of Medicare could not be accomplished by tinkering with the revenue stream or payment mechanism. They sought radical reform by shifting to a more market-oriented philosophy.[26]

Led by Speaker Newt Gingrich in the House, the new conservative Republican majority in Congress sought to change the fundamental nature of Medicare. The 1995 Report of the Board of Trustees of the Federal Hospital Insurance Fund (Trustees Report) projected depletion of the Medicare Part A Trust Fund in seven years. This was the impetus for moving forward the conservative policy ideas for Medicare reform. The ensuing legislation incorporated large spending cuts, a future cap on government funding of the fee-for-service (FFS) segment, and expanding use of private insurance.[27] Use of the term was avoided, but the concept was to transform Medicare from its social insurance base to a voucher program. The legislation passed, but was vetoed by President Clinton.

Two years later, some of the ideas reappeared in the Balanced Budget Act of 1997 (BBA-97) and were enacted into law with bipartisan support. The BBA-97 instituted significant savings by reducing hospital payments and restructuring reimbursement for rehabilitation hospitals, skilled nursing facilities, home health agencies, and outpatient services.[28] A new name, Medicare+Choice, signaled an expanded array of alternatives to traditional FFS Medicare. A sustainable growth rate (SGR) formula for physician fees sought to impose a global limit on the growth rate of fees. This provided the mechanism, but not the will, to actually limit the growth of fees.

As the Clinton administration ended, the partisan division over the future of Medicare had grown into a chasm. Both market-oriented reformers and President Clinton had begun to recognize that the absence of systematic prescription drug coverage was a glaring benefit weakness because drug costs were rapidly rising. A Medicare prescription drug benefit would be the next battle as George W. Bush took office in 2001.

Prescription Drugs Take Center Stage: 2001–2008

A final report of the Commission on the Future of Medicare was not adopted by the necessary supermajority, but in the process of attempting to fashion an agreement, a prescription drug benefit became part of the discussion. In his 1999 State of the Union message, President Clinton proposed a new Medicare drug benefit with financing from the emerging budget surplus. In the 2000 election campaign, candidates George W. Bush and Al Gore both proposed expanding Medicare benefits to include prescription drugs. Medicare benefit expansion had been only a minor element in Clinton's first-term major health reform plan. In the several years that followed, the long ideological consensus on Medicare had been shattered and Clinton's proposal signaled a renewed policy debate. A prescription drug benefit was the center of attention, but the fundamental engagement was a philosophical contest over the future of Medicare.

In the 1990s prescription drugs had become more important as a therapeutic tool, but they also grew more expensive. The average number of prescriptions used by Medicare recipients as well as their costs rose rapidly in the late 1990s. Medicare HMOs were less likely to offer free drug benefits, employment-based retirement health benefits were declining, and Medigap policies with drug coverage were becoming expensive.[29] Drug costs were an escalating problem for beneficiaries. The problem was placed on the political agenda by both Democrats and Republicans.

For Republicans who occupied the White House and held a congressional majority after the 2000 election, a prescription drug benefit was the carrot to be used for market-based Medicare reform. For Democrats, it was a more tactical than strategic question. How could this major Medicare benefit be extended without an excessive cost increase? A drug benefit had been considered but not pursued within a year after Medicare began. The 1988 Catastrophic Coverage Act included it under Part B; it was repealed the following year.

Beginning with the 1999 Clinton proposal, there was a steady stream of drug benefit proposals from political leaders and a wide range of policy studies on the subject. The culmination of these efforts was the passage of the Medicare Modernization Act of 2003. Along the way, various policy options were scrutinized and debated. The George W. Bush administration and some congressional Republicans wanted the benefit to be part of a broader transformation of Medicare into a system of competing private insurance plans, but a congressional majority did not exist to support this idea. This left two broad strategic options: adding a drug benefit to Part B or creating a stand-alone drug plan with private insurance companies. The latter emerged as the preferred approach.

The Congressional Budget Office (CBO) estimated total drug spending by Medicare beneficiaries in 2002 to be $87 billion, of which 40% was out-of-pocket. One-quarter of all beneficiaries had no drug coverage. Others were covered in part by Medicaid, Medigap, an HMO, or employment-based retirement coverage. Less than 20% of Medicare beneficiaries spent more than $5,000, but this constituted one-half of the total spending.[30] This concentration of spending symbolized the formidable policy design challenge in constructing a new Medicare benefit. The CBO projected total prescription drug spending to be $128 billion by 2005. The Bush administration budgeted $350 billion to $400 billion for Medicare prescription drugs over a decade. Without significant new money, it was impossible to fully cover Medicare drug costs. The CBO summarized the policy design choices as:

- How large should the deductible be? (amount to be spent before coverage begins)
- What should the cost sharing be? (share of the cost paid by beneficiary)
- Should there be a benefit cap? (amount beyond which the enrollee must pay full cost)
- What should be the stop-loss? (level beyond which beneficiary pays nothing)[31]

The stand-alone proposals presumed a premium for all with a subsidy for low-income individuals, voluntary participation but no ability to opt in and out, and administration by pharmacy benefit managers. Should the ultimate risk be borne by the government or the insurance plans? The entity at risk has the greatest incentive to pursue cost-containment strategies.

In June 2003, the Senate Finance Committee developed a bipartisan agreement for a drug plan that included two options. The first was to join a new preferred provider organization with drug benefits and other services, or to receive drug benefits from private insurance plans if the beneficiary opted to stay in FFS Medicare. The price tag was $400 billion over ten years. The two committees with jurisdiction in the House announced an agreement on a drug plan that included subsidies for low-income beneficiaries as well as a differential catastrophic limit based on income. In June, both the House and Senate passed their versions of a drug bill.

As the ultimate plan emerged in the legislative process, the "doughnut hole" became a strange policy device. The compromise was to set a copayment at 25% after the deductible of $250, until total drug expenses reach $2,250. Then, the beneficiary is fully responsible for payments until $5,100 at which point 95% is covered. Figure 3.2 shows the doughnut hole, which is the $3,610 in between that is wholly the responsibility of the beneficiary.[32] The average monthly premium in 2010 was about $40, but premiums vary across plans.

There are 1,600 drug plans across the country, with forty to fifty different plans in each state from which beneficiaries select one. The monthly premium is set to cover 25% of the cost of standard drug coverage. The balance is paid by Medicare from general revenue funds.

The close votes and internal disputes among Republicans within the House and Senate, as well as significant differences between the House and Senate versions, were in some ways a preview of the more comprehensive health reform bill taken up by Congress in 2010. Unless there is a major change in the composition of Congress in the decade ahead, future Medicare policy decisions are likely to offer similar struggles.[33]

Figure 3.2
The Medicare Prescription Drug Benefit (2010)

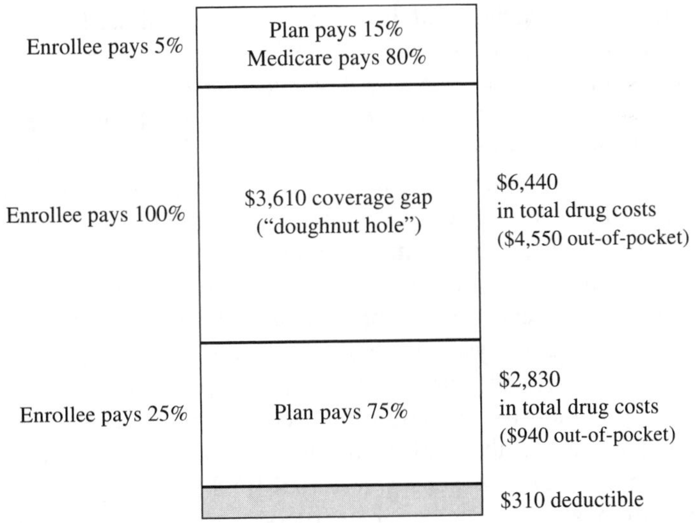

Source: "Medicare: A Primer" (Washington, DC: Kaiser Commission on Medicaid and the Uninsured, June 2010).

Core Policy Issues

By the middle of this decade, Medicare will be fifty years old. Prescription drug coverage added a significant new benefit, and the 2010 health reform bill initiated a path to reducing the doughnut hole as well as improving coverage of preventive services.[34] In the first part of this chapter, I traced the development of Medicare over its first four decades. In the next part, I examine several key policy issues looming on the horizon.

The perception of a problem can propel an issue onto the decision agenda, but only when the problem grabs the attention of voters and political leaders. In the last part, I showed how the absence of prescription drug coverage was perceived as a problem shortly after the enactment of Medicare in 1965, yet forty years passed before there was a legislative fix. There is no certainty that the five issues I describe below will move to center stage in the next few years, but at least some are likely to do so.

Social Insurance Versus Private Insurance

Ideas matter. In the decade before the enactment of Medicare, the philosophical debate over health insurance for older people focused on a welfare versus social insurance approach. At the time, few thought private insurance companies were interested or able to provide comprehensive health insurance for retired people. Those who favored a welfare approach argued that the government had an obligation only to those too poor to afford health insurance. Social insurance proponents prevailed in Congress, and Medicare as social insurance was enacted into law. This meant risk was to be spread over the entire older population, with all entitled to the same benefits and program eligibility based on a history of contributions while in the workforce. With social insurance, the government assumes the ultimate risk for a population when the private insurance system cannot do so for all at an affordable rate. Since older people and people with disabilities have lower incomes and potentially higher medical costs, their coverage has been earned by past participation in the workforce. Medicare premiums cover only a part of their medical expenses.[35] Actual funding in a given year is derived from taxes paid by current workers. The Medicare social insurance system is best characterized as an intergenerational transfer from workers to retirees. For the first three decades, there was a consensus among policymakers around the social insurance principle as the basis for Medicare. Then, in the mid-1990s, the common philosophical approach was lost as an alternative conceptualization emerged. This new approach rejected the premise that private insurance companies were unable or uninterested in providing the financial structure for Medicare. Conservative policy analysts and political leaders came to believe and advocate a major shift in the basic way of thinking about Medicare. Often citing as an example the success of the Federal Employees Health Benefit Program (FEHBP), the system for providing federal workers private health insurance, an alternative organizational approach emerged as a policy idea.[36]

Called "privatization" by its opponents and "premium support" by its supporters, this redesign of the Medicare system is based on the managed competition ideas advanced by economist Alan Enthoven.[37] Most current recipients participate in FFS or traditional Medicare. Providers deliver health care services and bill Medicare for payment, which the government pays based on established fee systems. Since the 1970s, there has been an HMO option within Medicare. Private health insurance plans or integrated delivery systems guarantee beneficiaries a package of services equal to or better than FFS Medicare and receive a lump-sum payment from Medicare. The private plan must deliver the promised services for that amount. Medicare does not make any additional payments during the year.

BBA-97 significantly expanded private plan choices. In the following decade, between 13% and 23% of Medicare beneficiaries were enrolled annually in private plans. In 2009, nearly one-quarter were in Medicare Advantage, the current name for the system of private insurance plans. The annual payments are set by a legislatively established formula that, after 2003, sought to encourage use of private plans by enhancing payments. In 2009, these Medicare Advantage plan payments averaged 114% of FFS costs. The 2010 reform law will set in motion changes over time in the payment formula intended to bring Medicare Advantage payments in line with average FFS costs. This may reduce the share of recipients in those plans.[38]

There are a number of critical design elements in a premium support system. In this proposal, Congress would set a common dollar figure that is made available to both FFS Medicare and private plans. The dollar amount would be determined by bids submitted by the participating plans. Recipients could choose among plans or stay in the FFS system. The benefit package could be standard, or plans might be allowed to vary the covered benefits.[39] This is similar to the current system, with a critical difference. Depending on design details, the Medicare Advantage plans might engage in selective recruitment of healthier participants. The FFS option would retain a disproportionate number of higher-cost beneficiaries, and have difficulty maintaining the current level of benefits at the average bid price.[40] Premium support advocates maintain that, in the long run, a system of private plans would be more innovative and flexible in their benefit structure and better able to maintain a lower rate of expenditure growth.

This debate is nearly two decades old. Arguments are often made in terms of technical details, but the fundamental issue is the role of government. Today, the Medicare organizing idea remains the same as it was forty-five years ago at adoption. Medicare is a social insurance program. All beneficiaries receive the same services regardless of income. High-income recipients, the top 5%, pay an additional income-related premium, but this is only a small deviation from the social insurance idea because services are the same. Poor recipients are also eligible for Medicaid. One in five beneficiaries are thus dual eligibles whose premiums and cost sharing are paid for by Medicaid. The higher premium for the wealthy and income-related assistance for the poor have introduced welfare approach elements.

Those who wish to move Medicare toward a premium support system of private plans are convinced government's role should be limited to collecting revenue and organizing the bidding system, with private plans managing benefit structure and payment systems. The Medicare Advantage system used by one in four beneficiaries introduces an extensive system of private health plans as an integral part of Medicare. Social insurance advocates still believe the government is in the best position to balance service access and costs in a fair way. They continue to be committed to Medicare as social insurance. This debate about the fundamental idea of Medicare is likely to continue whenever Medicare policy is on the decision agenda in the decade ahead. A shift in the organizing idea could lead to major changes in the structure and operation of Medicare.

Long-term Fiscal Viability

In the beginning there were a few voices of concern about the long-term fiscal viability of Medicare, but within a couple of years alarm bells began to sound in several places around Washington, DC. The 1967 report of the Medicare trustees projected exhaustion of the Part A Trust Fund in 1991, a quarter-century away. Two years later the trustees revised their outlook to project exhaustion in 1976, less than a decade ahead. Table 3.1 shows the subsequent annual reports, which resemble a roller coaster as insolvency projections vary from a high of twenty-four years to a low of six years. The pattern is cyclical rather than linear, and reflects both program adjustments and changes in the economy.

The Part A Hospital Insurance Trust Fund revenues are primarily derived from the payroll tax, 1.45% paid by both employees and employers for a total of 2.9%. Since 1994, there has been no upper limit on the wage base for the Medicare payroll tax. When revenue exceeds expenditures in a given year, the balance is retained in the Part A Trust Fund. The exhaustion point is the year that the trustees project expenditures will exceed the balance, which is the combination of annual revenue and accumulated surplus, not the complete depletion of the trust fund.

The Part B Supplementary Medical Insurance Trust Fund is organized differently. Its primary source of revenue is the federal general fund, which accounted for almost 80% of dollars spent from the Part B Trust Fund in 2009. The balance is from Part B and Part D premiums, which are adjusted each year to reflect growth in costs.

Table 3.1   Part A: The Hospital Insurance Trust Fund (1970–2010)

Report Year	Project Insolvent	Years Remaining
1970	1972	2
1980	1994	14
1990	2003	13
1991	2005	14
1993	1999	6
1995	2001	6
1997	2001	4
1999	2015	16
2001	2029	28
2003	2026	23
2005	2020	15
2007	2019	12
2009	2017	8
2010	2029	20

Source: Annual Report of the Board of Trustees of the Federal Hospital Insurance Trust Fund (Washington, DC: US Government Printing Office, 1966–2010).

Thus, it is a misnomer to refer to the exhaustion of the Part B Trust Fund. Sufficient resources are transferred from federal general operating funds to meet expenditures in a given year.

The trust funds are, in the words of Eric Patashnik, commitment devices: "Trust funds embody attempts to precommit the government to a particular policy direction, typically for long or indefinite periods of time."[41] He argues that Ways and Means Committee chairman Mills in 1966 constructed the trust funds to be both a commitment to financing Medicare and a device to restrain spending.[42] The trust funds separate Medicare from the routine appropriations process, but the potential for exhaustion of the Hospital Insurance Trust Fund forces Congress and the public to constantly be concerned about financial trends.

Medicare's long-term financial crisis is not the danger of exhaustion of the Part A Trust Fund, but the relentless escalation of costs in the health system. Current Medicare spending represents about 20% of total health spending and 3.5% of GDP. Over the next twenty years, the share of GDP is expected to nearly double. For decades, private and public spending per beneficiary has been similar and health expenditures have increased faster than general economic growth. Demographic changes associated with the aging of the population will shift more of the total health expenditures to Medicare as the share of the population aged sixty-five years and older increases in the decades ahead. Because Medicare spending is inevitably linked to the price of services in the health market, its rate of increase is coupled to the rest of the system.

There are two scenarios found in public discussion about the future of Medicare. The loudest voice warns of future Medicare bankruptcy. This view of the future projects recent price escalations at historic growth rates and adds the demographic dimension to find unsustainable demands on federal funds to maintain Medicare. In this scenario, the options are to significantly increase revenues or reduce the entitlement benefits. Major program change is advocated as the solution, and the sooner the better.[43]

An alternative scenario is offered by political scientist Joseph White. He argues that the history of Medicare trust fund prognosis resembles a roller-coaster ride because, when the trustees begin to project trust fund exhaustion in single digits, policymakers fashion incremental adjustments in provider payments or benefits, or both, to extend the fund. White says that "control of Medicare costs twenty or thirty years from now is not a rational goal that actual human beings could pursue with any semblance of rational calculation."[44] He contends that the seventy-five-year long-range projections required of the Medicare trustees are the equivalent of trying to anticipate military needs that far into the future.[45] For example, that would have meant estimating the requirements for World War II immediately after the Civil War.

White's incremental perspective is an apt description of the way adjustments have been made over the years to sustain Medicare. Political leaders tend to be more comfortable with a series of short-term incremental policy steps rather than major changes in a popular program. Those who fear fiscal Armageddon from an aging population and escalating health care system costs per person envision a time when Medicare crowds out other essential national spending priorities.

Three institutions are engaged in official projections and assessments concerning the fiscal future of Medicare: the Medicare trustees/Office of the Centers for Medicare and Medicaid Services Actuary, the Congressional Budget Office, and the Medicare Payment Advisory Commission (MedPac). If we accept White's skepticism about the value of projections for more than ten years into the future, we still find these independent agencies each offering warnings about the rate of growth of Medicare spending over the next decade. According to the CBO, total Medicare spending will rise over the next decade, from $499 billion in 2009 to $962 billion in 2019. This represents an annual rate of growth of about 7%, and as a percentage of GDP it is anticipated to increase from the present 3.5% to 4.6% in a decade. Medicare currently represents 15% of the total federal budget and that will increase to 20% by 2019. The net spending numbers are slightly lower when Part B and D premiums are subtracted, but the fundamental problem is clear and generally not a point of dispute.[46]

The 2010 report of the Medicare trustees projects the Part A Trust Fund to remain solvent until 2030, which is a twelve-year improvement over the 2009 projection. The year's difference is a reflection of the health reform legislation passed by Congress in 2010.[47] However, the Office of the Actuary published a report that took issue with the projection. It argued that the existing law payment updates were unrealistically low, and likely to be modified by Congress.[48] The dispute primarily involves technical questions about methodology. It illustrates the broad truth that Medicare reimbursement in the future is unlikely to trend sharply lower than private insurance plans because physicians and hospitals are part of the same health care system. If the cost trajectory is not lowered for the rest of the system, it is unlikely to be lowered for Medicare alone.

Part of the increase can be attributed to the aging of the population as the baby boom generation begins to reach the age of sixty-five, but this will not be the major contributory factor over the next decade. The rate of growth of the cost of medical services is the principal reason for the increase. Without some change in public policy, Medicare will consume a greater share of both federal general revenue and national wealth over the next decade. The following decade will be worse if no action is taken in the next few years. The 2010 health reform legislation contained provisions intended to reduce the rate of growth of Medicare spending by reducing payments to Medicare Advantage plans, reducing the annual updates for provider payments, and fostering delivery system reforms. The law also established a new Independent Payment Advisory Board to recommend policies to reduce Medicare spending.

The solvency status of the Part A Trust Fund does remain the "canary in the mine" for Medicare finances, as perhaps Wilbur Mills intended. If the economy grows over the next several years as it did in the late 1990s, the additional payroll tax revenue will improve the status of the Part A Trust Fund. If this is accompanied by some slowing of the rate of growth of provider payments, then the Medicare trustees will project depletion of the fund into the next decade. The pressure for major reform will decline in the short run. However, a prediction that, sometime in the next ten years, Medicare finance issues will return to the decision agenda is a good bet. When that happens the debate between the radical reformers and the incrementalists will again be joined. The next subsection, on cost control measures, features the issues at the heart of this policy debate.

Cost-control Strategies

Whether the problems with Medicare financing that stem from the growth of expenditures is seen as a Part A Trust Fund problem or a budget problem, at some point in the next few years there will be a need to address it. Gail Wilensky, an economist and former head of Medicare as administrator of the Health Care Financing Administration, suggests strategic cost control approaches for addressing Medicare's long-term financial prospects. They include constraining provider payments, reducing benefits by charging beneficiaries more in copayments or increasing the age of eligibility, enhancing program funding by tax increases, and increasing efficiency in the delivery of services by payment incentives or delivery system reform.[49]

In the 1980s, the changes in payment policies for hospitals and physicians created a system of administratively determined prices. This did succeed in slowing the rate of growth of costs, especially for hospitals. Eventually, other services were also moved from cost-based to prospective payment systems. With the PPS for hospitals and the resource-based relative value scale for physician fees and other similar systems, the MedPac and Congress have the technical ability to restrict the rate of growth of payments to providers. However, it is more difficult to control the volume of services, which can be used to game the system for providers to enhance revenue.

The current practice is for MedPac to recommend to Congress the annual increment adjustment for the hospital and physician payments. Over time, the tightening of this adjustment could reduce the rate of growth. But the increment is ultimately determined by Congress, and providers use their legitimate right to lobby Congress to increase the annual adjustment. The common argument is that Medicare fees should be equal to those of private insurance plans or some Medicare beneficiaries will not be able to find physicians willing to treat them. Hospitals already complain that Medicare payments do not fully cover costs, and it is alleged that cost shifting occurs with private insurance payments for the non-older patients subsidizing Medicare patients because payments are below cost. A recent MedPac study refutes this argument by asserting that hospitals with a strong market position have higher costs per unit of service and hospitals with less market share constrain costs, thus generating profits on Medicare patients.[50]

As part of the Balanced Budget Act of 1997, Congress introduced the sustainable growth rate concept as part of the mechanism for controlling the rate of growth of physician fees. The idea is to set an aggregate target for total Medicare spending on physician fees in a given year. If that target is exceeded, the difference is subtracted from next year's total. This was perceived as a deterrent. In fact from 2002 forward, the cumulative differential has been huge and, if applied, would result in substantial fee reductions. But each year, Congress has fixed the problem with short-term extensions. The latest was during the lame duck session after the 2010 midterm elections. The current system is now widely perceived as badly flawed, but expensive to fix on a permanent basis.[51]

The experience of the past three decades, since the enactment of the prospective payment system for hospitals and fee schedule for physicians, points to the limits of constraining provider payments as the sole cost control strategy. Medicare is the largest purchaser of health care services, but ultimately Congress determines the rate of payment increase. Hospitals, physicians, and other providers have continued to successfully make the case to elected officials that Medicare payments should be equivalent to those of private insurance companies to make certain recipients have equal access to health care services. The prospective payment system provides the technical tools to significantly constrain the rate of expenditure growth by limiting the reimbursement growth, but it is not clear that Medicare by itself will be able to achieve this if such restraints do not also include payments from private insurance companies. Restraining growth of Medicare provider payments appears to be a necessary, but not sufficient, approach to restraining cost increases.

Cost-control Options

From a budget perspective, the federal government could manage its costs by forcing beneficiaries to pay more in the form of copayments or premiums. Some have suggested this approach, but it seems unlikely to be enacted by Congress. Half of all Medicare recipients have incomes below 200% of poverty. Higher-income beneficiaries are already paying a higher Part B premium. It does not seem feasible to attempt to solve Medicare's financial problems by charging beneficiaries more. Medicare now pays on average only about half of the total medical expenses of beneficiaries. Other third parties pay a quarter and beneficiaries themselves a quarter. Significant increases in beneficiary copayments do not seem politically feasible.

Part of the 1982 rescue legislation for Social Security was the gradual increase in the age of eligibility for full benefits to age sixty-seven. Some have suggested a similar approach for Medicare. This action would take at least two decades or more to fully implement, and the cost savings may not be worth the political cost of seeking to put such a policy into place. Medicare costs are not evenly distributed across beneficiaries. In a given year 10% of beneficiaries generate 58% of the total spending, for a 2006 average of $48,210 per person. The average cost for the remaining 90% was $3,910. Someone who is sixty-five years old is much more likely to be in the latter category.

One of the fastest-growing categories of the uninsured has been the pre-Medicare group of those between the ages of fifty-five and sixty-five years. Layoffs and forced early retirements have contributed to this decline in workplace insurance within this age group. With the 2010 health reform law many of these individuals will be forced to seek private insurance, perhaps with a federal subsidy to bridge the gap until they are eligible for Medicare at the age of sixty-five. The net savings for the federal government may be relatively small.

Major tax increases or diversions of federal funds from areas such as national defense are also unlikely. The CBO estimates that a 10% increase in the payroll tax rate would raise almost $600 billion total over the next decade.[52] For a worker making $60,000, this represents a tax increase of about $300. In the current anti-tax environment, it seems unlikely this will be enacted by Congress.

Those who favor shifting to a premium support system argue that it will lead to major reductions in the rate of growth of Medicare expenses. This will be true if the system is designed in such a way that high-cost beneficiaries remain in traditional FFS Medicare with increased cost sharing. Such a change reduces the rate of growth of federal budget obligations, but does not necessarily slow the medical spending by Medicare recipients. There is a belief among premium support advocates about the cost-saving prospects of this change, but little evidence to support the assertion.

The 2010 health reform legislation establishes a new Center for Medicare and Medicaid Innovation to test and implement new service delivery and payment innovations. There is a hope that this system reform approach will reduce the rate of growth of Medicare expenditures by lowering basic costs. These transformations of existing practices offer prospects for success, but the US health system is large and diverse. Reform models will diffuse slowly across the country, even if successful in some locations.

Benefit Redesign

Policy change usually begins to occur when a long-standing condition is perceived as a problem. The Medicare benefit structure is almost fifty years old, with relatively few changes over time despite major shifts in the configuration of private insurance over the past several decades. For a number of years, the most glaring omission in Medicare services was the absence of prescription drug coverage.

The Medicare Modernization Act of 2003 established Part D, but this was quickly regarded as an inadequate response to the problem. In order to constrain costs and provide some assistance to many Medicare recipients, the structure of the drug benefit created a doughnut hole in which beneficiaries receive payment for drugs until the total drug costs incurred reaches $2,800. Then, Medicare covers no further costs until the total surpasses $6,400. The absurdity of this policy design led to incremental changes as part of the Patient Protection and Affordable Care Act of 2010 so that the coverage gap will gradually be reduced and ultimately eliminated in 2020. The law also improves the low-income subsidy provision in Part D.[53]

At the time of Medicare enactment, congressional and administrative leaders decided that nursing home coverage would be limited to those in temporary transition from hospital care back to their home. For those whose chronic illness required institutionalization, the per diem costs were not considered medical care and, therefore, not part of the Medicare benefit. Medicare later added significant home health benefits to assist the chronically ill. In a later chapter the issues surrounding the financing of long-term care are considered in depth.

In the 1970s Medicare coverage was extended to those aged sixty-four years and younger who receive disability payments, subject to a two-year wait before Medicare eligibility. This was instituted to utilize employment-based insurance as long as possible and confirm that the disability was permanent.[54] It is estimated that nearly 500,000 people are certified as disabled, but do not have health insurance.[55] Elimination of the waiting period would represent a Medicare benefit improvement.

Modifying the antiquated Medicare cost-sharing provisions represents the greatest benefit modification challenge. In addition to the Part B and D premiums, beneficiaries pay deductibles under Parts A, B, and D. They are also responsible for coinsurance on many but not all services, and there is no stop-loss provision that limits the total payments that a beneficiary might be charged. A stop-loss is common in private insurance today, but it was not in 1965. Because these cost-sharing payments could become very high, a private insurance market has developed to protect beneficiaries. Almost 90% of FFS beneficiaries have some type of supplemental coverage. For one-third of beneficiaries, supplemental coverage is subsidized by their former employer. Another one-quarter have Medicare Advantage plans that provide protection. The low-income 15% are dual eligibles also covered by Medicaid, and 16% purchase individual Medigap policies.[56]

A recent analysis by MedPac found a concentration of cost-sharing liability in FFS Medicare. The top 22% of beneficiaries incurred two-thirds of all cost sharing. There was little difference in use of emergency service or essential hospitalization between those with and without supplemental coverage, but there were significant differences in preventive care.[57] The Catastrophic Coverage Act of 1988 attempted to rationalize and improve the cost-sharing structure, but did so by high-income beneficiaries subsidizing low-income beneficiaries. The resulting opposition forced repeal of the law. With former employers subsidizing supplemental insurance for one in three recipients, it is difficult to redesign the system without either major new public expenditures or causing some beneficiaries to pay more. This category is declining because fewer employers are willing to provide this benefit. At some point, the distortions and inequities in the cost-sharing system will need to be addressed.

Who Should Pay for Medicare?

Most of the questions addressed in this chapter revolve around money. Who should pay for Medicare is a fundamental issue. Today current workers pay about 40% of Medicare costs through the payroll tax, taxpayers pay 39% that goes to the general revenue, and beneficiaries pay 12% in premiums.[58]

Over the next twenty years, the number of Medicare beneficiaries will nearly double. Even if cost-containment strategies succeed in slowing the growth rate of the average cost per beneficiary, additional resources will be needed to sustain the program unless the economy grows at a pace to significantly increase tax revenues. Should these new revenues come in the form of cost-share payments from beneficiaries who use the services? The individuals who use the most services are generally older, sicker, and poorer than the average beneficiary. Or should all beneficiaries pay more in the form of premiums, which are now the same for most individuals regardless of income? Perhaps current workers should pay a slightly higher payroll tax rate on the premise that ultimately they will be Medicare beneficiaries and can better afford a small tax increase while they are employed. If the share of general revenue support for Medicare is to grow, either the income tax rate will need to increase or funds will need to be taken from some other budget category.

Important policy choices are rarely easy or clearly provide the best option. Before this decade ends, Congress will likely address the major Medicare issues. The resulting legislation will probably contain a mixture of elements to address the long-term Medicare problems.

Medicare in the Postreform Future

Medicare has been in place for almost a half-century. Changes in the program have been relatively modest, and supporters have resisted the recent proposals for radical redesign. Since its inception, alarm has been expressed from time to time about the fiscal future of the program, especially given the frequent projections of the imminent demise of the Part A Hospital Insurance Trust Fund. After three decades of relative consensus around the basic idea of the program as social insurance, a significant philosophical divide has developed between those who want to see Medicare continue its social insurance roots and reformers who are convinced Medicare will better serve its beneficiaries and the taxpayers by transformation into a system of private insurance plans supported by premium contributions from the federal government. This philosophical divide has been evident in every major Medicare policy discussion over the past fifteen years, and is likely to continue.

Notes

1. John D. Norris, "President Signs Medicare Bill; Praises Truman," *New York Times,* July 31, 1965, p. 1.
2. "Medicare at a Glance," Issue Brief (Washington, DC: Henry J. Kaiser Family Foundation, January 2010).
3. For additional information on Medicare, see "Medicare: A Primer" (Washington, DC: Kaiser Commission on Medicaid and the Uninsured, April 2010).
4. Theodore Marmor, *The Politics of Medicare,* 2nd ed. (New York: Aldine de Gruyter, 1970), p. 50.
5. David Blumenthal and James Morone, *The Heart of Power: Health and Politics in the Oval Office* (Berkeley: University of California Press, 2009), p. 229.
6. Judith M. Feder, *Medicare: The Politics of Federal Hospital Insurance* (Lexington, MA: Lexington Books, 1977).
7. Ibid.

8. Jonathan Oberlander, *The Political Life of Medicare* (Chicago: University of Chicago Press, 2003), pp. 114–115; Feder, *Medicare.*

9. Herman M. Somers and Anne R. Somers, *Medicare and the Hospitals: Issues and Prospects* (Washington, DC: Brookings Institution, 1967), pp. 259–260.

10. Feder, *Medicare,* p. 12.

11. Oberlander, *The Political Life of Medicare,* pp. 40–43.

12. Stacy Dale and James Verdier, "Elimination of Medicare's Waiting Period for Seriously Disabled Adults: Impact on Coverage and Costs" (New York: Commonwealth Fund, July 2003).

13. Oberlander, *The Political Life of Medicare,* pp. 40–43, 40–47.

14. Ibid., p. 47.

15. Charles L. Schultze, Edward K. Hamilton, and Allen Shick, *Setting National Priorities: The 1971 Budget* (Washington, DC: Brookings Institution, 1970), p. 72.

16. Rick Mayes and Robert A. Berenson, *Medicare Prospective Payment and the Shaping of US Health Care* (Baltimore: Johns Hopkins University Press, 2006), pp. 19–21.

17. David G. Smith, *Paying for Medicare: The Politics of Reform* (New York: Aldine de Gruyter, 1992).

18. Mayes and Berenson, *Medicare Prospective Payment,* pp. 38–39.

19. Louise B. Russel, *Medicare's New Hospital Payment System* (Washington, DC: Brookings Institution, 1989), p. 7.

20. Mayes and Berenson, *Medicare Prospective Payment,* pp. 42–46.

21. Smith, *Paying for Medicare.*

22. MedPac, *Physician Services Payment System* (Washington, DC: MedPac, 2009).

23. Mayes and Berenson, *Medicare Prospective Payment,* pp. 87–92.

24. *Annual Report of the Board of Trustees of the Federal Hospital Insurance Trust Fund* (Washington, DC: US Government Printing Office, 1993).

25. Oberlander, *The Political Life of Medicare.*

26. For example, D. Brandow and M. Tanner, "The Wrong and Right Ways to Reform Medicare," Policy Analysis no. 230 (Washington, DC: Cato Institute, June 8, 1965); and Stuart M. Butler and Robert E. Moffit, "The FEHBP as a Model for a New Medicare Program," *Health Affairs* 14, no. 4 (1995): 47–61.

27. Oberlander, *The Political Life of Medicare,* pp. 171–176.

28. Marilyn Moon, *Medicare: A Policy Primer* (Washington, DC: Urban Institute Press, 2006), pp. 71–72.

29. Andrea L. Campbell and Kimberly Morgan, "The Medicare Modernization Act and the New Politics of Medicare," paper prepared for the annual meeting of the American Political Science Association, Philadelphia, August 31–September 3, 2006, p. 10.

30. Congressional Budget Office, *Issues in Designing a Prescription Drug Benefit for Medicare* (Washington, DC: CBO Publications Office, 2002).

31. Ibid.
32. "The Medicare Prescription Drug Law," Fact Sheet (Washington, DC: Henry J. Kaiser Family Foundation, March 2004).
33. This account draws heavily on Thomas R. Oliver, Philip R. Lee, and Helene L. Lipton, "A Political History of Medicare and Prescription Drug Coverage," *Milbank Quarterly* 82, no. 2 (2004): 283–343; Campbell and Morgan, "The Medicare Modernization Act and the New Politics of Medicare"; and Jonathan Oberlander, "Through the Looking Glass: The Politics of the Medicare Prescription Drug, Improvement, and Modernization Act," *Journal of Health Politics, Policy and Law* 32, no. 2 (2007): 187–219.
34. "Prescription Drug Coverage for Medicare Beneficiaries: A Summary of the Medicare Prescription Drug, Improvement, and Modernization Act of 2003" (Washington, DC: Kaiser Commission on Medicaid and the Uninsured, December 10, 2003), pp. 1–11.
35. "Medicare and the American Social Contract: Final Report of the Study Panel on Medicare's Larger Social Role" (Washington, DC: National Academy of Social Insurance, February 1999).
36. Stan Jones, "Building a Sound Infrastructure for Choice," in *Medicare: Preparing for the Challenges of the 21st Century,* eds. Robert D. Reischauer et al. (Washington, DC: National Academy of Social Insurance, 1998), p. 61.
37. Alain Enthoven, "Managed Competition: An Agenda for Action," *Health Affairs* 7, no. 3 (1988): 25–47.
38. "Explaining Health Reform: Key Changes in the Medicare Advantage Program," *Focus on Health Reform* (Washington, DC: Henry J. Kaiser Family Foundation, May 2010).
39. Congressional Budget Office, *Issues in Designing.*
40. Ibid.
41. Eric Patashnik, "Unfolding Promises: Trust Funds and the Politics of Precommitment," *Political Science Quarterly* 112, no. 3 (1997).
42. Eric Patashnik, "Paying for Medicare: Benefits, Budgets, and Wilbur Mills's Policy Legacy," *Journal of Health Politics, Policy and Law* 26, no. 1 (2001): 7–36.
43. Gail Wilensky, "The Challenge of Medicare," in *Restoring Fiscal Sanity 2007: The Health Spending Challenge,* ed. Alice Rivlin and Joseph Antos (Washington, DC: Brookings Institution, 2007), pp. 81–103.
44. Joseph White, "Protecting Medicare: The Best Defense Is a Good Offense," *Journal of Health Politics, Policy and Law* 32, no. 2 (2007): 221–246.
45. Joseph White, "Uses and Abuses of Long-term Medicare Cost Estimates," *Health Affairs* 18, no. 1 (1999): 63–79.
46. Congressional Budget Office, *The Long-Term Budget Outlook* (Washington, DC: CBO Publications Office, June 2010).
47. Boards of Trustees, Federal Hospital Insurance and Federal Supplementary Medical Insurance Trust Funds, *The 2010 Annual Report of the Boards of Trustees of the Federal Hospital Insurance and Federal Supplementary Medical Insurance Trust Funds* (Washington, DC: Government Printing Office, 2010).

48. J. Shatto and M. Clemens, *Projected Medicare Expenditures Under an Illustrative Scenario with Alternative Payment Updates to Medicare Providers* (Baltimore, MD: Center for Medicare and Medicaid Services, 2010).

49. Gail R. Wilensky, *The Challenge of Medicare* (Washington, DC: Brookings Institution, 2007), p. 8.

50. Jeffrey Stensland, Zachary R. Gaumer, and Mark E. Miller, "Private-Payer Profits Can Induce Negative Medicare Margins," *Health Affairs* 29, no. 5 (2010): 1–7.

51. Ewe E. Reinhardt, "The Annual Drama of the 'Doc Fix,'" *New York Times,* December 17, 2010, http://economix.blogs.nytimes.com/2010/12/17/the-annual-drama-of-the-doc-fix; Meghan McCarthy, "Unsustainable," *National Journal,* December 4, 2010, p. 62.

52. Congressional Budget Office, *Issues in Designing a Prescription Drug Benefit for Medicare.*

53. Amanda Cassidy, "Health Reform's Changes in Medicare," Health Policy Brief, *Health Affairs* (May 20, 2010), www.healthaffairs.org/health policybriefs/brief.php?brief_id=17.

54. Stacy Dale and James Verdier, "Elimination of Medicare's Waiting Period for Seriously Disabled Adults: Impact on Coverage and Costs" (New York: Commonwealth Fund, July 2003).

55. Moon, *Medicare,* p. 177.

56. "Medicare: A Primer" (Washington, DC: Kaiser Commission on Medicaid and the Uninsured, 2010), pp. 11–12.

57. MedPac, "Improving Traditional Medicare's Benefits Design, Report to the Congress: Improving Incentives in the Medicare Program" (Washington, DC: Government Printing Office, June 2009).

58. Lisa Potetz and Juliette Cubanski, "A Primer on Medicare Financing" (Washington, DC: Henry J. Kaiser Family Foundation, July 2009).

4

Medicaid:
The Accidental Program

In late August 1965 Howard Rusk, medical reporter for the *New York Times,* began a Sunday column with these words: "The correlation between low incomes and poorer health has long recognized that the chance a Negro baby born today will not live to his first birthday is almost twice as great as for a white baby born at exactly the same time."[1] Rusk concluded that provisions in the recently passed Medicare law would extend the Medical Assistance for the Aged Act (Kerr-Mills) to recipients of federally aided public assistance programs and be a fundamental step in the attack on poverty. As a result of the attention surrounding the controversial Medicare law, little consideration had been given to this part of the law.

Medicaid began as an almost unnoticed incremental expansion of welfare system policy. Over the past forty-five years the program has grown step by step to rival Medicare in its size and scope. Few who read the Rusk column that Sunday morning in 1965 would have imagined Medicaid's future.

The Early Years: 1966–1980

The implementation of Medicare was a public administration success. In less than a year, the program had put a Medicare administrative system in place and was fully ready for the first patients on July 1, 1966. The implementation of Medicaid was rockier. Medicare was a national program that utilized Blue Cross–Blue Shield as a fiscal intermediary to handle payments. One set of administrative rules applied to the whole country. For Medicaid, the Division of Medical Services had only six months to write regulatory rules and send instructions to the states about how they were to submit their plan for administration of Medicaid. Each state plan had to be individually approved in Washington, DC. Most state governments were not prepared to distribute medical vendor payments on the necessary scale. Initially a handful of large states, such as New York and California, moved quickly to adopt the program. But computer systems were primitive or nonexistent. Payments often were late or incorrect, or both. Without effective control systems, fraud was rampant at times. Since payment policies were the province of the state governments, there was little control that could be exerted by federal officials to contain costs.

The Social Security Amendments of 1972 represented a significant modification of Medicaid. With the exception of mothers with children, welfare recipients were placed in the new Supplemental Security Income (SSI) program. Most SSI recipients were eligible for Medicaid. There were provisions designed to uncover fraud, provisions for utilization and capital expenditure control systems, and provisions to broaden the authorization for participation of health maintenance organizations (HMOs) in Medicaid.

Early in his term, President Jimmy Carter proposed a Children's Health Assurance Program (CHAP) that would have ultimately expanded Medicaid coverage to additional poor children. Congress did not enact this legislation, but it was to be the first of several attempts to broaden Medicaid coverage of poor children. For both Presidents Richard M. Nixon and Carter, Medicaid as a program, was legislatively less important than attempts to create a national health insurance system. Coverage expansion was secondary to general cost control measures in the Carter administration.[2] Congress successfully pursued additional legislative authority to combat fraud and abuse. Administratively, during the Carter administration Medicare and Medicaid were brought together in a new agency, the Health Care Financing Administration (HCFA).

In the first fifteen years of its existence, Medicaid grew and established deep roots in the health care system as the major public method for financing the welfare poor and older people in nursing homes. Each subsequent administration appeared to treat Medicaid as a temporary program. Medicaid was to be a bridge to a future in which some type of national health insurance would eventually replace Medicaid. No president or any Congress was willing to expend political capital to do more than make incremental changes to a Medicaid program that had been widely seen as inadequate, but temporary.

Medicaid During the Reagan Revolution: 1981–1993

President Ronald Reagan entered office with a mission to dismantle the Great Society welfare system that had grown exponentially since 1960. In the Omnibus Budget Reconciliation Act of 1981 (OBRA-81), the Reagan administration achieved some Medicaid savings when eligibility for Aid to Families with Dependent Children (AFDC) was tightened. President Ronald Reagan also sought to transform Medicaid into a block grant in which the federal government paid states a fixed amount per year to run their Medicaid program. Congress rejected the block grant approach and temporarily set a 5% cap on annual increases in the federal share of Medicaid. The Reagan administration briefly flirted with the idea of trading a federalization of Medicaid for giving the states responsibility for the welfare program, but governors rejected the idea and it was dropped.[3]

A realistic observer might have concluded in early 1982 that Medicaid would be unrecognizable by the end of the Reagan presidency. The unpredictable factor was Congressman Henry Waxman. The resistance of the governors to a block grant approach and the reluctance of Congress to pass too many budget cuts back to the states are understandable. Local voters elect members of Congress. Waxman, a liberal Democrat from Los Angeles and chair of the House Subcommittee on Health and Environment of the Commerce Committee, devised a strategy to expand Medicaid participation. Over several years, he methodically built support for broadening eligibility to include additional poor women and children. The expansion occurred incrementally over several years and the legislative changes were incorporated into budget reconciliation acts. This incorporation effectively rendered the amendments veto-proof because it would have required rejecting a major part of the budget for the year. Despite the fact that federal grants to states and local governments were a special target in the Reagan administration, it was unable to change the Medicaid spending trajectory. Medicaid participation was actually liberalized. The block grant idea, however, did not die. To this day, conservative health policy thinkers have continued to argue for a new approach to Medicaid that centers on shifting to a block grant approach.[4]

The Medicaid Showdown: 1993–2001

The great Medicaid showdown of 1995 had all of the ingredients of a Western movie shoot-out. This confrontation between President William J. Clinton and Republicans in Congress was part of a larger battle over the future direction of federal spending, especially on entitlements. At no other time in the history of Medicaid was the program on the verge of such fundamental change as it was in the fall of 1995, when it was part of the confrontation that led to the shutdown of the federal government.

Despite the initial efforts of the Reagan administration to substantially change Medicaid, the program had grown significantly. The number of Medicaid recipients increased by 34% between 1988 and 1992. Many new enrollees were eligible because of the Waxman amendments approved during the 1980s. Spending more than doubled during this time, although the new beneficiaries were not the most significant cause of the increase.[5] The new conservative Republican majority in Congress, led by Speaker Newt Gingrich, sought to institute a conservative revolution, including the Medicaid reform that had eluded the Reagan administration.

The prequel to the 1995 showdown was the Clinton health reform plan. Under the plan, Medicaid would have been integrated into the new managed competition system. After the failure of the health reform plan in 1994, a major Republican victory in the November elections shifted the majority in Congress and created a potential majority coalition to support conservative policy ideas. Gingrich sought a number of significant changes, including Medicaid reform, in a single major bill, the Balanced Budget Act of 1995 (BBA-95).

Despite initial discussion about treating Medicaid in the same fashion as the welfare program by transforming it into a block grant, there was disagreement among Republican governors. Instead, the Reagan-era concept of a "capped entitlement" was resurrected and proposed at 5% per year. This would be the amount of growth allowed in the federal share. It was close to the most recent year's increase, but considerably below the annual increase a few years earlier. The projected seven-year budget reductions were large, with one-half coming from Medicare and Medicaid.[6] In the legislative discussions and negotiations among congressional leaders and governors, there was movement toward a general consensus on a capped entitlement approach, with a 5% cap on annual growth of federal Medicaid spending. With this change, there was also some sentiment to modify the basic formula used to determine the federal share per state. If future federal increases were to be limited, a status quo formula was unacceptable to some states whose governors believed they were entitled to a larger base federal share.

Medicaid has never enjoyed Medicare's broad interest group support and defense. However, it gained an important ally when the American Hospital Association began to question the direction of the Republican-sponsored Medicaid reform. Hospitals, especially those serving poor urban and rural communities, are dependent on Medicaid reimbursement. Hospitals would bear the largest burden in the future if states cut reimbursement in the face of budget problems and increases from the federal government were limited.

As mentioned above, President Clinton's veto of the BBA-95 led to a government shutdown at the end of 1995. The battle around the BBA-95 ended with the Gingrich side retreating on the Medicaid and Medicare changes for 1995. In early 1996, there was an initial effort to combine the same Medicaid reforms with the welfare reform bill, but the prospects of a second Clinton veto forced the Republicans to separate the two by dropping the major Medicaid changes.

The failure of the Medicaid radical reform effort in 1995 ironically led in 1997 to a major expansion of public coverage of children in the form of the State Children's Health Insurance Program (SCHIP). The Balanced Budget Act of 1997 (BBA-97) was, like its 1995 predecessor, comprehensive reconciliation legislation that featured Medicare and Medicaid provisions. The BBA-97 was successful because it was bipartisan and did not seek radical change.[7]

There had long been a general recognition among policymakers across the political spectrum that on average children generated low health care costs, that employer-offered insurance was declining or costing more in premium cost sharing (especially family coverage), and that small sums spent on childhood medical care could provide huge long-term savings in the prevention of expensive adult conditions. Between the children in low-income families covered under Medicaid and the middle-class families typically covered by employment-based health insurance, near-poor or working-poor families too often fell into the cracks of the system. Many of the uninsured children were in this category. The welfare reform legislation enacted in 1996 could exacerbate the situation in a few years. Because former AFDC recipients were phased out of that income support program and forced to take part-time and low-income jobs that did not provide health insurance, the ranks of the uninsured would grow, especially among children. Still, family income levels would put these children above Medicaid eligibility. They were destined to join the ranks of the uninsured working poor.

In the previous decade, some bipartisan support for the Waxman amendments demonstrated that incremental expansions of public coverage for children might be possible in an environment in which comprehensive reform was unlikely. The perception of a growing problem of coverage for children presented an opportunity. From opposite ends of the political spectrum, Senators Orrin Hatch and Ted Kennedy jointly proposed a block grant for the states to expand coverage for children. The next month a different bipartisan pair, Senators Lincoln Chafee and Jay Rockefeller, proposed expanding Medicaid to cover children in families up to 150% of the federal poverty level; this would be an increase from 133% and the states would receive a higher Medicaid matching rate for this group.

Unlike the showdown two years earlier, both sides were willing to find a compromise, and it came in the form of a combination of the two ideas. For those who did not wish to expand the traditional Medicaid entitlement, the block grant feature was a step in the right direction. The law made clear that this was not an individual entitlement, but money to help states develop a program reflecting their situation. For those who believed Medicaid expansion was the best route to efficient and effective coverage for these children, states would be allowed to expand their Medicaid program to include this additional group, but the federal SCHIP contribution would be capped per year. Thus, states had the option of choosing either to use their allocated SCHIP funds to start a new program, to integrate the newly covered into Medicaid, or to do some of each. While the total federal funds per year were fixed, the states were induced to participate by a high federal share of the total expenses. State financial participation was still required, but at a lower rate.[8]

According to Alan Weil, SCHIP was a "carefully crafted compromise" that provided the states a great deal of flexibility in the use of significant additional funds for expanding health insurance coverage for children. Not only was the match rate better than Medicaid's, but critical design decisions were left to the states.[9] It was a solution that did not completely satisfy any of the major actors, but left all believing that the compromise was better than nothing.

In the midst of the epic battles over the future of Medicaid, a significant structural modification was taking place. There was no defining moment, but a steady growth in the use of managed care for the Medicaid population occurred in the 1990s. Only 3% were in managed care in 1983, but by 1995 that had increased to over 30%.[10] By the end of the decade, the percentage in managed care had risen to nearly 60%.[11] Because beneficiaries in Medicaid managed care are mostly families with children, they represent a large share of enrollees, but a much smaller percentage of total program spending.

Medicaid and Health Reform: 2001–2010

With the beginning of the first decade of the twenty-first century, the new Republican president George W. Bush had returned to old Medicaid ideas. Early in the Bush administration, attempts were made to work with the National Governor's Association (NGA) to shift Medicaid to a block grant approach. The term was a flash point so the effort was called "modernization" rather than "block grant."[12] The thrust of the discussions over multiple years was to convert all of Medicaid to resemble SCHIP. Governors tended to support this model as long as SCHIP's more generous federal contribution was part of the plan. When the Bush administration emphasized federal budget savings as a key component, support from the NGA waned. In the early part of the decade, the recession following the September 11 attacks put added pressure on state Medicaid budgets. Governors were reluctant to support a plan in which they had more administrative flexibility but the prospect of less federal revenue in the future.

After the 2006 election, the Democrats regained control of Congress and major Medicaid structural change became a dead issue. The Medicaid issue for the new Congress was the renewal of SCHIP, which was set to expire after ten years. Republicans as well as Democrats viewed it as a success in expanding coverage for children. Governors and major health care provider groups supported renewal and expansion. A five-year reauthorization bill with an additional $35 billion passed Congress in September 2007 by a comfortable bipartisan majority. But President Bush vetoed the bill. Unable to override the president's veto, Congress made adjustments and passed a second bill, which he also vetoed in December. With a stalemate on the issue, Congress postponed action until after the 2008 presidential election by extending the program until March 2009.[13]

The renewal of SCHIP became one of the first major pieces of legislation for the Barack Obama administration, with a reauthorization of four and one-half years in the legislation.[14] Under the reauthorization, the renamed Children's Health Insurance Program (CHIP) continues to cap federal funds with an enhanced matching rate. The Congressional Budget Office (CBO) estimates that an additional 4 million children will be covered by 2013. New options to cover pregnant women and poor adults without children were also included in the legislation.[15]

The CHIP renewal represented the completion of old business. This set the table for the beginning of a major new effort to enact comprehensive health reform with Medicaid and CHIP at the center of the discussion. This effort extended into early 2010 before resolution. The story and details of the 2010 health reform act, the Patient Protection and Affordable Care Act (ACA), are provided in Chapter 7. Medicaid expansion is a key component of the new law, with a national floor of 133% of poverty and full federal funding for states from 2014 to 2016 to cover those newly eligible.

Policies That Will Shape Medicaid's Future

Medicaid has grown up. For decades it was like a younger sibling, never enjoying the attention and acclaim given to Medicare. Little more than a decade ago, Medicaid appeared to be on the brink of extinction as opponents attempted to shove it into the coffin called a block grant. Indeed, for decades Medicaid had experienced many narrow escapes. Liberals sought to blend Medicaid into a national health insurance program and conservatives attempted to push it back into a narrow welfare-oriented program. It was no one's favorite health care program. In a 2003 analysis, Colleen Grogan and Eric Patashnik found Medicaid to be at a political crossroads, with one fork in the road leading back to its welfare origins and the other forward toward an expanded role in providing coverage for poor and near-poor families who are outside the employment-based system.[16] With the 2010 passage of ACA, it seems that Medicaid has begun to move forward into the wide path to universal coverage. There continues to be a segment of elite opinion opposed to Medicaid expansion, and another change in the congressional majority might again pose a roadblock to Medicaid as a major vehicle for universal coverage for the poor.

Two elements of the ACA appear to open the path for Medicaid to become the preferred vehicle for achieving universal coverage for the poor and near poor. One is the enhanced matching rate for enrollees absorbed into Medicaid through the expanded eligibility. The other is the final break from its historic link to the welfare system. As Medicaid emerged from the ashes of Kerr-Mills in 1965, its core beneficiaries were the poor, whose life situation made them part of a defined category in the welfare system. By ending this categorical link in 2010, Medicaid is poised to become the primary source of financial access for all poor people. In the rest of this chapter, I examine three policy dynamics that likely will shape the future path for Medicaid as the major financing vehicle for care of the poor and near poor. These three policy dynamics are the need for states to balance their budgets, the size of Medicaid as a constraint on radical change, and the impact of federalism as a core design feature.

The federal government can and often does spend more money in a year than it collects, but state constitutions typically mandate a balanced budget. This basic difference shapes the perception of Medicaid in governors' mansions and state legislatures. Critics in Washington, DC, may condemn deficit spending, but usually they blame someone else's program as the culprit. State elected officials cannot duck hard budget trade-offs by creating a deficit. Additional money spent on health care may mean less for education or roads. Medicaid is a double whammy for states. In an economic downturn, more citizens become eligible for Medicaid because they have lost their jobs and state tax revenues decline. A recent study found a 1-percentage-point rise in national unemployment increases in Medicaid and CHIP enrollment by 1 million, leading to $3.4 billion of additional Medicaid spending of which $1.4 billion is incurred by the states. The rise in unemployment also caused a 3% or 4% decline in revenue. This dynamic puts a major squeeze on state budgets.[17]

According to the Kaiser Commission, states across the country cut provider payments or limited benefits, or both, in 2009 as a response to the global financial crisis.[18] Several years earlier when the bursting of the technology boom and the slowdown following 9/11 contributed to an economic downturn, the pattern was the same. Those on the margins of Medicaid eligibility typically are most affected. This creates coverage instability and is an obvious weakness in the policy approach featuring expanded use of Medicaid. During recent economic downturns, states have had relatively few policy options for finding new revenue to finance the expanded Medicaid enrollment. In addition to the state action to reduce enrollment and cut provider costs, the federal government has frequently developed additional revenue sharing with states in the form of special economic stimulus assistance targeted to assist states. The result is a series of ad hoc onetime measures to help the states with their extra Medicaid budget shortfalls.

The original Medicaid financial structure did not provide a safety valve for a recession safeguard. Because states have more limited flexibility, the federal government needs to either pay a larger share of the total cost by using a permanently higher matching rate or find a different approach that avoids the cyclical financial pressure on the states.

Since the early 1980s, those in Washington, DC, who have wished to slow the rate of growth of federal spending on Medicaid and other entitlements have advocated the block grant or its close cousin, the capped entitlement. With both, the concept is similar. The federal government's financial obligation is limited and states must react to rising costs by cutting expenses or paying a larger share of the total. Ultimately, states will reach a cost-cutting limit on reducing Medicaid provider reimbursement and find ways to cut program enrollment. SCHIP and the 2010 ACA were the last two major legislative expansions of Medicaid, and they addressed this potential problem by increasing the federal matching share. For the initial years in the implementation of the ACA, the federal government will pay almost 100% of the cost to provide care for newly eligible Medicaid recipients.[19] The CHIP renewal in 2009 continued a matching rate more favorable than that of traditional Medicaid.[20] Total available funds were limited, but states pay a smaller share of the costs under CHIP.

If, over the next decade, the federal government continues to be willing to pay a larger share of the total Medicaid bill, then states will be less inclined to either cut benefits or dramatically squeeze provider reimbursement at the first sign of an economic downturn. In this scenario, program stability will be more likely and, thus, Medicaid can march down the road to broad expansion. The alternative scenario is a renewed determination in Washington to reduce the rate of growth on federal entitlement spending, including federal health care programs. This perspective represents an ideological opposition to the national subsidy of health services for the poor and near poor. A closely related concern is the long-term federal deficit projections, which are heavily driven by health care and Social Security expenditures.

The various campaigns by Washington conservatives to shift Medicaid from the traditional entitlement program to a block grant usually have met with strenuous opposition from governors, even Republicans. Policy change happens when a problem is serious enough to be on the decision agenda, there is an idea that appears to be feasible, and a majority coalition is available. If Medicaid's road is to be an expansionist path, federal policymakers will need to recognize the trade-off between cost and access that states cannot avoid. Most governors want more flexibility and greater federal funds. They see this as the only way to ultimately smooth the boom and bust cycle, balance their budgets, and provide health care access to the poor and near-poor citizens of their states.

Is Medicaid Too Big to Fail?

Medicaid is large and complex, and invades almost every nook and cranny of the US health care system. My brief review of the scope of the program demonstrates the sweep of Medicaid.

As Table 4.1 illustrates, Medicaid is a significant force in the financial structure of US health care. Medicaid covers 15% of the total population, with much higher coverage for selected needy populations. The $339 billion spent on Medicaid in 2008 financed health care services for 58 million people, which is 15% of the population. One-half of Medicaid enrollees are children. One child out of every four in the United States is in Medicaid. Medicaid pays for almost 20% of all hospital care and 40% of all nursing home care. Over the past forty years, Medicaid has moved from a little-noticed Medicare legislation add-on to a huge sprawling program that is projected to spend 80% as much as Medicare by 2019, up from 75% in 2009.[21] Medicaid has become critical for both key population groups and health care institutions.

Children

Medicaid and CHIP are critical to the health insurance coverage of children. In 2009 private insurance covered 58% of the nation's 79 million children, and 31% were covered by Medicaid and public programs. Usually coverage for children is relatively inexpensive on a cost-per-recipient basis, and cost effective since preventive care often has health benefits for a lifetime. Children covered by Medicaid and CHIP have the same level of access to care as those with private insurance. Children who are uninsured are much more likely to have no usual source of care or to go without care because of cost.[22]

Table 4.1   Medicaid Coverage for Selected Populations

Selected Population	Percentage of Medicaid Coverage
Total population	15
The poor	41
African Americans	24
Hispanics	23
All children	28
Low-income children	53
Low-income parents	20
Births (pregnant women)	41
Medicare beneficiaries	19
People with severe disabilities	20
People with HIV/AIDS	44
Nursing homes	65

Source: "Medicaid: A Primer" (Washington, DC: Kaiser Commission on Medicaid and the Uninsured, June 2010).

The Disabled

Medicaid provides coverage for nearly 9 million non-older people with disabilities, of which 4 million are children. They represent 16% of enrollees, but generate 43% of the total cost. Enrollees with disabilities generate seven times the yearly expenses of an average child.[23] Children and adults with disabilities require special services and more intensive medical care. For them, Medicaid is often the financial support of last resort.

Pregnant Women

Medicaid funds four of ten births and pays for the prenatal and postpartum care associated with these births. Some funds also cover pregnancy-related counseling services or breast-feeding support. In a number of states, the share of women dependent on Medicaid for pregnancy-related services is much greater than 25%; for example, in Louisiana, it is 63%.[24]

Low-income Beneficiaries

Dual eligibles are low-income Medicare beneficiaries who are covered by both programs. They represent 18% of all Medicaid enrollees.

One in three of the 9 million dual eligibles are aged sixty-four years or younger and covered by Medicare because of disability status. For some, Medicaid serves as supplementary coverage to fill the Medicare benefit gaps and cost sharing, but most receive full Medicaid benefits. While representing only 18% of Medicaid enrollment, dual eligibles account for 46% of total program costs.[25]

Each of these categories of enrollees depends on Medicaid in a critical way to finance essential medical services. A significant reduction in program spending or scope of activity would ripple through these communities of low-income and often health-challenged individuals. A major decrease in Medicaid spending would also have a devastating impact on those who provide services to these populations. Medicaid reimbursement is usually lower than that of Medicare or private plans, but institutions such as hospitals would, in the absence of Medicaid, still provide many of the services as charity care with no payment. For hospitals, nursing homes, and similar institutions, Medicaid contributes critical income, even if the rate of payment is below that of other forms. Social safety net providers, such as public hospitals, also rely on Medicaid payments. Health centers and public hospitals receive one-third of their revenue from Medicaid.[26] In 2007, over 16 million poor patients were served by 7,200 federally qualified health centers. One-third of the revenue received by these centers comes from Medicaid.[27]

How Serious Is the Problem?

For at least two decades, there has been episodic discussion about the impact of growing entitlement spending on the federal budget. Many have sounded alarms about the dire consequences of the growth rate of Social Security and Medicare spending, especially as the baby boom generation begins to retire. Although each program has a different trajectory, Medicaid is typically included in the discussion as part of a triumvirate of uncontrolled spending that threatens the nation.

For some, the obvious response is to take significant steps to slow the rate of growth of federal Medicaid funds by transforming the program into a block grant that limits annual federal expenditures to the states. This would allow states to make up the shortfall, but most do not have the financial resources to do so. Over the next decade, Medicaid spending will grow as the ACA offers expanded coverage of the uninsured. In its 2010 pre-ACA projection of Medicaid expenditures, the CBO projects total federal Medicaid outlays to increase from $276 billion in 2010 to $444 billion in 2020, representing an average annual increase of 5%.[28] It predicts Medicaid spending in 2020 to represent 8% of federal spending, up from 7% in 2007.

Is the Medicaid increase from 7% to 8% of federal spending over a decade enough to cause policymakers to make fundamental structural changes, or has Medicaid become too big and important to allow the drastic change that some seek? This level of increased spending is not likely to be the key factor. Many have a philosophical objection to the basic assumption of a federal entitlement to finance health care for the poor. Because of Medicaid's size and scope, few legislators are likely to urge a sudden repeal, but a capped entitlement or block grant would incrementally slow the rate of growth of the federal commitment to Medicaid by shifting more financial responsibility to the states. Medicaid sprawls over many different types of beneficiaries and services, and therefore it is difficult to identify a quick and easy way to flatten the growth curve. In the past, state governments seeking to reduce their Medicaid costs reduced provider payments, restricted eligibility standards, and reduced benefits. The latter two actions will be increasingly difficult to achieve because of the greater standardization resulting from ACA. While older people and people with disabilities account for 28% of total enrollees, they spend 67% of all funds.[29]

It is increased enrollment rather than per-enrollee cost that drives the Medicaid cost increases.[30] The CBO expects an average annual growth of 3% in older Medicaid beneficiaries. The 2007 average cost per enrollee among older people was $14,000, compared to $2,400 for children.[31] This reflects the significant nursing home use among older beneficiaries.

Federalism: Every State Is Different

From the beginning, Medicare has been a national program, but Medicaid's origins are in the federal-state welfare system established by the Social Security Act of 1935. Medicaid was passed in 1965, but is officially Title XIX of the Social Security Act of 1935. It established minimum federal eligibility and benefit standards, and left it to the states to specify their individual mix. States set up their own administrative systems for determining eligibility and paying providers. Medicaid has never been a national program, but fifty different state programs. The stark variations from state to state are jarring when examined.

Using 1994 data, John Holahan of the Urban Institute investigated state variations in Medicaid and found that levels of spending for low-income individuals averaged about $2,000 per person but with a wide variation. New York, for example, spent over $4,000 per person while Arkansas spent less than $1,300. Acute care spending ranged from $1,800 per person in New York to $700 in Arkansas.

The extent of coverage of the low-income population of a state was another basis for comparison. Nationally, Medicaid covered 46% of all individuals below 150% of poverty. High-income states (like New York) covered more than 60% of their low-income population in 1994, but more rural southern and western states (like Arkansas) covered less than 40%.[32]

In 2007, the Public Citizen Health Research Group conducted a similar study based on 2003 data and reached equivalent conclusions. It ranked the states based on a numerical scoring system using eligibility, scope of services, quality of care, and reimbursement to arrive at a composite score. Vermont had the highest rank, followed by New York. Virginia was lowest, with a ranking score half that of Vermont. Overall, New York ranked the highest at two and one-half times the lowest-ranking, Mississippi.[33] A recent Kaiser Commission data summary showed a payment per enrollee for people with disabilities in 2006 as $26,500 in New York, which was three and one-half times greater than in Arizona, with the lowest payment.[34]

These are analytic snapshots in time that serve to illustrate one of the starkest examples of federalism. States have used their flexibility to determine eligibility standards and scope of services to offer different ranges of coverage. A person with the same life characteristics in Arkansas is likely to have access to Medicaid coverage very different from that of a person in New York in the same situation. A continuing challenge for Medicaid, as a federal health coverage system, is to balance the system's individual state differences with the concern of all citizens to be treated equitably.

The differences among states in critical Medicaid eligibility and coverage far exceed state income or cost of living differences. A central policy question is whether or not the United States should have such substantial variations in a critical national health program. Medicaid was not an experimental program that developed in the states. It was instead the product of national law with an invitation to participate offered to states. More than one-half of Medicaid funds come from the national income tax. Should we move away from the differences and toward a national standard of eligibility and coverage? Or have we become so accustomed to these differences that we take them for granted?

The Federal Medical Assistance Percentage Formula

When Medicaid was enacted into law in 1965, Congress established a formula, the federal medical assistance percentage (FMAP), which begins with the rolling three-year average per capita income of a state. The square of the state's per capita income is divided by the square of the US per capita income and multiplied by 0.45. The minimum federal share is 50% irrespective of the formula outcome. At the minimum match, the federal government pays one dollar for every dollar spent by the state for Medicaid. At a 75% match, the federal government pays three dollars for every state dollar spent. The formula is recalculated every year, but the basic components have remained the same. In 2008, there were twelve states at the minimum 50% share. Some of these states would be considerably below without the minimum match. The highest federal payment scale was for Mississippi at 76%.[35]

A variety of critics have argued that the formula's use of per capita income as the key variable has a distorting effect since it does not reflect concentrations of low-income people or service delivery costs.[36] In 2003, the General Accounting Office (GAO), an agency of Congress, found in a study of FMAP that "because of the formula's current structure, in many instances, two states devoting the same proportion of their own resources toward funding Medicaid services are unable, after receiving federal matching aid, to spend the same amounts per person in poverty, adjusted for cost differences related to age and geographic location."[37] In a 2004 study, Vic Miller and Andy Schneider identified options for changing the formula that would better reflect state tax capacity, be more responsive to economic cycles, and better take into account concentrations of people living in poverty.[38]

As with any formula-based distribution of money, even when most of the participants recognize problems with the structure, any change will create winners and losers. Those who have a high match under the current system are unlikely to support a change, even if the abstract logic of the change seems compelling. Despite the current partisan rancor over health policy issues, the congressional delegation from a state with a high match is likely to unite in favor of the status quo rather than lose a share of federal funds. Some proposals for change have called for elimination of the 50% minimum on the grounds that wealthy states could pay a larger share. Legislators from those states, such as New York, will resist such reform. To create a new formula in which the winners significantly outnumber the losers would cost more than the current system. Yet those who want to change the system usually envision saving money, not spending more. In this instance, the federal system mitigates against a modification of this critical financial component of Medicaid.

Medicaid Managed Care

In the early 1980s, less than 2% of Medicaid beneficiaries were enrolled in managed care. As this form of service delivery began to be utilized more widely by employer group plans, state Medicaid officials saw it as a way to control costs, limit utilization by system management, and increase the availability of primary care providers to Medicaid recipients. By 1997, over 50% of Medicaid recipients were in managed care.[39] Until the BBA-97, most states had to obtain a waiver from the federal government in order to require Medicaid recipients to be in the Medicaid managed care system. The BBA-97 legislation allowed states to contract with managed care organizations (MCOs) to provide services, and established standards for plan quality and patient protection. Bolstered by the states, the managed care trend has continued and 71% of Medicaid recipients were in some type of managed care by 2008.[40]

The MCO model is a risk-based capitation model in which the organization is responsible for the financial risk associated with delivering basic services for a monthly fee. In 2008, one-half of all Medicaid enrollees were in MCOs. The primary care case management model with about 16% Medicaid beneficiaries is the other approach. It is predominant in rural areas lacking the population density needed for MCOs. Since 2003, Medicaid-dominated MCOs have become the most typical approach. Some are organized by safety net hospitals, but corporations specializing in this market organize others. Use of commercial MCOs with a mixed population has declined.[41]

In the initial wave of states adopting managed care for their Medicaid program, children and families were the focus. More recently, intensive case management programs have begun to emerge to serve people with disabilities and chronic illnesses. These are high-risk and high-cost groups, and Medicaid officials hope that managed care organizations and primary care case management organizations can be induced to move beyond routine care for children and families to special arrangements to provide for the more intense needs of people with disabilities. To do so effectively, states must develop risk-adjusted payments for people with disabilities.[42] Many states are also now moving dual eligibles into managed care arrangements.

Within a little more than a decade, states have moved most of the Medicaid population into managed care organizations for service delivery. This has been accomplished with a minimum of political conflict at the same time that there has been active rebellion against managed care in employment-based private health plans. It is a political success story for state Medicaid officials.

Disproportionate Share Payments

The Boren Amendment was part of the Omnibus Budget Reconciliation Act of 1981. One feature was the authorization for states to make extra payments to hospitals with a disproportionate number of Medicaid patients. These were called disproportionate share hospitals (DSHs). Thus began a saga of financial federalism that can be viewed as either a "Medicaid scam" or an example of creative financing on the part of public program entrepreneurs who were struggling to find enough money to serve the medically indigent of their states.

Because few states were utilizing DSHs, Congress in 1986 additionally authorized Medicaid payments to hospitals with high volumes of low-income patients exceeding the Medicare upper payment limit (UPL).[43] By 1990, DSH payments were still less than $1 billion. In 1991, they had jumped to $4.7 billion, an almost 400% increase. The following year they totaled $17.4 billion, and reached their maximum in 1995 at $19 billion.[44]

What happened? It began in West Virginia as an attempt by state officials to find additional funds in a cash-strapped state with many Medicaid recipients. Hospitals donated money to the state, which the state Medicaid agency then used to pay the hospitals for Medicaid services. When the donated dollars were paid back to the states, they were used to generate federal reimbursement. For example, a $10 million donation generated a $12 million DSH payment, of which $6 million was paid by the federal government. The hospital gained $2 million, the state gained $6 million, and the federal government paid $6 million that would not have otherwise been spent. Other states adopted provider tax programs similar to the West Virginia donation. Within two years, the number of states with DSH programs jumped from six to thirty-nine.[45] In some instances, states were not using their net gain dollars for care of the poor or even for health care. They applied the net state gain to other state expenditures.

To stem the hemorrhaging of federal DSH funds, Congress over several years took a series of steps to limit future DSH growth. These included rules for provider taxes and donations, a limit of DSH payments in each state to 12% of total Medicaid spending, facility-specific ceilings on DSH payments, and imposition of national and state specific allotments for DSH payments.[46] States continue to have flexibility in designating DSHs and establishing the payment as long as the allocations are not exceeded. In 2005, the federal share of DSH payments was almost $10 billion. This amounted to about 5.5% of total Medicaid benefits, down from 15% in 1992. These DSH payments still represented about 40% of regular Medicaid payments for inpatient care. The payments have continued to be concentrated. The 2011 allotment for the top five states was 40% of the total, and 58% for the top ten states.[47]

The imagination of state Medicaid officials seeking to maximize federal payments was not limited to DSHs. A related approach was to utilize UPL rules along with intergovernmental transfers to increase federal payments beyond what they would have been. States made extra payments to a set of providers, usually county-operated facilities. These extra payments were greater than the actual cost to provide services for the Medicaid beneficiaries, and did not violate the federal regulations as long as aggregate payments were not in excess of the Medicare UPL for a class of institutions. The county public institution would then transfer back the extra payment to the state in the form of an intergovernmental transfer.[48] Once again the state would gain extra revenue that might be spent in a variety of ways, not limited to health expenditures for the poor. This was in effect a higher matching rate paid by the federal government. The GAO, an agency of Congress, criticized some of these arrangements. Figure 4.1 offers a diagram of one real case to illustrate how the state government gained additional matching money from the federal Medicaid agency.[49]

These innovative financing arrangements resulted in the transfer of billions of dollars from the federal government to the states, and are an example of the opportunity for manipulating the federal system. They were not illegal, nor were individuals benefiting by the financial

Figure 4.1
State Financing Arrangement in Which
Provider Did Not Retain the Full Supplemental Payment

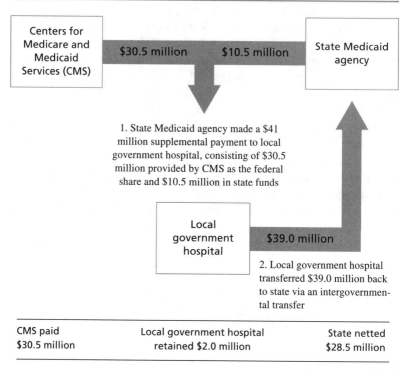

Centers for Medicare and Medicaid Services (CMS)

$30.5 million $10.5 million

State Medicaid agency

1. State Medicaid agency made a $41 million supplemental payment to local government hospital, consisting of $30.5 million provided by CMS as the federal share and $10.5 million in state funds

Local government hospital

$39.0 million

2. Local government hospital transferred $39.0 million back to state via an intergovernmental transfer

CMS paid $30.5 million	Local government hospital retained $2.0 million	State netted $28.5 million

Source: Government Accounting Office, Report no. GOA-07-214 (2007), www.gao.gov/new.items/d07214.pdf.

manipulation. Rather state officials used loopholes in the federal laws and regulations to gain additional reimbursement. Once states and provider institutions had become accustomed to these funds, it was difficult for Congress to end the payments. DSH funds increased fivefold in a few years, but Congress was not prepared in the early 1990s to suddenly terminate them. The allocations exist today at the same dollar amount as nearly fifteen years ago. Although relatively smaller, they still represent important sources of money for Medicaid hospitals. The generally lower rate of hospital reimbursement for Medicaid compared to Medicare and private plans offered justification for everyone involved to manipulate the system to collect extra federal funds.

Under ACA, the secretary of health and human services is given authority to target Medicaid DSH reductions based on the share of uninsured in the state, whether the state DSH targets hospitals with high Medicaid patient loads, and to provide smaller reductions for low-DSH states. However, the aggregate allotment for 2014 will increase from $11 billion to $13 billion. The new law also provides various incentives for safety net hospitals to prepare for what could be an increase in Medicaid patients. We might expect that this will provide opportunities for new imaginative approaches to Medicaid fiscal federalism.

There has also been a Medicare DSH payment system, but these funds have been distributed to hospitals on the basis of a formula that has not been subject to the same type of manipulation. ACA scales back future Medicare DSH funds because the number of uninsured is expected to decline.

1115 Waivers

Medicaid is a federal-state program whose basic structure allows for flexibility and innovation at the state level. Nevertheless, state officials have often found the federal regulations restrictive. There has always been the desire on the part of the federal government, both Congress and the program administrators, to have rules to prevent state governments from pursuing policies that either allow too much program divergence from the national norms or do not serve the interest of program recipients. Waivers of national program requirements have provided system flexibility. Section 1115 waivers allow for research and demonstration projects that depart from normal rules. The secretary of health and human services can issue such waivers. The law does not require that the project be budget neutral, but this has been a long-standing practice. It has meant that states seeking waivers must demonstrate that federal costs as a result of the waiver must be no more than they would have been if there had been no waiver.[50]

Until the early 1990s, waivers tended to be small in scope and state officials viewed the process as cumbersome. In the 1990s President Clinton, a former governor, sought to provide more flexibility for states in the administration of Medicaid. Thus, from the mid-1990s forward, the scope and pace of waivers increased and tended to broaden coverage expansion by allowing states to include within their Medicaid population other groups or approaches. This expansion included mandating managed care and eligibility expansion, especially for pregnant women and children. The fiscal balance often came from redirecting DSH funds or using savings from mandated managed care.[51] In the George W. Bush administration, after 2001, waivers more often sought state flexibility to reduce benefits and charge cost-sharing fees to help ease the pressure on state budgets. The changed approach was the result of economic downturn and active debate about the future direction of the program. Broad program restructuring waivers were sought after 2005 and the waivers became a critical element for the 2006 Massachusetts health reform legislation; it granted a Section 1115 waiver for use of Medicaid funds.

The other waiver provision is Section 1915, which was approved by Congress in 1981. This is a programmatic rather than demonstration waiver. It opened the way for managed care expansion and use of home health care as an alternative to nursing homes for older people.[52] Despite the early history of waivers as approval for demonstration projects, there has been little formal evaluation of them.[53]

In the decade after 1995 almost every state sought at least one waiver, and a total of 149 out of 195 were approved. Often the waiver was in fact negotiated between state and federal officials. The administrative flexibility provided by many of the waivers tended to erode any residual support among state officials for moving Medicaid to a block grant system with capped yearly increases. Block grant flexibility, not reduced funds, was the original inducement for what support existed among governors for a capped entitlement or block grant approach. Increased use of the Section 1115 waiver approach in essence released federal control and provided a corrective adjustment to a system that many state officials thought was too federalized while still requiring them to raise a substantial amount of revenue to pay program costs.

Medicaid's Next Half- or Maybe Quarter-Century

Several years ago, Grogan and Patashnik saw Medicaid at a crossroads. The program could continue to develop as a broad-based social welfare entitlement used by even many middle-class Americans, or it could take the path back to a narrow program repeatedly threatened with retrenchment.[54] The 2010 enactment of ACA appears to have sent the program down the broader path. As with the origins of

Medicaid, this was not a clear choice made at the center of the legislative spotlight. Given their central role in this new health reform package, the Medicaid provisions received surprisingly little media attention. The headlines in the days leading to enactment were filled with mentions of abortion and other issues that were not central to the legislative goal of expanding insurance coverage. Medicaid expansion accounts for about one-half of the uninsured who will be extended coverage under ACA.

For some time, Medicaid has been incrementally modified to move away from its origins as a health care program for only the welfare poor. The most important Medicaid provision in ACA extends Medicaid coverage to everyone with an income below 133% of poverty. This will include adults aged sixty-four years and younger without children, who had not been eligible. The determination will be made on the basis of income without an asset test. To protect states against a sudden jump in their Medicaid share, the federal government will fully cover the first two years (2014–2016), and then incrementally add a state share until 2020, when the federal share becomes 90% permanently. The CBO estimated that the new federal cost over the decade will be $434 billion, with only a $20 billion state increase.[55]

Will ACA end policy discussions about the future of Medicaid? On the contrary, it is likely to propel key issues to the agenda before the end of this decade. Reducing the size and role of the federal government in Medicaid by either program shrinkage or some type of privatization remains a policy goal for many conservatives. Over the next decade, a new congressional majority, combined with a change in the White House, might lead to a different and more narrow direction for the future of Medicaid. Representative Paul Ryan, a Wisconsin Republican, is chairman of the House Budget Committee. He has once again introduced the idea of shifting Medicaid from an entitlement to a block grant. The budget plan passed by the House in April 2011 would transform Medicaid into a block grant. This plan would significantly reduce federal Medicaid funding within a decade.[56] Neither the Senate nor the Obama administration supports this approach, but the idea of transforming Medicaid into a block grant is likely to remain a subject of serious discussion.

Another issue is the federal match formula. Many have argued about its policy obsolescence and technical inadequacy. Any attempt to incrementally change the formula creates state winners and losers, with the latter unwilling to support change. With the federal government now about to pay nearly all the costs of Medicaid expansion on a permanent basis, it will not be long before the states conclude that this would be a good arrangement for the rest of Medicaid. A movement, perhaps incremental, toward 85% or 90% federal funding for Medicaid would make actual adjustment of the formula easier because in essence all states would win, some more than others.

If the federal government were to ultimately assume most of the costs of the program, significant differences in benefit structure and eligibility would be impossible to justify. Any new policy movement is likely to be in the direction of national set standards. States would still be responsible for the day-to-day administration of the program, which now includes the critical element of arranging for and supervising the managed care system in which three of every four participants will participate. Moving Medicaid clients with disabilities and special needs effectively and fairly into managed care will require more focused attention than can be provided with a waiver process. Congress will no doubt be asked to provide legislative ground rules for the continued process of state agency organization and oversight of Medicaid managed care. Since the program will remain based on the principle of federalism with joint responsibilities, the policy choices will need to reflect an accommodation between consistent policy tendencies of the federal government and the desire of state officials to maintain administrative flexibility to deal with local differences. The resolution of these issues will not be simple, but if accomplished in the congressional arena they will be less likely to create the administrative game playing that has characterized the DSH payment system over the past two decades.

Finally, Medicaid is notorious for its low rate of provider reimbursement. Without attempting to judge the adequacy of reimbursement, it seems clear that providers, especially physicians, do not receive compensation for services to Medicaid patients commensurate with Medicare or private insurance plans. This leads many providers to limit the number of Medicaid patients that they are willing to accept. If Medicaid continues to take the broad path toward a more comprehensive system for low- and moderate-income individuals and families, is it possible to do so without a reimbursement modification that at least tethers fees to those paid by Medicare? It seems not, but this is a critical policy question.

If Wilbur Mills was to return to observe the path of the Medicaid program that he almost single-handedly created forty-five years ago, he probably would not be surprised by the scope and reach today. He would no doubt find it appropriate that members of Congress will likely have to find compromises and policy accommodations to put Medicaid firmly on its path for the next fifty years.

Notes

1. Howard A. Rusk, "Caring for the Poor: Social Security's Medical Provisions Could Help Solve Poverty Problems," *New York Times,* August 22, 1965, p. 58.

2. Jonathan Engle, *Poor People's Medicine: Medicaid and American Charity Care Since 1965* (Durham, NC: Duke University Press, 2006), chap 8.

3. Robert Pear, "Reagan Said to Ask States to Assume Food Stamp Costs: US Would Pay Medicaid," *New York Times,* January 22, 1982, p. A1; Robert Pear, "White House Halts Attempts to Shift Welfare to States," *New York Times,* April 7, 1982, p. A1.

4. See, for example, Michael F. Cannon, "Medicaid's Unseen Costs," Policy Analysis no. 548 (Washington, DC: Cato Institute, August 18, 2005).

5. John F. Holahan and Joel W. Cohen, *Medicaid: The Trade-off Between Cost Containment and Access to Care* (Washington, DC: Urban Institute Press, 1986), p. 93.

6. David G. Smith, *Entitlement Politics: Medicare and Medicaid, 1995–2001* (New York: Aldine de Gruyter, 2002), pp. 39–66.

7. David G. Smith and Judith D. Moore, *Medicaid Politics and Policy* (New Brunswick, NJ: Transaction, 2008), pp. 248–251.

8. Ibid., pp. 261–265; Sara Rosenbaum et al., "The Children's Hour: The State Children's Health Insurance Program," *Health Affairs* 17, no. 1 (1998): 75–89.

9. Alan Weil, "The New Child Health Insurance Program: A Carefully Crafted Compromise" (Washington, DC: Urban Institute, October 1999).

10. Diane Rowland and Kristina Hanson, "Medicaid: Moving to Managed Care," *Health Affairs* 15, no. 3 (2003): 150–152.

11. "Medicaid and Managed Care: Key Data, Trends, and Issues" (Washington, DC: Kaiser Commission on Medicaid and the Uninsured, February 2010), pp. 1–7.

12. Smith and Moore, *Medicaid Politics and Policy,* p. 280.

13. Jonathan B. Oberlander and Barbara Lyons, "Beyond Incrementalism? SCHIP and the Politics of Health Reform," *Health Affairs* 28, no. 3 (2009): 404–406.

14. Robert Pear, "Obama Signs Children's Health Insurance Bill," *New York Times,* February 5, 2009, p. NA(L), www.nytimes.com/2009/02/05/us/politics/05health.html.

15. "Children's Health Insurance Program Reauthorization Act of 2009" (Washington, DC: Kaiser Commission on Medicaid and the Uninsured, February 2009), pp. 1–2.

16. Colleen Grogan and Eric Patashnik, "Between Welfare Medicine and Mainstream Entitlement: Medicaid at the Political Crossroads," *Journal of Health Politics, Policy and Law* 28, no. 5 (2003): 821–858.

17. Stan Dorn, Bowen Garrett, John Holahan, and Aimee Williams, "Medicaid, SCHIP, and Economic Downturn: Policy Challenges and Policy Responses" (Washington, DC: Kaiser Commission on Medicaid and the Uninsured, April 2008), pp. 3–5.

18. "State Fiscal Conditions and Medicaid" (Washington, DC: Kaiser Commission on Medicaid and the Uninsured, February 2010), pp. 1–4.

19. January Angeles, "Health Reform Is a Good Deal for States" (Washington, DC: Center on Budget and Policy Priorities, April 2010), pp. 1–2.

20. "Children's Health Insurance Program Reauthorization Act of 2009" (Washington, DC: Kaiser Commission on Medicaid and the Uninsured, February 2007).

21. Christopher J. Truffer, "Health Spending Projections Through 2019: The Recession's Impact Continues," *Health Affairs* 29, no. 3 (2010): 522–529.

22. "Health Coverage of Children: The Role of Medicaid and CHIP" (Washington, DC: Kaiser Commission on Medicaid and the Uninsured, October 2009).

23. "Medicaid: A Primer" (Washington, DC: Kaiser Commission on Medicaid and the Uninsured, June 2010), p. 10; Jeffrey S. Crowley and Risa Elias, "Medicaid's Role for People with Disabilities" (Washington, DC: Kaiser Commission on Medicaid and the Uninsured, August 2003).

24. "State Medicaid Coverage of Perinatal Services: Summary of State Survey Findings" (Washington, DC: Kaiser Commission on Medicaid and the Uninsured, November 2009).

25. "Dual Eligibles: Medicaid's Role for Low-Income Medicare Beneficiaries" (Washington, DC: Kaiser Commission on Medicaid and the Uninsured, February 2009), pp. 1–2.

26. Kaiser Commission on Medicaid and the Uninsured, *Medicaid,* pp. 1–42.

27. "Community Health Centers" (Washington, DC: Kaiser Commission on Medicaid and the Uninsured, March 2009), pp. 1–2.

28. Congressional Budget Office, *Spending and Enrollment Detail for CBO, March 2010, Baseline: Medicaid* (Washington, DC: CBO Publications Office, March 2010).

29. "Report on the Financial Outlook for Medicaid" (Baltimore, MD: Centers for Medicare and Medicaid Services, Office of the Actuary, October 17, 2008).

30. John Houlahan and Alshadye Yemane, "Enrollment Is Driving Medicaid Costs, but Two Targets Can Yield Savings," *Health Affairs* 28, no. 5 (2009): 1453–1465.

31. "Report on the Financial Outlook for Medicaid," p. 11.

32. John Houlahan and David Liska, "Variations in Medicaid Spending Among States," New Federalism Brief No. 3 (Washington, DC: Urban Institute, January 1997).

33. Annette B. Ramirez and Sidney M. Wolfe, "Unsettling Scores: A Ranking of State Medicaid Programs" (Washington, DC: Public Citizen Health Research Group, April 2007).

34. "State Variation and Health Reform: A Chartbook" (Washington, DC: Kaiser Commission on Medicaid and the Uninsured, October 2009), pp. 1–19.

35. Christie P. Peters, "Medicaid Financing: How the FMAP Formula Works and Why It Falls Short," Issue Brief No. 828 (Washington, DC: National Health Policy Forum, December 2008), pp. 1–9.

36. Peters, "Medicaid Financing"; Robert B. Helms, "The Medicaid Commission Report: A Dissent," Health Policy Brief No. 2 (Washington, DC: American Enterprise Institute for Public Policy Research, January 2007), pp. 1–7.

37. US General Accounting Office, *Report to the Honorable Dianne Feinstein, US Senate on Medicaid Formula*, GAO Report No. 03-620 (Washington, DC: GAO, July 2003).

38. Vic Miller and Andy Schneider, "The Medicaid Matching Formula: Policy Considerations and Options for Modification" (Washington, DC: AARP Public Policy Institute, September 2009), p. 24.

39. Etienne E. Pracht, "State Medicaid Managed Care Enrollment: Understanding the Political Calculus That Drives Medicaid Managed Care Reforms," *Journal of Health Politics, Policy and Law* 32, no. 4 (2007): 686–701.

40. "Medicaid and Managed Care: Key Data, Trends, and Issues" (Washington, DC: Kaiser Commission on Medicaid and the Uninsured, February 2010), pp. 1–7.

41. Ibid.

42. Bruce C. Vladek, "Where the Action Really Is: Medicaid and the Disabled," *Health Affairs* 22, no. 1 (2003): 90–100.

43. Teresa A. Coughlin and David Liska, "The Medicaid Disproportionate Share Hospital Payment Program: Background and Issues," Issue Brief No. 14 (Washington, DC: Kaiser Commission on Medicaid and the Uninsured, October 1997).

44. Jean Hearne, "Medicaid Disproportionate Share Payments," *CRS Report for Congress* (Washington DC: Congressional Research Service, Library of Congress, Order Code 97-483, January 10, 2005).

45. Coughlin and Liska, "The Medicaid Disproportionate Share," p. 2.

46. David Rousseau and Andy Schneider, "Current Issues in Medicaid Financing: An Overview of IGTs, UPLs, and DSH" (Washington, DC: Kaiser Commission on Medicaid and the Uninsured, April 2004).

47. Kaiser Commission on Medicaid and the Uninsured, www.kff.org; State Health Facts.org, "Federal Medicaid Disproportionate Share Hospital (DSH) Allotments," www.statehealthfacts.org/comparemaptable.jsp?ind =185&cat=4&sort=a&gsa=2.

48. Teresa A. Coughlin, Brian K. Bruen, and Jennifer King, "States' Use of Medicaid UPL and DSH Financing Mechanisms," *Health Affairs* 23, no. 2 (2004): 245–257; Teresa A. Coughlin, Stephen Zuckerman, and Joshua McFeeters, "Restoring Fiscal Integrity to Medicaid Financing?" *Health Affairs* 26, no. 5 (2007): 1469–1480.

49. US Government Accountability Office, *Report to the Committee on Finance,* GOA Report No. 07-214 (Washington, DC: GAO, March 2007).

50. "The Role of Section 115 Waivers in Medicaid and CHIP: Looking Back and Looking Forward" (Washington, DC: Kaiser Commission on Medicaid and the Uninsured, March 2009).

51. Frank J. Thompson and Courtney Burke, "Executive Federalism and Medicaid Demonstration Waivers: Implications for Policy and Democratic Process," *Journal of Health Politics, Policy and Law* 32, no. 6 (2007): 971–1004.

52. Ibid., p. 974.

53. "The Role of Section 115 Waivers in Medicaid and CHIP."

54. Grogan and Patashnik, "Between Welfare Medicine and Mainstream Entitlement," p. 821.

55. "Medicaid and Children's Health Insurance Program Provisions in the New Health Reform Law" (Washington, DC: Kaiser Commission on Medicaid and the Uninsured, April 2010), pp. 1–8.

56. January Angeles, *Ryan Medicaid Block Grant Would Cause Severe Reductions in Health Care and Long-Term Care for Seniors, People with Disabilities, and Children* (Washington, DC: Center on Budget and Policy Priorities, May 3, 2011).

5

Too Much Money: Uncontrolled Costs

***

Every dollar of health-care expenditures is also a dollar of someone's income.
—*Robert Evans, Department of Economics, University of British Columbia*

Across the developed world, administrators of health care systems grapple with the problem of containing costs. Some have been more successful than others. In this chapter, I offer a snapshot of health care system costs across the developed countries, look at policy approaches used to control the rate of growth, and review three possible scenarios for the United States in the decade ahead.

A century ago, the health care system in the United States consisted of marginally educated physicians practicing mainly in the small towns. There was limited capability for surgery, hospitals were unable to do more than provide a bed for poor and sick patients, and pharmacists dispensed medicine in much the same way as a century earlier. Even by 1930, health care in the United States consumed only about 3% of gross national product (GNP). Today, the cost to provide health care services is approaching one dollar out of every five.

The system developed for health care service delivery is complex. It requires vast amounts of expensive equipment, utilizes the services of a wide range of well-paid professionals, involves hospitals that provide around-the-clock care to many very ill patients, and cares for a population whose average age is steadily rising. All health care systems are inexorably linked to both national and regional governments. Each nation has a different public and private mix within its health care system. Every dollar spent must first be collected from individuals and businesses. As the rate of spending increases, rising taxes or insurance premiums cause other goods and services to be deferred to pay for health care.

Why Is Health Care in the United States So Expensive?

Table 5.1 compares the United States and selected Organisation for Economic Co-operation and Development (OECD) countries on the basis of per capita health care expenditures. The US total expenditures are considerably higher than those of the other countries. Why? Does the US health care system offer better care with more efficacious outcomes? Do US citizens live longer as a result of the greater national investment in health care? Do patients in the United States receive care more quickly and therefore experience less pain, anguish, and threat to life? Reasonably good data regarding the cost of care are available for most developed countries. To simplify, I focus on four other countries (the United Kingdom, France, Germany, and Canada) to address these questions.

Diet, lifestyle, environment, and medical care all contribute to life expectancy. The major increase in life expectancy among developed countries in the twentieth century was probably attributable more to improved sanitation systems and public health responses to infectious disease than to application of routine medical care. Table

Table 5.1   Health Care Expenditures in Selected OECD Countries (2006)

	Per Capita Health Care Spending (dollars)	Percentage of Gross Domestic Product
Canada	3,678	10.0
France	3,449	11.1
Germany	3,371	10.6
United Kingdom	2,760	8.4
United States	6,714	15.3

Source: Karen Davis, Cathy Schoen, and Kristof Stremikis, *Mirror, Mirror on the Wall: How the Performance of the US Health Care System Compares Internationally* (New York: Commonwealth Fund, 2010), update from OECD data.

5.2 demonstrates that the much greater per capita spending in the United States has not produced either greater general life expectancy or a better age-standardized death rate per 100,000 from conditions such as ischemic heart disease, diabetes, stroke, and bacterial infections. It is easier to measure resources (e.g., hospital beds, physicians, magnetic resonance imaging [MRI]) or procedures (e.g., knee replacements) than to measure outcomes.

As shown in Table 5.3, there are fewer physicians per 1,000 people in the United States than anywhere except Canada, and fewer physician visits per capita. The MRIs per 1 million residents, knee replacements per 100,000, and dialysis per 100,000 are considerably higher in the United States. Only France has fewer nurses per capita than the United States. In a 2008 comparative study of health costs in the United States, the McKinsey consulting firm concludes that "the United States carries out 40 to 90 percent more PCIs (percutaneous coronary intervention), knee replacements, coronary bypasses, and cardiac catheterizations than other OECD countries, even when adjusting for prevalence. Above-average volume of these four procedures alone accounts for an estimated $21 billion in additional inpatient care costs."[1]

One of the few systematic attempts to measure comparative outcomes was a 2004 Commonwealth Fund study that examined such measures as cancer survival rates, asthma mortality rates, and thirty-

Table 5.2 Life Expectancy in Selected OECD Countries

	2008 Life Expectancy from Birth (years)	Percentage Change, 1986–2006	Mortality Amenable to Health Care, Age-standardized Death Rate per 100,000 Individuals, 1989–1999	Mortality Amenable to Health Care, Age-standardized Death Rate per 100,000 Individuals, 2002–2003
Canada	80.4	+3.9%	88.9	76.8
France	80.9	5.3%	75.6	64.8
Germany	79.8	5.2 %	106.2	90.1
United Kingdom	79.1	4.4%	130.0	102.8
United States	77.8	3.1%	114.7	109.7

Source: Karen Davis, Cathy Schoen, and Kristof Stremikis, *Mirror, Mirror on the Wall: How the Performance of the US Health Care System Compares Internationally* (New York: Commonwealth Fund, 2010), update from OECD data.

Table 5.3   Health Resources and Procedures in Selected OECD Countries

	Physicians per 1,000	Average Visits per Capita	Nurses per Capita	Beds per 1,000	MRIs per 1 Million Residents	Knee Replacements per 100,000 Residents	Dialysis per 100,000 Residents
Canada	2.1	5.9	9.4	2.8	6.2	130	63
France	3.4	6.4	7.2	3.7	5.3	95	59
Germany	3.6	7.0	9.9	6.2	7.7	121	80
United Kingdom	2.5	5.1	9.2	2.7	5.6	118	39
United States	2.4	4.0	7.9	3.4	26.5	176	114

Source: Karen Davis, Cathy Schoen, and Kristof Stremikis, *Mirror, Mirror on the Wall: How the Performance of the US Health Care System Compares Internationally* (New York: Commonwealth Fund, 2010), update from OECD data.

day case fatality rates after acute myocardial infarction and stroke.[2] The study found relatively little difference in the measures among the five countries, although all did well on some measures and poorly on others. A 2005 patient survey of adults with health problems in five countries identified problems with safety risks, care coordination, and chronic condition care. None of the countries were consistently better or worse on the items measured.

Over several years, the Commonwealth Fund has produced a report on care experiences and ratings of dimensions of care in seven countries. Its 2010 update found that the United States ranks last or next to last on five dimensions: quality, access, efficiency, equity, and healthy lives. The United States ranks high on some dimensions (e.g., prevention), but poorly on items such as chronic care and coordination.[3]

Whenever the international comparative numbers are discussed, the question of nonurgent surgical wait lists is brought up. This is rarely a problem in the United States. But it is perceived by the public as a problem in countries such as the United Kingdom and Canada. However, in a 2005 article, Gerard Anderson and colleagues offer a cogent argument about why this can explain only a small piece of the expenditure differences. A comprehensive study of surgical waiting times in OECD countries found this to be a problem for countries such as Canada and the United Kingdom, but not Germany, France, or the United States.

Waiting lists do not explain the difference in spending between the United States and Germany, which performs most of the cited procedures at considerably higher rates with one-half the per capita spending. A 2005 study calculated the total 2001 costs of the procedures that accounted for most of the United Kingdom and Canada waiting lists. It found this to explain only 3% of US spending.[4]

It appears that the higher rate of health care spending in the United States does not result in longer life expectancy, better quality of care, or quicker response than in any other country. A US patient receives a quicker hip replacement than a patient in the United Kingdom, but more Germans receive hip replacements without a waiting period.

Anderson and colleagues are among a number of scholars who have undertaken a comparative analysis of health care spending in the United States and other developed nations. They titled a 2003 article "It's the Prices, Stupid."[5] The article demonstrates that compensation for health care professionals, both wages and fees, is higher in the United States. Hospitals are more service intensive and the system less efficient. Jonathan Oberlander and Joseph White examined the US system and drew similar conclusions.[6] Anderson et al. point out that physician supply in the United States grew by only 1% from 1991 to 2001, and US medical schools in 2000 graduated about the same number as in the 1970s.[7]

M. K. Bundorf, Anne Royalty, and Laurence C. Baker's study of private insurance found outpatient and drug costs the most significant driver of cost in the period 2001–2006. They determined the number of procedures per patient, rather than an increase in patients, to be the key factor in rising outpatient costs. The price of brand-name drugs and volume per enrollee for generics were critical factors in drug price increases. In real dollars, hospital admissions and associated costs declined over the period.[8]

The Dartmouth Studies on Medicare Spending

In a 2009 piece in *The New Yorker*, Atul Gawande featured the town of McAllen, Texas. McAllen is located along the Mexican border in Hidalgo County, which has the lowest household income in the country. Medicare spends more per capita in McAllen than anywhere in the country, except Miami. El Paso County, also along the border, has similar demographics with half the average Medicare spending. In both towns the available technology, Medicare quality metrics, and supply of physicians are about average. An analysis of the utilization data points to the likely cause. McAllen patients had more specialist visits, ultrasound, bone density studies, stress tests, gallbladder operations, knee replacements, home health visits, and cardiac bypass operations than patients in El Paso County. Hospital officials and physicians in McAllen each thought the other hospitals were the culprit. Gawande in the end concludes that the difference between McAllen and El Paso County was the aggressive nature of the local physicians in ordering tests and procedures. The financial structure rewarded them when volume was up. This did not appear to be a problem of fraud or completely unnecessary procedures. Rather it was the "very aggressive" and "push to the limit" type of medicine that produced more services per patient than were found elsewhere in the country.[9]

Since 1996, a research team under the leadership of John Wennberg of the Dartmouth Medical School has been publishing and updating a large dataset of Medicare expenditures, called the Dartmouth Atlas, that is now available on the team's website. In the introduction to the most recent version, Wennberg and his colleagues offer the following conclusions from their study of regional variations in Medicare spending:

- Variations are not due to difference in the prevalence of serious illnesses.
- Variations are due to supply-sensitive care such as the number of physicians and hospital beds.
- Higher spending and greater supply of physicians and hospital beds are not associated with better care.
- Variations in spending range from 20% above the national average to 25% below.[10]

The link between supply of hospital beds and utilization was first studied and articulated by Milton Roemer, who succinctly states, "A bed built is a bed filled."[11] He found a direct correlation between bed capacity and utilization. The Dartmouth Atlas project is a sophisticated continuation of that tradition of scholarship.

Many who are concerned about rising health care costs and seeking policy approaches to address the problem have used the Dartmouth Atlas and the conclusions drawn by the Wennberg team to support various cost-containment policies. Others have been critical of the implications drawn, especially the reduction of provider payment rates for high-cost areas. The Atlas has statistically demonstrated that there are significant differences in both Medicare service levels and spending in different counties across the country, even when adjusted for other factors such as income differences, health of the local population, and local prices. One set of inescapable implications from the data is that excess supply leads to overuse of services.

The next step is to draw policy change implications. Many of the high-cost hospitals are located in urban areas such as Manhattan. They are among the major health institutions in the country associated with medical schools, not a small hospital owned by physicians in a Texas border town. If the policy suggestion drawn from the Dartmouth Atlas data is to reduce rates of payment to major medical centers, a strong negative reaction is likely.

How to Control the Rate of Increase

The problem of rising costs is large and critical to the future of health care service delivery and the economic stability of the country. There is no shortage of ideas and suggestions about how to address the issue. In this section, I organize these ideas into five categories: price control approaches, capital expenditure regulation, market approaches, system reorganization, and payment ideas. In each category, I discuss relevant policy ideas for addressing the growth of health care spending.

In 2009, national health spending was estimated to be $2.4 trillion. The Office of the Actuary of the Centers for Medicare and Medicaid Services projects this will grow by 6.1% on average, which is 1.7% faster than gross domestic product (GDP). It projects total health care spending to be $4.5 trillion in a decade, which would be an 81% increase. During that time the population will grow 9%, and GDP will grow 63%.[12] Table 5.4 shows the increases by service category.

The Office of the Actuary projects private health insurance expenditures will grow at an annual rate of 5.1%, which is less than total health care spending. Medicare will grow at 6.9% annually and Medicaid at 7.5% annually. By the end of the decade, the public share of health care spending is expected to be 52% of the total. Michael E. Chernew, Richard A. Hirth, and David M. Cutler conclude that the increase in health care spending between 1999 and 2007 means that 35% of the increase in per capita income during the period was devot-

Table 5.4   Projected Health Care Expenditures (2009–2019)

	2009 ($billions)	2014 ($billions)	2019 ($billions)	Percentage Share	Percentage Growth, 2009–2019
Hospital	760.6	996.3	1,374.5	31	81
Physician and clinical	527.6	646.8	882.0	21	67
Other professional	69.6	90.0	123.7	3	78
Dental	104.4	135.7	180.4	4	73
Other personal health care	75.7	117.2	184.6	3	144
Nursing home and home health	216.3	286.9	399.7	9	85
Prescription drugs	246.3	322.1	457.8	10	86
Medical equipment	27.0	32.6	43.0	1	59
Nondurable medical products	40.8	49.5	63.3	2	55
Program and INS administration	162.8	225.1	320.3	7	97
Public health	75.2	101.0	140.3	3	87
Total	2,472.3	3,225.3	4,482.6		81
Population	307.2	321.0	334.8		9
GDP	14,282.5	18,488.2	23,283.0		63
National health expenditures as percentage of gross domestic product	17.3	17.4	19.3		

Sources: Centers for Medicare and Medicaid Services, National Health Expenditure Data, www.cms.gov/NationalHealthExpendData/downloads/NHEProjections 2009to2019.pdf; Christopher J. Truffer et al., "Health Spending Projections Through 2019: The Recession's Impact Continues," *Health Affairs* 29, no. 3 (2010): 522–529.

ed to health care.[13] The higher the gap between the health care expenses and GDP growth, the larger the share of all new real income devoted to health care. This is a concern not only for government budgets but for corporate financial health and individual consumer preferences. Across the political spectrum, this is a recognized problem. The proposed solutions are varied, with no clear consensus choice.

Price Control Approaches

For a long time, social insurance advocates have contended that the best approach to limit the growth of health care spending is to have the government collect all or most of the money to be spent in the form of taxes and distribute it as part of a central budget process. This came to be called a "single-payer system," and is exemplified by the UK and Canadian systems.[14] Both systems have experienced controversial waits for elective surgery and some recent citizen dissatisfaction over the adequacy of innovation in delivering care. Given the intensity of the debate around the issue of the appropriate role of government in health care resource decisions that preceded adoption of the Patient Protection and Affordable Care Act of 2010 (ACA), it seems unlikely that the United States will adopt either a UK- or Canadian-style single-payer system.

Medicare prospective payment system. Interestingly, for three-quarters of older Americans, Medicare provides a single-payer system. The remaining one-quarter of older people participate in Medicare Advantage, which consists of private health plans that receive an allotment from Medicare for each enrollee and use those funds to pay providers. With the enactment in the 1980s of the prospective payment system (PPS) for hospital payment and the resource-based relative value scale (RBRVS) for physician fees, Medicare payment strategy shifted from cost reimbursement to an administered price system. If price of services is indeed the critical factor in determining escalating costs, then for Medicare enrollees the federal government has the policy tool to slow the rate of increasing expenses. If Congress held the annual increases for the hospital and physician fees to the rate of general inflation, it would appear to maintain Medicare cost growth at the level of inflation in the economy. Congress, however, has been unable to resolve the increasing gap between the recommended physician fee adjustment and the argument of physicians for a higher rate.

The process of continuing the review to extend the status quo from year to year, without resolving the basic issue, does not bode well for use of administrative prices as a Medicare cost control mechanism. Additionally, as the McAllen, Texas, example vividly illustrates, total spending is the product of both price and volume. If the reimbursement system cannot control volume as well as price, then aggregate expenditures will rise.

With Medicare there is the added factor of an aging population and a declining ratio of workers to retirees, especially since a significant share of total program revenue is derived from the payroll tax. Over the past two decades, there have been periods of time when Medicare costs have risen more slowly than private insurance and other spans of time when the opposite has happened. On average, the two have tracked fairly closely in the growth rate of spending per enrollee.[15] Despite different populations and benefit structures, both pay the same hospitals, physicians, and other providers. Over time, it will be difficult for Medicare to pay substantially lower rates, especially since it represents such a large share of total hospital payments with 30% of all hospital revenue and also 20% of all physician and clinical services. Medicaid, on the other hand, has historically accounted for a much smaller share of total hospital and physician payments.

To some extent, the Medicare payment system has been the trendsetter for private insurance negotiation with providers. It can be a standard against which payments are benchmarked by private plans. However, if a price control system is to be effective, it must apply to all payers. Joseph White has made a compelling case for an all-payer rate system. He argues for a system in which both hospital and physician rates of payment are common across all payers. Thus Medicare, private insurance plans, and Medicaid would all pay the same amount for similar delivered services. Among other things, this system would lower provider administrative costs since there would be no need for a bewildering array of different forms and procedures for reimbursement. Electronic record systems and provider cost analysis would be simpler without multiple payment systems.[16]

Maryland's Health Services Cost Review Commission. A long-standing example of an all-payer system is the state of Maryland's Health Services Cost Review Commission. It was established by the state legislature in 1971 to restrain costs, ensure access for all, and provide financial stability for the hospitals. Maryland uses a system somewhat similar to the Medicare PPS to establish yearly rates for hospitals in the state. All payers (Medicare, Medicaid, and private plans) pay the same rate for the same service category. There is no need for cost shifting since costs incurred by the uninsured are spread across all hospitals and are not the sole responsibility of the serving institution. In 1976, Maryland hospital costs were 26% above the national average, but in 2007 they were 2% below it.[17]

The Maryland commission is moving from fee-for-service (FFS) to bundled payments for outpatient services and has experimented with pay-for-performance (P4P) initiatives. Maryland also has a long-standing Certificate of Need (CON) program to limit hospital capital expenditures; this also serves to contain costs. In the history of US health policy development, states have frequently served as experimental laboratories, testing an idea before it is adopted on a national scale. The Massachusetts health reform plan recently served as a model for ACA. The Medicare PPS system and the Maryland commission are both working examples of how establishing an administrative price system might help contain the growth of costs.

Capital Expenditure Regulation

The intellectual foundation for capital expenditure regulation is found in the 1959 articulation of Roemer's law. Milton Roemer postulated that an excess supply of hospital beds in a region leads to greater utilization.[18] As far back as the 1930s, some in the hospital industry called for state regulation to control the tendency of hospitals to overbuild. In the 1950s, civic leaders in cities such as Cleveland and Rochester, New York, instituted planning processes in an attempt to determine the ideal number of hospital beds for the community. In 1964, the New York legislature established the first state CON program. Any new hospital construction needed to be reviewed by a regional planning agency and approved, ultimately, by the state public health department. The new construction would not be licensed as a hospital without an approved certificate showing the need: no institution could build or expand without first receiving a certificate of need.

In 1968, Congress established a grant program to assist regions in establishing health care planning agencies. In states with CON laws, Comprehensive Health Planning (CHP) agencies performed the local review of hospital capital projects. Later, in the mid-1970s, Congress replaced CHP agencies with Health Systems Agencies (HSAs). Under this 1974 health planning law, each region was required to have a planning agency and review capital projects. States were mandated to establish CON agencies, but in the interim, failure to gain HSA approval would result in reduced Medicare and Medicaid reimbursement for services provided in the new facilities.

During the 1970s, most states and regions adopted a comprehensive planning process, including CON legislation. The results were mixed. Powerful local institutions often were able to gain approval for their projects, even if they did not meet the guidelines. Planning agencies also wrestled with how to regulate new technology such as computerized tomography (CT) scanners.[19] The CON process seemed to be more successful at controlling the entry of new institutions (especially, for-profit hospitals) into the market.

The Jimmy Carter administration sought what would have amounted to a national CON program administered by the HSAs with regional limits on the amount of capital spending. Institutions would have had to compete for limited health care capital dollars. But Congress did not approve this proposal. The Ronald Reagan administration shifted the emphasis in health policy toward market-oriented approaches and ended federal support for HSAs and the regional planning process. CON programs have survived in a number of states, but they have not been a key part of the national cost-containment strategy for thirty years.

The Dartmouth Atlas identifies excess capacity as a major factor in the Medicare regional spending disparities.[20] If this is found to be a major contributor to escalation of health care costs, the regional health planning and CON process should be revisited.

Market Approaches

At the other end of the continuum is the argument that more government intervention in the health care marketplace would be counterproductive in controlling costs. This point of view emerges from the consumer choice advocacy coalition. Coalition advocates firmly believe that government is the problem, not the solution. According to this approach, government should reduce or eliminate its role in regulating, purchasing, and subsidizing health services. Consumer choice becomes the key to more effective cost control. But since health care is a service purchased in the marketplace, if consumers ultimately wish to purchase more rather than less service, this is a choice to be respected.[21]

The proposal begins with the elimination of the dominant existing approaches to health insurance. Employer-sponsored insurance and its income tax subsidy would be eliminated and replaced with individual medical savings accounts (MSAs). These are high-deductible plans with catastrophic insurance. Employers would contribute to the MSA and probably pay for most of the catastrophic insurance. Thus, the individual exercises greater personal choice about whether to pursue medical treatments and which ones are most valuable. The consumer makes the choice based on a calculation of the value of the medical services received for the dollars spent. This market-based consumer choice is assumed to produce the "right" amount of medical services at the appropriate price.

Under the consumer choice cost-containment approach, state regulation of insurance by benefit mandate would be eliminated. Interstate sale of insurance would be allowed with only the home state regulating the product. The safety net for those whose medical conditions effectively exclude them from the regular insurance market is the strengthening of state high-risk pools and more extensive tax credits for those who donate money to providers who offer charity care.[22]

The role of government would not be completely eliminated, but Medicare would move exclusively to a premium support plan and parts of Medicaid would be converted into a cash subsidy for the purchase of private insurance. Government would be needed to ensure the functioning of the marketplace by promoting competition and preventing fraud.[23]

Consumer choice champions place great faith in the health care markets to produce long-term cost containment, and general acceptance of whatever level of spending is the result of individual decisionmaking about desired level of health care. What this approach does not appear to address is the growing concentration of power in both the hospital and insurance sectors. Even in major markets today, there are often only a handful of medical centers and insurance companies that appear relatively immune to competition.[24] Choice among providers at the entry level will do little to mitigate the costs associated with long periods of intensive and costly treatments. Even with only catastrophic insurance, the premiums could become unacceptably high.

System Reorganization

Any discussion of cost containment inevitably finds agreement from both ends of the spectrum. The fragmented and disorganized nature of the US health care system is a major component of the problem. System reorganization is central to the discussions within health reform debate. Various reorganizational concepts have been proposed as an answer, or the answer. Some of the concepts have previously circulated under different names; others have been recently proposed.

These concepts are categorized below as ideas about payments or about service delivery.

Payment Ideas

Pay-for-performance. The basic P4P idea is to pay health care providers to provide quality. Of course, the first response might be incredulity: we should assume that health care providers wish to serve the interest of patients with quality care. Sandra J. Tanenbaum has traced the development of these concepts within Medicare over the past fifteen years and found broad support for the idea. She found relatively little evidence to demonstrate that P4P makes any difference in a series of demonstration projects.[25] "Quality" is operationally defined as a target level of performance using process or outcome measures against a baseline.[26] Medicare, and other payers, reimburse on the basis of services rendered. In the current system, poor quality in a hospital could lead to an additional payment because of hospital readmission. This payment might be as low as 1% or 2% of current payments.[27]

Issues involved in the design of a P4P system include the size of the bonus payment, the accuracy of the measures used to determine quality, employment of relative or absolute targets, and the entity receiving the payment. For example, in a fragmented system, a patient with a chronic illness may be seen by multiple and uncoordinated physicians or hospitals. If outcome measures are used, it will be impossible to determine which entity was responsible for the outcome. Process measures are under greater institutional control, but may have a tenuous relation to quality. Unless all payers use the same metrics for P4P systems, institutions will find themselves pursuing different goals or just abandoning the system as being not worth the effort.

Bonus systems are notorious for rewarding what is easiest to measure rather than most important. If P4P systems are to be successful, it will likely be the result of system reorganization to take advantage of the bonus potential rather than a change of behavior within the existing structure.

Bundled payments. Bundled payments occur when a payer combines a set of normal reimbursements for an episode of care into a single package. The presumption is that bundled payments for both the physician and hospital will reduce total spending by providing a disincentive for unnecessary and uncoordinated care. The ultimate result will be both reduced cost and better-quality care. Medicare demonstration projects have employed a bundled services concept. The projects showed promise of both quality improvement and lower cost, but there has been strong resistance to the combination of physician fees and hospital payments into one bundle.[28]

The Prometheus model is a Robert Woods Johnson Foundation–sponsored set of pilot projects that uses bundled payments to encourage physician-hospital collaboration and the reduction of avoidable complications.[29]

The design of the bundled payment system offers key choices. But if the payment does not account for disease severity, hospitals may be reluctant to care for patients with a more serious problem or with multiple interrelated health issues. If post–acute care is included in the bundle, there are additional cost and quality improvement opportunities. Yet post–acute care may pose greater risk for providers because of uncertainty, and it may offer more opportunities to game the system by pushing some services beyond the time covered by the bundling.

A RAND Corporation study of the potential of bundled payments concluded that treatment of seven chronic conditions by bundling payments could save the system 5.5% in costs over ten years.[30] As with P4P, bundling payments alone is unlikely to produce momentous change. Any payment mechanism must produce new organizational arrangements to be truly effective.

Reorganization Ideas

Accountable care organizations. Accountable care organizations (ACOs) are "providers who are jointly held accountable for achieving measured quality improvements and reductions in the rate of spending growth."[31] These producers serve a defined subset of Medicare beneficiaries or insurance plan subscribers. ACOs manage patients with a continuum of care across institutional settings, plan budgets, and complete performance measurement. There has not been universal agreement among ACO advocates about the precise organizational structure, and one of the elements of the model is the flexibility that allows for adaptation to local areas. These ACOs can be physician-centered organizations such as independent practice associations (IPAs), hospital-centered organizations, or health care provider networks. The organizations are voluntary, with eligible entities agreeing to participate in exchange for meeting quality performance standards.

The organizations may also be mandatory. With mandatory ACOs, hospitals and physicians are assigned to virtual ACOs based on a sharing of patients assigned by claims data. Participation of primary care physicians is central to the ACO accountability concept and the management of cost and quality.

In either instance, the key incentive for quality improvement is a shared savings program in which the ACO receives the standard FFS Medicare Part A and B reimbursement, but is eligible for retrospective bonus payments based on the difference between expected and actual spending for the beneficiaries in the ACO.[32]

ACA authorized the use of ACOs with a shared savings program for Medicare providers. Steven M. Lieberman and John M. Bertko argue this is an attempt to create a middle ground between fee-for-service payments and capitation plans, which pay providers a flat fee for each participant. Success will depend on the flexibility of the regulatory rules governing the creation of Medicare ACOs.[33]

In Grand Junction, Colorado, in the 1970s a group of primary care physicians took the lead in developing an integrated system with shared savings and cost control incentives. This system has succeeded in maintaining expenditures and usage considerably below the national average.[34]

ACOs represent an attempt to bind providers serving the same beneficiary population in an attempt to improve quality and reduce costs through better coordination of services. It uses shared savings as the participation incentive. The generation of significant savings may be difficult because it is dependent on a significant modification in health care systems that have long resisted change.

Comparative effectiveness research. What works best for the treatment dollars spent? This obvious question does not have a simple answer. Physicians make clinical decisions based on their medical education, clinical experience, and study of the current literature in the field. When a patient has an identifiable problem, the physician selects diagnostic tests and a course of treatment most likely to be successful. Usually, the physician does not have access to scientifically developed information on the comparative effectiveness of treatment options. There are often alternative modes of treatment for a given disease or medical problem and the cost difference among them may be significant. In the United Kingdom, the National Institute for Health and Clinical Excellence makes recommendations to the National Health Service based on research concerning the cost-effectiveness of treatments or technologies.

Comparative effectiveness research "compares two or more different methods for preventing, diagnosing, and treating health conditions."[35] There has been some private sector research funding of comparative effectiveness as well as limited studies sponsored by the National Institutes of Health. The most rigorous approach to this research is the use of clinical trials, but this approach is also expensive. The Congressional Budget Office (CBO) concluded that the comparative effectiveness of clinical trials could lead to reductions in federal health spending, but not by as much as the cost of the research.[36] Analysis of medical claims data or reviews of treatment evidence is a less expensive method of comparison, but these conclusions are more prone to inaccuracy because other factors are not held constant.

While some have lauded the possibilities for significant cost savings and improved quality of care from the application of comparative effectiveness research, the actual impact of the studies on cost have not been proven. The American Recovery and Reinvestment Act of 2009 allocated $1 billion for the sponsorship of this research. The resulting studies may, in the future, provide an indication as to whether or not this cost-containment approach will work.

Electronic medical records. Across the US health care system a vast array of modern technology is employed to treat disease. Amazingly, the patient records of that care are still often written by hand. Information technology systems are far more developed in other major US industries as well as in the European health care systems. Information technology systems can be used to maintain a personal health record for individuals, exchange clinical data among providers, and keep the institutional records of services provided to patients. The Geisinger Health System in Pennsylvania utilizes an electronic record system as an integral part of its attempt to improve quality and maintain cost-effective service delivery.[37]

Those advocating a massive effort to move health care institutions into the digital era argue that a comprehensive electronic medical record system would improve patient care coordination, reduce medical errors, facilitate reimbursement, and generate cost savings.[38] If the US health care system was more integrated, it would be easier to implement electronic records. The most consolidated system in the United States is that of the Veterans Administration, which has developed an extensive electronic record system. The National Health Service in the United Kingdom has also developed an electronic record system. Electronic records assist in the development of integrated systems, but the motivation to network is an essential first step. The computerized systems themselves will not generate integration.

Many physicians are opposed to the implementation of electronic records because of cost barriers, simple resistance to changing established practices, fear of selecting an obsolete system, and, perhaps more importantly, resistance to the network effect. Technology, in this case electronic recordkeeping, becomes essential only when others in the network are also using it. A fax machine was not useful in an office until most other offices possessed one. At that point, it became essential technology.[39] A recent CBO study of the issue states that "research indicates that in certain settings, health IT [information technology] appears to make it easier to reduce health spending if other steps in the broader health care system are also taken. By itself, the adoption of more health IT is generally not sufficient to produce significant cost savings."[40]

Despite some skeptics, there has been broad support for providing incentives to providers to adopt electronic record systems. Advocates cite quality improvements in addition to cost savings as the rationale for much broader use of electronic medical records. Since there are significant costs associated with the adoption of electronic records, some type of financial incentive may be essential. The CBO estimates a cost of $3,000 to $9,000 annually per physician to implement a system in office practice.[41] Without some type of incentive, the pace of adoption may be slow. Financial assistance from the federal government might increase the pace of development. The broader the implementation of electronic records, the greater opportunity to achieve the network effect.

Rationing

Any US health policy debate can be enlivened by interjecting the word "rationing." In the summer of 2009, reform opponents generated press and attention by accusing the Barack Obama administration of wanting to institute death panels to ration care for the dying. It is difficult to have a serious discussion about what all scholars will admit: every health care system rations, in some fashion. No society is willing to pay for all possible treatments that might be given to anyone. In his book, Henry Aaron states that rationing refers to "the situation in which people who can afford a commodity are unable to buy it because of scarcity, which results because some nonmarket allocation system—ration coupons or queues, for example, limits demand to available supply."[42]

The National Health Service in the United Kingdom has more aggressively rationed certain types of care, such as kidney dialysis, than has the US health care system. Prior to Medicare coverage of dialysis in the late 1960s, there was limited availability of machines. Because of the high cost and lack of insurance coverage, hospitals did not have the capacity to provide dialysis to all who might benefit from the service. Panels were established to review applicants, and those whose age and lifestyle best fit the criteria were allowed to undergo dialysis. For the others, rejection was a likely death sentence.

A more recent example of rationing is organ transplants. The limited supply of organs is less than the number of patients who might benefit. A strict criterion is used to select those who receive available organs. If artificial organs became available, even at a steep price, should we ration them and provide to some and not others?

It is not unusual for analysts, such as Aaron, to say "the United States will be forced by sharply rising public and private health care spending to consider the adoption of such limits."[43] This usually is not offered as the preferred policy approach, but as a threat. If cost containment is not achieved, the evil of rationing will be imposed. Rationing typically does not occur universally, but with respect to particular services that are expensive to offer and perhaps of questionable value. The difficulty with the discussion of rationing is that it implicitly puts a value on human life; our society is uncomfortable with this.

In a class several years ago, I asked my students how many would pay $1 to provide lifesaving treatment to a stranger. Everyone raised their hand. How about $10? A few hands went down. How about $100 or $1,000? As the cost escalated, the hands were lowered. We all recognize rationing as an essential economic tool to address a world of limited resources, but we are uncomfortable discussing it. Because of this discomfort, it seems unlikely that rationing will be explicitly used as a policy tool for addressing the rising costs of health care.

Three Scenarios for the Future

The continued increase in health care spending is a serious national problem. On that point, there is little disagreement. The problem has been recognized for years. If there was an easy answer, it would have been solved long ago. In this chapter, I examined many of the remedial policy ideas that have been suggested. In conclusion, I suggest three possible scenarios.

As national health expenditures creep toward 20% of GDP, pressure will grow on the government, the insurance industry, and the providers to take action to mitigate the absorption of large amounts of the annual economic growth subsumed by the health care system. Even many supporters of health reform have argued the cost control elements of ACA may not be strong enough to effectively bend the cost curve.[44] The three scenarios that I describe below assume that the rate of growth of national health care expenditures will continue moving toward 20% of GDP by the end of the decade, with no end in sight to the cost escalation.

Incremental Adjustments

Despite broad concern about the negative economic impact of a steady escalation of health care spending, neither the government nor businesses are able to put policies in place to stem the growth. Providers publicly lament the cost growth, but privately resist any major changes to either their income or ways of doing business. The continued consolidation of both the medical and insurance sectors makes it easier for them to reach an accommodation than undertake decisive action. By the end of the decade, the federal government will be responsible for raising more than half of the total revenue spent in the health care system. Decisive public action is impossible because of partisan divisions, provider lobbying strength, and citizen resistance to either tax increases or hints at service reduction.

The only viable strategy for the federal government is adjustment on the margins. Some of the cost-containment demonstration projects authorized by ACA will be efforts to improve system efficiency, such as the expansion of electronic medical records. The major emphasis now has become the solvency of the Medicare Part A Trust Fund. The hospital reimbursement growth rate is marginally controlled, and economic recovery plus some shifting of general tax revenue into Part A will allow the fund to remain in balance into the next decade.

No new Medicare benefits have been added; Medicaid continues to experience temporary cost saving on the margins by eligibility adjustments at the state level. The insurance exchanges, ACA insurance regulation, and the individual mandate are some help in controlling premium costs in the growing individual market. Private insurance plan costs, however, continue to rise faster than inflation, causing households to spend more of their income for health care. Even employers who self-insure have found the only way to contain their own budget costs is to impose more cost sharing on workers.

The various incremental adjustments do not bend the cost curve, but tweak it just enough to keep the system from imploding. As the baby boom population grows, there are increasing calls for drastic policy change. Yet none of the proposed solutions are politically acceptable and the ultimate crisis appears to be at least a decade into the future.

All-payer Reimbursement

The inability of the cost control provisions of ACA to significantly alter the national health spending trajectory has caused a realization on the part of leaders in government, the health care industry, the insurance industry, and business that unless some type of cooperative action is taken, the entire economy will be threatened. With providers unable or unwilling to make significant changes in the basic structure of the health care delivery system and some fearful of a government takeover, providers decide to support government establishment of an all-payer reimbursement system.

To accomplish this, a national commission with responsibility to set payment rates that apply to all providers for hospitals, physician fees, nursing homes, and home health is established. This basic approach is similar to the Medicare payment system. The starting point for this payment system is the historic price averages. Yearly increments are based on statistical analysis by commission staff. The commission is responsible for setting the increments after public hearings in which major provider and consumer groups testify and present evidence. Congress has the ability within ninety days to veto a proposed increment, but will not be able to initiate an increase. Since the commission is composed of provider representatives as well as health finance experts, it effectively becomes a bargaining place over annual increments as well as any shifts in resources among the categories of provider groups.

While providers are somewhat apprehensive about a government body controlling the revenue flow, the commission creates stability in a system in which instability is becoming a growing possibility. A common reimbursement system means much less administrative difficulty for both hospitals and physician offices because of a single online system to submit claims. Large private plans are not able to negotiate special discounts with providers, but also are not subject to cost shifting as each payer is responsible for the services generated by its enrollees. In the past, all but the largest private plans found it increasingly difficult to negotiate deep discounts because of the market concentration of large hospital systems and physician groups in major metropolitan areas.

The all-payer rate system can modestly bend the cost curve by restricting price increases, yet only marginally control volume. The commission staff would need to continue to refine the payment systems leading toward bundling of payments around an episode of care; bundling does help restrict volume abuse. One must keep in mind, however, that putting physician and hospital payments into a single package is difficult to achieve because of the inevitable strong physician opposition. On the other hand, the all-payer system benefits the providers because the government's emphasis is on negotiating a price for services instead of a government push for external reorganization of providers. If the all-payer rate system is implemented incrementally, little system change will take place around care management or coordination of care. An advantage of the all-payer system for providers is the government's emphasis on negotiating a price for services and not pushing for internal reorganization of providers. Thus, relatively little system change takes place around care management or coordination of care.

System Reorganization

In his landmark 1982 book, Paul Starr predicts the growth of vertically integrated health care systems in the years ahead.[45] The subsequent decade saw the rise and decline of health maintenance organizations (HMOs) as an effort to reorganize the delivery of health care to achieve better quality with a decline in the rate of expenditure growth. During that period, the model design for many was the California-based Kaiser Permanente integrated HMO. This model did not spread across the country, and vertical system integration did not occur at the pace Starr anticipated.

In this third scenario, it is assumed that the current round of attempts to integrate and rationalize a fragmented health care delivery system succeeds in implementing major changes. ACA provides for the development of accountable care organizations with ACOs receiving bonus payments for successfully achieving better coordination of care.

As the decade progresses and cost concerns grow, the fragmentation of the health care system is perceived as a problem of cost and quality. The federal government begins to pursue a strategy of pushing reorganization to address cost and quality. If ACOs inevitably become mandatory, bonus payments will be linked to performance on process and outcome measurements. Those ACOs not able to meet these metrics will be penalized not only by failing to receive bonuses, but also penalized on existing reimbursement.

Medicare payment systems will be increasingly bundled and combined with P4P metrics. Major public spending to subsidize start-up costs results in exponential growth in electronic medical records, and soon the network effect will begin to provide an incentive for the remaining holdouts to adopt the emerging universal use. As the investment in comparative effectiveness research begins to produce a substantial literature comparing the cost-effectiveness of alternative treatments, payment systems will reflect this understanding.

The size and scope of Medicare with the authorization to aggressively pursue these approaches will cause private insurance plans serving both Medicare Advantage and others to emulate this approach and pressure physicians and hospitals toward ACOs that serve all patients. The combination of financial pressure and bonus rewards for better organizational delivery of services to patients with chronic illnesses succeeds in inducing hospitals and physicians to better integrate. For most, this is not the tight organization arrangement of the Kaiser Permanente HMO integrated staff model, but rather a networked organization led only by physicians and not administrators. Based on the better data available from electronic records, it will be easier to track and measure both process and outcome for the identified high-expense patients with multiple chronic conditions. As the network systems are developed and tied to reimbursement, physicians and hospitals will be driven by financial incentives to integrate patient care, even if remaining organizationally separate.

Since patients with chronic illnesses generate a huge share of total costs, the virtual network integrated system emphasizes the management of care for these individuals and partially succeeds in bending the cost curve for both Medicare and private plans. However, the costs of maintaining electronic records, verifying effectiveness research, and paying bonuses do limit the amount of total savings. A dollar saved in hospital care is worth only fifty cents if half of the savings are used to pay for the system reorganization.

* * *

In none of the three scenarios is the adoption of a cost-containment strategy completely successful in reducing the cost trajectory at or below the rate of inflation. In each scenario, the curve is bent enough that the immediate crisis is avoided and usually accompanied by an optimism that things will get even better. After more than a half-century of health care spending growth above the rate of inflation, an incremental shift of the cost curve may be the best achievement.

Notes

1. Diana M. Farrell, Eric S. Jensen, and Bob Kocher, "Why Americans Pay More for Health Care," p. 58, McKinsey Quarterly, McKinsey Global Institute Report, December 2008, www.mckinseyquarterly.com/Why _Americans_pay_more_for_health_care_2275.

2. Peter S. Hussey et al., "How Does the Quality of Care Compare in Five Countries?" *Health Affairs* 23, no. 3 (2004): 89–97.

3. Karen Davis, Catch Schoen, and Kristof Stremikis, *The Commonwealth Fund Report: How the Performance of the US Health Care System Compares Internationally,* June 2010, www.commonwealthfund .org/~/media/Files/Publications/Fund%20Report/2010/Jun/1400_Davis _Mirror_Mirror_on_the_wall_2010.pdf.

4. Gerard F. Anderson, Peter S. Hussey, Bianca K. Frogner, and Hugh R. Waters, "Health Spending in the United States and the Rest of the World," *Health Affairs* 24, no. 4 (2005): 903–912.

5. Gerard F. Anderson, Uwe E. Reinhardt, Peter S. Hussey, and Varduhi Petrosyan, "It's the Prices, Stupid: Why the United States Is So Different from Other Countries," *Health Affairs* 22, no. 3 (2003): 89–105.

6. Jonathan Oberlander and Joseph White, "Public Attitudes Toward Health Care Spending Aren't the Problem; Prices Are," *Health Affairs* 28, no. 5 (2009): 1285–1286.

7. Anderson et al., "It's the Prices, Stupid," p. 96.

8. M. K. Bundorf, Anne Royalty, and Laurence C. Baker, "Health Care Costs Growth Among the Privately Insured," *Health Affairs* 28, no. 5 (2009): 1294–1304.

9. Atul Gawande, "The Cost Conundrum," *The New Yorker,* June 1, 2009, www.newyorker.com/reporting/2009/06/01/090601fa_fact_gawande.

10. John E. Wennberg, Elliot Fisher, David Goodman, and Jonathan Skinner, "Tracking the Care of Patients with Severe Chronic Illness" (Lebanon, NH: Dartmouth Institute for Health Policy, April 2008), www.dartmouthatlas.org/downloads/atlases/2008_Chronic_Care_Atlas.pdf.

11. M. Shain and M. I. Roemer, "Hospital Costs Relate to the Supply of Beds," *Modern Hospital* 92, no. 4 (1959): 71–73.

12. Christopher J. Truffer et al., "Health Spending Projections Through 2019: The Recession's Impact Continues," *Health Affairs* 29, no. 3 (2010): 522–529.

13. Michael E. Chernew, Richard A. Hirth, and David M. Cutler, "Increased Spending on Health Care: Long-term Implications for the Nation," *Health Affairs* 28, no. 5 (2009): 1253–1254.

14. Carolyn H. Tuohy, "Single Players, Multiple Systems: The Scope and Limits of Subnational Variation Under a Federal Health Policy Framework," *Journal of Health Politics, Policy and Law* 34, no. 4 (2009): 453–492; Adam Oliver, "The Single-Payer Option: A Reconsideration," *Journal of Health Politics, Policy and Law* 34, no. 4 (2009): 509–529.

15. *A Data Book: Healthcare Spending and the Medicare Program Report* (Washington, DC: Medicare Payment Advisory Commission, June 2010), p. 9, www.medpac.gov/documents/Jun10DataBookEntireReport.pdf.

16. Joseph White, *Implementing Health Care Reform with All-Payer Regulation, Private Insurers, and a Voluntary Public Insurance Plan,* pp. 1–26, www.ourfuture.org/files/JWhiteAllPayerImplementing.pdf.

17. Robert Murray, "Setting Hospital Rates to Control Costs and Boost Quality: The Maryland Experience," *Health Affairs* 28, no. 5 (2009): 1395–1404.

18. Shain and Roemer, "Hospital Costs Relate to the Supply of Beds."

19. James M. Brasfield, "Health Planning Reform: A Proposal for the Eighties," *Journal of Health Politics, Policy and Law* 6, no. 4 (1982): 718–738.

20. David Goodman, Elliot Fisher, and Kristen Bronner, "Hospital and Physician Capacity Update," *Dartmouth Atlas of Health Care,* March 30, 2009, www.dartmouthatlas.org/downloads/reports/Capacity_Report_2009.pdf.

21. R. Glenn Hubbard, John F. Cogan, and Daniel P. Kessler, *Healthy, Wealthy, and Wise* (Washington, DC: American Enterprise Institute Press, 2011).

22. Tom Miller, "Rising Health Care Costs," testimony before the Committee on Health of the Wisconsin Assembly, August 13, 2002, Cato Institute, www.cato.org/testimony/ct-tm081302.html.

23. Joseph Antos and Thomas Miller, "A Better Prescription: AEI Scholars on Realistic Health Reform" (Washington, DC: American Enterprise Institute for Public Policy Research, 2010), p. 3, www.aei.org/docLib/ABetterPrescription.pdf.

24. Paul Ginsberg, "Wide Variation in Hospital and Physician Payment Rates Evidence of Provider Market Power," Research Brief no. 16 (Washington, DC: Center for Studying Health System Change, November 2010).

25. Sandra J. Tanenbaum, "Pay for Performance in Medicare: Evidentiary Irony and the Politics of Value," *Journal of Health Politics, Policy and Law* 34, no. 5 (2009): 717–743.

26. Mark Merlis, "Health Care Cost Containment and Coverage Expansion" (Washington, DC: National Academy of Social Insurance, January 2009), p. 15.

27. Karen Milgate and Sharon Bee Cheng, "Pay-for-Performance: The MedPac Perspective," *Health Affairs* 25, no. 2 (2006): 415–419.

28. Jeff Goldsmith, "Analyzing Shifts in Economic Risks to Providers in Proposed Payment and Delivery System Reforms," *Health Affairs* 29, no. 7 (2010): 1301.

29. Francois de Brantes et al., "Building a Bridge from Fragmentation to Accountability: The Prometheus Payment Model," *New England Journal of Medicine* 361 (2009): 1033–1036.

30. Peter Hussey et al., "Controlling US Health Care Spending: Separating Promising from Unpromising Approaches," *New England Journal of Medicine* 361, no. 22 (2009): 2109–2112.

31. Mark McClellan et al., "A National Strategy to Put Accountable Care into Practice," *Health Affairs* 29, no. 5 (2010): 982–990.

32. Kelly Devers and Robert Berenson, "Can Accountable Care Organizations Improve the Value of Health Care by Solving the Cost and Quality Quandaries?" (Washington, DC: Urban Institute, October 2009).

33. Steven M. Lieberman and John M. Bertko, "Building Regulatory and Operational Flexibility into Accountable Care Organizations and 'Shared Savings,'" *Health Affairs* 30, no. 1 (2011): 23–31.

34. Thomas Bodenheimer, "Low Cost Lessons from Grand Junction, Colorado," *New England Journal of Medicine* 363 (2010): 1391–1393.

35. "Explaining Health Reform: What Is Comparative Effectiveness Research?" (Washington, DC: Kaiser Commission on Medicaid and the Uninsured, October 2009).

36. Congressional Budget Office, *Research on the Comparative Effectiveness of Medical Treatments: Issues and Options for an Expanded Federal Role* (Washington, DC: CBO Publications Office, 2007).

37. Ronald Paulus et al., "Continuous Innovation in Health Care: Implications of the Geisinger Experience," *Health Affairs* 27, no. 5 (2005): 1235–1245.

38. Darrell M. West and Edward Alan Miller, *Digital Medicine: Health Care in the Internet Era* (Washington, DC: Brookings Institution Press, 2009).

39. Michael C. Christensen and Dahlia Remler, "Information and Communications Technology in US Health Care: Why Is Adoption So Slow and Is Slower Better?" *Journal of Health Politics, Policy and Law* 34, no. 6 (December 2009): 1011–1034.

40. Congressional Budget Office, *Evidence on the Costs and Benefits of Health Information Technology* (Washington, DC: CBO Publications Office, 2008), p. 3.

41. Congressional Budget Office, *Key Issues in Analyzing Major Health Insurance Proposals* (Washington, DC: CBO Publications Office, 2008), p. 149.

42. Henry J. Aaron and William B. Schwartz, *Can We Say No? The Challenge of Rationing Health Care* (Washington, DC: Brookings Institution, 2005), p. 6.

43. Ibid., p. 7.

44. Jonathan Oberlander, "Long Time Coming: Why Health Reform Finally Passed," *Health Affairs* 29, no. 6 (2010): 1116.

45. Paul Starr, *The Social Transformation of American Medicine* (New York: Basic Books, 1982), pp. 430–436.

6

Long-term Care:
The Sleeping Giant

A number of years ago, there was a student from Nigeria in the health policy class that I taught. He was attentive, but not very vocal in expressing his opinion on class issues. Toward the end of the class, we spent an evening discussing the long-term care readings. After about an hour, he stood up and launched into an impassioned speech about caring for one's parents. He told his classmates that, in Africa, it would be unthinkable to place elderly parents in an institution like a nursing home. He said it was the duty of children to care for the parents who had brought them into the world and raised them. His unexpected oratory certainly changed the tenor of the discussion that evening.

In this chapter, I address the policy questions, institutional arrangements, and societal responsibilities that have developed around care for those who cannot live on their own. Until the middle of the twentieth century, the model described by the Nigerian student was the norm. Children, grandchildren, and extended family cared for the elderly and people with disabilities in the home. Women were the primary caregivers, and typically they were not employed outside the home. This provided time, but did not diminish the burdens of the task. Average life expectancy was much shorter in the nineteenth and early twentieth centuries. A century ago, 0.2% of the population was aged eighty-five years and older. In 2000, this percentage was 1.5%, and 11.0% of the population was aged sixty-five years and older. The medical technology to prolong life for the people with severe chronic illnesses did not exist at the beginning of the twentieth century. Caregiving years were short, but still a burden.

Today, a complex system has evolved to care for people with disabilities who are dependent on others. Some of the responsibilities involve tasks that can be legally performed only by licensed medical personnel. Others require little formal training, but infinite patience and concern. When professional institutions and individuals are engaged in caring for people with disabilities, money must be raised to compensate them. Whether this should be public funds, private out-of-pocket funds, or aggregated as part of an insurance mechanism is at the heart of the policy questions surrounding care of dependent people.

The Elderly and the Rise of the Nursing Home

It is relatively easy to count the number of people who live in nursing homes. It is harder to precisely define the institution, since the line between assisted living and nursing home is not always precise, especially if they are under the same roof. What is even more difficult is categorizing the level of disability for someone living independently or in the home of a relative. Disability is typically measured by the ability to perform activities of daily living (ADL) independently, such as bathing, and instrumental activities of daily living (IADL), such as housekeeping. Probably about 11 million people (4% of the population) need some help with one or more ADLs or IADLs. About one-half of these individuals, 4.7 million or 2% of the population, need assistance with ADLs. Those at an institutional level of need with multiple ADLs number about 3.2 million. The latter are at high risk of institutionalization if they do not live with someone who provides care.[1]

The group in greatest need is not restricted to the elderly because nearly one-half are aged sixty-four years and younger. The number of nursing home residents is about 1.8 million. This population is older and more likely to be women who are unmarried. Their income is lower than for people of a similar age without assistance needs.[2]

No one collected this kind of statistic 100 years ago, but we can assume that the impact of aging on the human body has not substantially changed. We have learned how to medically intervene to prolong life for those with deteriorating health, but the basic aging process has not been transformed. What has changed greatly in the past half-century is the development of institutional arrangements for assisting people with disabilities, especially older adults.

A policy genealogist could trace the Medicaid family tree back to Elizabethan poor laws in sixteenth-century England. More immediate ancestors are the early twentieth-century public assistance programs developed in many states. For example, Arizona enacted a program of cash payments to the elderly in 1915, and Wisconsin instituted a program for blind individuals in 1907.[3] Public policy is evolutionary. The Social Security Act of 1935 established the framework for the social welfare system. The public assistance programs in this law established support programs for the poor who were blind, elderly, or living with dependent children.

In the Social Security Act of 1935, Congress explicitly excluded from benefits those who were living in public institutions. The county public workhouses that sheltered some of the poor had a snake pit reputation. A 1925 Department of Labor report cited by Bruce C. Vladeck says, "Dilapidation, inadequacy, and even indecency are the outstanding physical features of many of our small almshouses. Ignorance, unfitness, and a complete lack of comprehension of the social element involved in the conduct of a public institution are characteristic of a large part of their managing personnel."[4] Congress did not wish to subsidize these institutions, and the modern nursing home industry can trace its beginnings from this decision. Private boardinghouses were established to serve the elderly who were eligible for subsistence payments under the public assistance programs.[5] Health insurance was not included in the original Social Security legislation. In 1950, the Social Security Board recommended and Congress authorized medical vendor payments for public assistance recipients under the Old Age Assistance (OAA) program.[6] Medical vendor payments were optional and, by 1960, spending for hospital and nursing home care totaled $514 million. Some medical vendor payments were used for nursing home expenses.

The Medical Assistance for the Aged Act (Kerr-Mills), passed in June 1960, proved to be an interim measure; Medicare replaced it five years later. There were two major provisions of the bill. First, it increased federal matching funds for medical vendor payments under the existing OAA. Second, it created a new program, Medical Assistance for the Aged (MAA). Under MAA, the federal government reimbursed states 50% to 80% of the cost of medical payments for medically needy persons aged sixty-five years and older. This new "concept of medically needy" referred to an individual who was not poor enough to qualify for OAA, but too poor to meet medical and other health care costs. MAA represented a significant increase in national responsibility, and for the first time the federal commitment was open ended. There were no limits on individual payments or total state expenditures. The control, administration, and limitations of the program were left to the states. Nursing home vendor payments were one of the allowable uses of MAA funds if the states opted to include them. In calendar year 1962, total nursing home payments under MAA were $117 million, which represented 47% of total program expenditures.

The nursing home industry began to grow because county poorhouses were unable to accept federal welfare payments and medical vendor payments were rising as an additional source of subsidy for the poor elderly people who were disabled. Between 1954 and 1961, nursing home beds increased 32%. Two additional policies were at work in this expansion. The Hill-Burton hospital construction program was modified to include nursing home projects. In 1956, Congress allowed the Small Business Administration to make loans to nursing home proprietors, and in 1959 the Federal Housing Administration was authorized to provide mortgage insurance for new nursing homes. The latter two actions assisted proprietary nursing homes, which represented almost three-fourths of the industry. The availability of public subsidy under OAA, and subsequently under MAA, enabled nursing home owners to build with confidence that future residents would have at least some public support for the cost of their care.

The importance of these factors in the growth of the nursing home industry was clearly stated by William Beaumont, president of the American Nursing Home Association. In his January 1964 testimony before the House Ways and Means Committee, he cited the federal legislation as a significant stimulation to nursing home construction and identified a positive relationship between the level of OAA payments and the availability of nursing home beds in the states:

> Government programs such as the mortgage loan program of the Federal housing administration, the nursing home program under the small business administration, and the Hill-Burton nonprofit nursing home Grant program, without a doubt, have provided the impetus for the rapid construction of nursing homes and the resultant improvements and facilities. . . . A computation made recently from health, education, and welfare trends, 1961 edition, showed decisively that where all OAA payments were highest, the availability of nursing home beds was greatest.[7]

Kerr-Mills has usually been seen as interim legislation representing the transition from limited medical vendor payments under the Social Security Amendments of 1950 to the expansive potential of Medicare and Medicaid entitlement programs. In the development of long-term care policy, Kerr-Mills should be seen as a true watershed. Vladeck estimated that, in 1960 when Kerr-Mills was adopted, there were about 10,000 nursing homes with 400,000 residents. Less than 50,000 residents were supported by vendor payments under OAA. By 1965 when Medicaid was established, payments under Kerr-Mills had increased fivefold and totaled half a billion dollars. Vendor payments for nursing homes represented one-third of an MAA program. More than one-half of all nursing home residents were supported by nursing home vendor payments.[8]

In 1960, when Kerr-Mills was enacted, there was an option to restrict or limit vendor payments for nursing homes, but the law did not exclude such payments. The inclusion of nursing home benefits under MAA, and the aggressiveness of at least some states in taking advantage of the new federal program, set the stage for greater expansion that was to take place under Medicaid. Federal policy directly and indirectly stimulated construction of new beds and facilities. The number of nursing home beds doubled between 1963 and 1971. The potential for public subsidy of nursing home care for older poor people was a major factor in this expansion.

Mental Illness and Public Policy

Mental illness is not new. Throughout history, some individuals have struggled to live and adapt to society. When such individuals appeared to be a threat, or perhaps a major inconvenience, institutions emerged to address the problem. As with other disabilities, relatives sometimes assumed responsibility to care for those whose behavior made employment difficult or impossible. Jail-type facilities were often used if the individual had no family members willing and available to provide care. In early nineteenth-century England, some institutions began to use moral treatment, which included spiritual advocacy and humane physical care. This innovation spread to the United States in the mid-nineteenth century. Reformer Dorothea Dix and others lobbied state governments to urge the building of large institutions in the rural parts of their states. Inmates who would otherwise have been a burden on their families or the county poorhouses were sent to the state institutions. These institutions sought to use religion and a healthy rural environment to change the lives of the mentally ill, who often were from the growing urban slums.

By the end of the nineteenth century, these institutions had taken on many more custodial characteristics. Staff were more likely to view their role as protectors of society by keeping people with mental illnesses institutionalized for life rather than attempting a cure and a return to the community. By the early twentieth century, these institutions were more like jails than treatment facilities. Once institutionalized, many never returned again to society. Freudian analysis introduced a more complex conceptual understanding of mental illness, but the labor-intensive work of analysis and the difficulty of using the technique for those with more serious problems led to two different worlds of treatment for mental illness. Rich people with neurosis could afford and benefit from Freudian analysis. The poor and the more seriously ill were shipped off to state mental institutions, often against their will.

A New Treatment for Mental Illness

The need to treat thousands of soldiers suffering from some level of mental illness during World War II led to a more sophisticated theory of mental illness in the postwar years. In 1946, Congress created the National Institute of Mental Health (NIMH) to foster more systematic research in the field. The major breakthrough in the approach to the treatment of mental illness came with the discovery of reserpine and chlorpromazine as effective tranquilizing drugs. These drugs did not offer a cure, but treated the symptoms in a way that allowed many patients to be considered for return to the community as long as the drug regime was maintained.[9] These drugs led to a shifting paradigm about the causes of mental illness and the possible treatment applications.

In 1961, the congressionally created Joint Commission on Mental Illness and Health published a report, *Action for Mental Health*.[10] Among other recommendations, it called for the development of local mental health clinics across the country. President John F. Kennedy supported this idea and, in 1963, Congress enacted the Community Mental Health Centers Act, which initially supported construction grants but later also included operating funds. At the state level, reformers began to target large state mental institutions as a result of the paradigm shift in the field. To legislatures and governors, the reformers argued that the return of institutional patients was possible with the new drugs and millions of dollars could be saved with the closing of facilities. To health care professionals, the reformers argued that these individuals could be safely returned to the community and, with family support and professional assistance from community mental health centers, the mentally ill could lead productive lives.

The deinstitutionalization movement rapidly spread across the country in the 1970s. Between 1974 and 1984, the bed capacity at state mental health facilities declined by over 50%.[11] The number of beds decreased from 500,000 in 1970 to 200,000 in 2000.[12] At the same time the campaign for parity of mental illness coverage in standard health insurance resulted in more inpatient mental health services at community hospitals. Over time, the characteristics of patients at state facilities changed. State facilities are now more likely to serve the poor, minorities, and men; middle-class patients use health insurance to pay for community hospital treatment.[13] The state facilities have come to serve a population that demographically resembles those incarcerated in prison.

Federal funding for the network of community mental health centers built in the 1960s and 1970s was turned into a block grant in the Ronald Reagan administration. Many states picked up the funding for these community-based institutions. Total mental health spending has kept pace with growth in gross domestic product (GDP), but at a lower rate of increase than overall health spending. In the past three decades, the financial mechanisms and institutional arrangements for delivery of mental health services have dramatically changed.

Medicaid and Care for People with Disabilities and Chronic Illnesses

People with disabilities is a broad category including people of all ages, levels of income, races, genders, and other demographics. Medicaid has become a common denominator in this category. Medicaid does not serve all people with disabilities, but it is a critical financial support system for many. For some, Medicaid pays the costs of institutionalization and, for others, it pays for essential home care to maintain life in the community. Medicaid's broad mandate to serve the poor, the long history of payments to nursing homes, and decentralized flexibility have placed it at the critical center of US society's response to care for people with disabilities.

In discussions as well as policy deliberations, there is a well-understood distinction between acute and long-term care, although it is clear that individuals with disabilities often consume larger than average amounts of both. "Long-term care" refers to the services rendered over an extended period of time to those who cannot by themselves perform activities of daily living. This assistance is sometimes provided by individuals with formal training, such as a nurse, but some types of assistance do not require any special training.

Various recent surveys generally conclude that about 5% of the adult population, 10 million individuals, require some assistance. A little over one-half of those requiring assistance are the elderly. The most common caregiver is one of the over 40 million individuals who provide some level of unpaid care to another adult. One-half of these unpaid caregivers assist one individual for eight hours or less a week, though almost 20% report more than forty hours of assistance per week. The need for caregiving typically lasts a little over four years. There is at least one caregiver in over 21% of all households, with relatives providing over 80% of all nonpaid caregiving. One-quarter of all recipients live in the same household as the caregiver, and almost 50% of caregivers live within a twenty-minute drive. A recent estimate is that 25 million caregivers provided 24 billion hours of care, with an estimated economic value of $200 billion.[14]

Women are twice as likely as men to be caregivers and, on average, provide more hours of care. Care recipients are mostly aged fifty years and older, with only 20% aged forty-nine years and younger. The need for caregiving for younger adults is more likely because of mental or emotional illnesses. For the recipients aged fifty years and older, Alzheimer's disease, diabetes, cancer, stroke, or just the ravages of aging cause the need for care.[15]

Caregiving by relatives in the home has been the norm for generations. This home-based care accounts for five times more help for those in need than does institutional care in a nursing home. In addition to the unpaid care provided by relatives, formal assistance provided by agencies has existed for decades and has exponentially expanded in the past two decades.

The History of Home Health Care

Some systems of outside assistance for the sick date as far back as early nineteenth-century Charleston, South Carolina, where the

Ladies Benevolent Society visited the poor who were sick to offer help. By the early twentieth century, many urban areas of the country had visiting nurse associations, which provided home visits on a charitable basis. In 1909, the Metropolitan Life Insurance Company began to contract with visiting nurse associations to provide home visits for their clients who had industrial life insurance policies. The company saw this as a way to prolong life and, therefore, delay the ultimate benefit payment. It also was a selling point for its insurance. Other insurance companies followed the lead. Not only were the nurse visits a good cause, but they also represented sound business practice. The program lasted until after World War II.[16]

Medicare initially had a limited home care benefit and, under Medicaid, this was an optional benefit. In the 1970s, the states were allowed to have a personal care services option for beneficiaries. For the first two decades of its existence, Medicaid long-term care spending was primarily for institutional services. In the Omnibus Budget Reconciliation Act of 1981 (OBRA-81), Congress authorized the expansion of home- and community-based services (HCBS) through Section 1915c waivers. This allows states to offer comprehensive services to beneficiaries who are eligible for institutionalization but can remain in the home with HCBS. The waivers also provide greater flexibility to the states in restricting services or limiting eligibility.[17] HCBS waivers now represent over 20% of Medicaid's long-term care spending. Medicaid spending on community-based care as a whole doubled from 1994 to 2004.

Medicare's provision of home care also grew exponentially in the 1980s as a result of legislative changes and court decisions. Medicare home care spending increased tenfold between 1987 and 1995. Because of the rapid growth and suspicion of fraud and overuse, Congress in the Balanced Budget Act of 1997 reduced Medicare payments to home health agencies and instituted measures to uncover fraud and abuse.[18]

Total long-term care expenditures in 2006 with the sources of funds are shown in Table 6.1. Nursing home expenses were 70% of total long-term care, and 43% of those dollars were spent by Medicaid. Of Medicare's $40 billion of expenditure about one-half was spent on nursing home care, representing short-term post-acute care, not chronic care. Medicare and Medicaid together account for 60% of nursing home care expenses representing different populations. And together they pay for over 70% of home care expenses.

Table 6.1   Sources of Payment for Long-term Care (2006)

	Total Long-term Care Expenditure, $billions (percentage)	Total National Health Expenditure, $billions (percentage)
Medicare	40.8 (23)	21.2 (17)
Medicaid	71.0 (40)	53.7 (43)
Out-of-pocket	39.1 (22)	32.5 (26)
Private insurance	16.0 (9)	11.2 (9)
Other public sources	5.3 (3)	2.5 (2)
Other private sources	5.3 (3)	5.0 (4)
Total	177.5	126.1

Source: Centers for Medicare and Medicaid Services, National Health Expenditures Data Tables, www.cms.gov/NationalHealthExpendData/downloads/tables.pdf.

Table 6.2 shows the distribution of 9.5 million people with long-term care needs in 2005. Those aged sixty-five years and older account for 63% of people with long-term care needs, and they are more likely to be in a nursing home. Most people aged sixty-four years and younger are children with disabilities or adults with long-term care needs who receive home- and community-based services.

Medicare has always paid for skilled nursing home care for up to thirty days as a transition from the hospital back to the home. And in the past three decades, Medicare has expanded home health visits that occur after a hospital stay. Medicare now finances one-quarter of all long-term care spending. It is Medicaid, however, that

Table 6.2   People with Long-term Care Needs (2005)

	Number of Individuals Aged 65 Years and Older (percentage)	Number of Individuals Aged 64 Years and Younger (percentage)
Community residents	4.5 (47)	3.4 (36)
Nursing home residents	1.5 (16)	0.17 (2)
Total	6.0	3.57

Source: Data from "Medicaid and Long-Term Care Services and Supports," Fact Sheet (Washington, DC: Kaiser Commission on Medicaid and the Uninsured, February 2009).

pays for 40% of all long-term care, and does so across a broad spectrum of categories of individuals and range of services. These long-term care payments represent one-third of all Medicaid expenditures. Until the early 1980s, Medicaid's long-term care spending was mostly for nursing home service. New home- and community-based services have become a substantial part of the Medicaid spending.

The categories of individuals eligible for Medicaid long-term care services include:

- the elderly with physical and cognitive impairments
- people with disabilities, including children and adults with developmental disabilities
- people who are severely mentally ill
- people with traumatic brain and spinal cord injury
- adults with debilitating illnesses such as multiple sclerosis
- people with AIDS
- children born with severe impairments[19]

Many of these individuals have extremely high total costs because of the severity of their condition. In 2007 the elderly represented 10% of Medicaid enrollees, but accounted for 25% of the spending. People with disabilities are an even more expensive group, as 15% of the enrollees accounted for 42% of Medicaid spending.[20] In a 2006 study for the Kaiser Commission, Jeffery S. Crowley and Molly O'Malley profiled Medicaid's high-cost populations to provide a synopsis of the disabled individuals, largely invisible to the average person, who are critically dependent on Medicaid for their survival and minimal quality of life.[21] When examining expenses by individuals rather than categories, a small percentage of the total Medicaid population (4%) accounted for 48% of total costs in 2001.

Preterm Births

Preterm births make up 12% of births per year. These births are characterized by low birth weight and often lifetime higher rates of chronic conditions. Medicaid does provide a wide range of services to these children with disabilities, and states can, under some circumstances, provide an institutional level of service.

Children in Foster Care

Almost 1 million children spend time in foster care each year. These children are at high risk for future mental and physical problems. In 2001, almost 900,000 children in foster care received Medicaid. The per capita cost for these children is more than three times the average Medicaid spending on children. A targeted care management system exists in thirty-eight states to coordinate the range of services required by these at-risk children.

Individuals with Spinal Cord and Traumatic Brain Injuries

There are about 250,000 Americans with spinal cord injuries, and about 5.3 million have a disability caused by traumatic brain injury. Costs for initial rehabilitation and ongoing maintenance are high. Often the individuals are not insured, or they lose their employment-based insurance with job loss after the injury. After injury, there is not likely to be a private insurance option for people with disabilities from these injuries. Even with some recovery success, these individuals are likely to have high medical bills for the rest of their lives.

People Who Have Mental Illness

Serious mental illness, such as schizophrenia or bipolar disorder, is experienced by 5% of the population. In recent decades pharmaceuticals have been effectively utilized to manage, but not cure, these mental illnesses. In 2001 Medicaid paid 27% of all spending on mental health services across the country, which is more than private insurance and Medicare. For those with these mental illnesses, Medicaid is often the only avenue of financial support for essential medication and treatment.

Individuals Who Have Developmental Disabilities

There are about 4.5 million Americans with developmental disabilities. Medicaid spent 78% of the total funds for developmental disability services, which amounts to 10% of all Medicaid spending. HCBS waivers are extensively used to provide a range of services in a community setting for people with developmental disabilities. Since 1971, Medicaid has also been able to provide services in intermediate care facilities for those with mental retardation (ICF/MR) and currently this represents about 4% of all Medicaid spending.

Individuals with Alzheimer's Disease

Alzheimer's is a devastating disease that impacts not only the individual, but the family members as well. It causes problems with memory, thinking, and behavior. The Alzheimer's Association estimates that 5.4 million people have Alzheimer's disease. Certainly many unpaid family caregivers are tending to people with Alzheimer's or some other form of dementia. But as the disease progresses, it becomes increasingly difficult to maintain the individuals in their homes. They need constant attention and monitoring to avoid injury or wandering. With the availability of community-based services to supplement unpaid care by relatives, many older individuals are able to remain in their homes and avoid institutionalization. This is less likely with Alzheimer's because the caregiving burden begins to exceed the ability of family to maintain the individual in the home as the disease progresses. The availability of Medicaid to fund nursing home coverage for this population remains a critical help for their families.

Combined Medicaid Populations

There are other high-cost Medicaid populations, such as organ transplant recipients, those with neurodegenerative diseases such as multiple sclerosis, and those with AIDS. In each instance, Medicaid has become the only realistic source of funding for assistance. Relatively small numbers of people in the community have these high-cost conditions, but for those individuals, Medicaid is essential for survival.

Categories of Medicaid Long-term Care Services

There are five categories of Medicaid long-term care services. Institutionalization in a nursing home is the oldest, dating from the start of Medicaid and even before with Kerr-Mills. Categorically eligible individuals are entitled to nursing home services as long as they meet the level-of-care criteria, but the states may also offer the service to others such as the medically needy. Home health service, including part-time nursing, home care agencies, and medical supplies and equipment, was initially an optional service, but it became mandatory in 1970. Eligible individuals are entitled to the services as long as the services are medically necessary. The home- and community-based services waiver was authorized by Congress in 1981. This allows services such as case management, home health aid, adult day care, habilitation, and psychosocial rehabilitation services. These services are necessary to avoid institutionalization and must be cost effective. Personal care services allow for assistance with ADLs or IADLs. This is an optional state service.[22] ICF/MR was established in 1971 as an optional Medicaid service for people with developmental disabilities who require extensive services and financially qualify for Medicaid assistance. Many are in small group homes with twenty-four-hour care and services.

Table 6.3 shows the relative distribution of enrollees and dollars spent for Medicaid community-based long-term care. From 1995 to 2006, these expenses grew from 19% to 41% of Medicaid long-term care dollars. As the HCBS program has grown significantly, many states have instituted cost control measures such as restrictive standards and enrollment limits.[23]

Medicaid beneficiaries receiving long-term care services represent 7% of enrollees, but account for 52% of the spending. One-third of the elderly use long-term care benefits and utilize 86% of all Medicaid spending on this group. Those receiving institutional care have much higher per enrollee costs.

Table 6.3   Medicaid Community-based Long-term Care: Participants and Costs (2006)

	Number of Participants (percentage)	Cost, in $billions (percentage)
Home health	873,607 (30)	4.6 (12)
Home- and community-based services waiver	1,107,358 (39)	25.0 (66)
Personal care	881,762 (31)	8.5 (22)
Total	2,860,000	38.1

Source: "Medicaid 1915(c) Home and Community-Based Service Programs: Data Update," Issue Paper (Washington, DC: Kaiser Commission on Medicaid and the Uninsured, December 2006).

Pathways into Medicaid

Medicaid is a means-tested program with complex criteria for eligibility at both state and federal levels. To qualify for Medicaid long-term care benefits, a recipient must also meet level-of-care criteria. Along the pathway to eligibility, one must meet categorical, financial, and functional criteria.[24] Categorically, those receiving Medicaid long-term care services are either elderly or disabled under federal or state definition. Of the total Medicaid population, about 16% are people with disabilities and 9% are elderly. People with disabilities include those with developmental disability, mental illness, spinal cord injury, AIDS, debilitating illness, and children with cognitive impairments.

The financial pathway for most people with disabilities is welfare related. Those in the Supplemental Security Income (SSI) program are eligible for Medicaid. These are individuals with low income and limited assets (rules are complex about which kinds of assets can be retained). Under some circumstances, for example, a home will not be counted as an asset. For older people a more common path to Medicaid is the medically needy option, which exists when a person's high medical expenses (e.g., nursing home) far exceed their income. Such individuals are expected to spend most of their available income and assets for the cost of care and usually retain only a meager living allowance.

The level-of-care criteria are determined by the states and tend to be more restrictive for nursing home and HCBS waiver services than for home health and optional personal services programs.[25] Because states establish the criteria and assessment mechanisms, there is wide variation in eligibility from state to state. Two individuals from different states with the same functional limits may differ in the Medicaid long-term care eligibility.

The Financial Structure of Long-term Care

The US long-term care system is complex, perhaps even Byzantine, in its financial and administrative structure. Of the estimated 11 million individuals with disabilities who need assistance for some ADLs, at least one-half receive some type of service from Medicaid or Medicare; the Medicare and Medicaid expenditures together account for almost 70% of long-term care spending.[26] This, of course, does not include the billions of dollars of uncompensated care provided by family members.

Medicare post-acute care spending grew by 75% between 1999 and 2007. Nursing home spending under Medicare grew from 23% of total nursing home spending in 1999 to 32% in 2007. Medicaid long-term care spending grew by 39% during the same period, and the community-based service segment was 95% higher in 2007.[27] There are now fewer nursing home residents over age sixty-five years than two decades ago.[28] This reflects the preference for remaining in the community as long as possible, restrictions on growth of nursing home beds by states, and the growth of assisted living facilities. A recent study estimated that there are over 800,000 assisted living units, which represent about one-half of the total nursing home residents.[29]

Because institutionalization is expensive, the per enrollee cost for those in nursing homes far exceeds that for individuals receiving community-based care. Only a small number of those needing some assistance are in a nursing home at a given point of time but they consume a large share of the total program costs.[30] As the population ages and family caregiving becomes more difficult because fewer children live nearby to provide care, it is likely the nursing home population will again increase. The question of whether or not the current financial administrative structure is adequate for the decades ahead and the policy challenges this poses are my topic for the final segment of this chapter.

Long-term Care Scenarios for 2030

We know for certain the population of older people will grow significantly over the next twenty years as the baby boom generation ages. While a majority of those who will need long-term care services in 2030 will be older people, those with developmental disabilities, degenerative disease, or spinal cord injury will also require nursing home and community-based services. The non-elderly recipients requiring long-term care services will continue to represent more than one-third of this population. Women eighty-five years and older will still be at the greatest risk for institutionalization near the end of life because they typically will be single, poorer, and less likely to have family assistance. While there is some dispute over the magnitude of the change, a number of recent studies have demonstrated a measurable decline in disability among the oldest cohorts of the population.[31] Assuming the trend continues, nursing home entry for many may be delayed, with a consequent reduction in total institutional care expenses that had not been anticipated. On the other hand, this may result in greater home care needs, adding strain to that segment of the long-term care system.

With Medicaid as the primary source of public funds for all types of long-term care, the fault line in the system moving toward 2030 is its structural weaknesses. As a federal-state program, Medicaid's long-term care services are inconsistent from state to state and across beneficiary eligibility categories. State governments tend to be subject to the boom and bust cycle of the economy. An economic downturn causes a reduction of state government revenues. With individual state determinations of eligibility and extent of service, states are likely to reduce services to avoid budget problems.[32] As the demand for long-term care services increases, these weaknesses in the Medicaid system will be magnified.

There are several policy options that might be considered to address these current and future problems. Examination of these options assumes that the current system needs change. The status quo may continue over the next two decades unless a service or budget crisis propels the issue to the top of the agenda. There are three distinct policy components of the systems to care for people with disabilities.

Public funding for nursing home care is primarily the responsibility of Medicaid. The Medicare nursing home reimbursements are intended for thirty days of short-term care for post-acute periods as a bridge between the hospital and the return home. The home health benefit is somewhat broader, but still linked to acute care episodes. Medicaid community-based care funding has grown rapidly in recent years and now represents the critical source of funding for these services.

Funding for mental health services is spread across a variety of payers, including private insurance plans, especially for employment-based group coverage. Medicaid in both institutional and community services provides funding for mental health–related problems. Medicare also funds some treatments for mental illness. As I review the major options, my focus is on nursing home and community-based services, with the assumption that some care for people with mental illness will also be included in the proposals.

Medicare Expansion: The Social Insurance Approach

When Medicare was enacted the two Wilburs (Representative Wilbur Mills and HEW Assistant Secretary Wilbur Cohen) were key architects who agreed that nursing home care for people with chronic illnesses was not a medical problem. It was an income issue. Wilbur Mills, first in the Kerr-Mills bill and then in Medicaid, created a pathway into the welfare system for those with disabilities too severe to live at home, but too poor to afford care. The medically needy category ensured that the route was not limited to those who had been poor all of their lives. The middle class, whose assets were depleted, could also have access to essential nursing home care with public support. Both feared an open-ended commitment to long-term care within Medicare would prove too expensive.

As the years passed, there were occasional attempts to reverse Medicare's thirty-day limit and expand Medicare to include a long-term care benefit beyond immediate post-acute care. Prior to the enactment of the Catastrophic Coverage Act in 1988, Representative Claude Pepper attempted to include a long-term care provision, but it was rejected as too expensive. Social insurance advocates continued to offer proposals that would incorporate a long-term care benefit into the core of Medicare.[33]

Such a Medicare Part E benefit might be structured in one of several ways. The most comprehensive would be to include a range of institutional and home care benefits currently offered under Medicaid and make them an entitlement for Medicare recipients. Many people aged sixty-four and younger who have disabilities would continue to require current Medicaid services, but the elderly with disabilities would have a new and more certain path to long-term care. This would be an expensive option requiring a new revenue source for funding.

The US Bipartisan Commission on Comprehensive Health Care (Pepper Commission) in the early 1990s proposed limited nursing home coverage (three months) and extensive home care funding with a more generous income and asset tests for Medicaid. This would have created an extensive home care benefit and a limited nursing home benefit as entitlements under Medicare while leaving Medicaid in place to cover, as a means-tested program, those in need of a long stay in the nursing home.

A Medicare Part E long-term care benefit might be financed from general revenue, a special tax on the entire working population, or revenue from only Medicare beneficiaries. A general revenue source of funding is not realistic in the near future because the mounting federal deficit is likely to exist for at least the rest of this decade.

Folding all or most of long-term care funding into Medicare as a new benefit would create a consistent and comprehensive policy and relieve what for many retirees is the worry about having enough assets for care at the end of life. As always, cost is the issue.

Private and Public Insurance Mix

Privately purchased insurance pays for less than 10% of all long-term care services. Most policies are sold in the individual market and the cost per year rises rapidly with age. In many ways, these policies resemble life insurance rather than health insurance. In addition to cost, there are a number of other barriers to expanding this approach to funding long-term care services. The largest is misunderstanding. Because Medicare covers post-acute care in nursing homes, many believe it will also cover extended nursing home care. Insurance underwriting, combined with lack of urgency by potential purchasers, keeps some people out of the market. When healthy and seemingly a long way from needing the services, people may consider even relatively small premiums to be a waste of money. When need is visible on the horizon, insurance carriers are reluctant to sell a policy at any price to someone who is a large near-term risk. Also, from the purchaser's perspective, even a relatively small premium may seem risky if one is not confident that an insurance company will remain in this line of business decades into the future. With the inflation factor unknown, the purchaser has no sense of whether the benefit expressed as dollars per day with a lifetime limit will be adequate when the services are needed. Most policies sold today have inflation protection and are comprehensive in covering both nursing home and home care.[34] Nevertheless, there is still a risk that the benefit will not be sufficient to cover nursing home expenses.

Cost, adverse selection, assumption of Medicare and Medicaid availability, and uncertainty about future benefit payments have all contributed to a low purchase rate for long-term care insurance.[35] A mixed system combining private long-term care insurance with existing or expanded public programs appears to offer promise. The Long-Term Care Partnership program was a small demonstration project for many years, but it was opened to every state by 2005 legislation. Individuals who purchase a qualifying long-term care insurance policy with limited duration of benefits are eligible for Medicaid coverage when their insurance expires, with more generous spend-down requirements. Because the insurance policy coverage is time limited, the cost will be lower and Medicaid obligations will be lower since many beneficiaries will not exhaust the insurance policy limits.[36]

One of the provisions of the Patient Protection and Affordable Care Act of 2010 (ACA) was to create a new, publicly sponsored long-term care insurance program, Community Living Assistance Services and Supports (CLASS). Working individuals can voluntarily sign up and make premium contributions. After five years of contributions, they will be eligible for payments for home or institutional care, although payments are unlikely to cover the full cost of a nursing home. There are no public funds spent for benefits, except for the premium collection. The CLASS program is designed to be self-sustaining. The average monthly premium is expected to be about $125, with an average daily payment of $75 without a lifetime limit.[37]

The obviously attractive feature of any approach that involves private long-term care is the collection of additional revenue with no requirement for new taxes. Existing insurance policies are mainly purchased in the individual market with high administrative costs. CLASS, which will be publicly managed, should be able to devote a higher share of premiums collected to service provision. Under the current structure, CLASS will not pay anywhere near the full cost of institutionalization. It is designed more to provide an alternative and flexible way of paying for community-based services. CLASS also is not likely to be an effective tool for those with a long-term disability or a birth defect. These individuals will not have the employment history, which is an essential part of the CLASS concept. The program will not begin until 2013, with no benefits paid until at least 2018. In the meantime some program modifications are likely.[38]

CLASS and private insurance offer options for alternative sources of revenue to finance long-term care, but their voluntary nature and relatively high premium costs will likely deter most individuals from utilizing these insurance approaches. At best, they seem to offer a partial solution.

Partial Federalization of Medicaid

In additional to the CLASS provision, ACA has several provisions related to Medicaid community-based long-term care services. It allows states to implement HCBS through a state plan option rather than a waiver. This includes an expanded scope of services and requires statewide coverage, removal of any cap on enrollment, ability to respond to a higher level of need, and targets for specific populations.[39] A series of other provisions are all designed to encourage home care as a substitute for institutionalization by encouraging nursing home residents to either return to the community (rebalancing) or remain longer in the community with services available to those whose incomes were previously too high to qualify.

Because Medicaid long-term care programs cover such a wide range of services for different categories of individuals, program resources are spread thin. The extent of financial responsibility for a state varies with its Medicaid match rate, which can be anywhere from 50% to nearly 80%. It is easier for states to cut back on some services than on others. HCBS services even under ACA are more likely to be cut than nursing home payments to an individual already in the system. ACA provided for Medicaid expansion to include everyone under 133% of the federal poverty level, regardless of category. Over the next decade and beyond, the federal government will pay most of the cost of this expansion. Some of these new recipients will be eligible for long-term care services, but for the others the states will continue to finance their share according to the match rate. It seems plausible to assume that, by 2020, there will be a movement toward a general change in the match rate, which will bring the federal contribution much higher. This probably will occur gradually over time, but will have the effect of freeing up state revenue for other purposes such as education. It should also standardize basic benefits and eligibility, even with continued state administration of the program.

This federalization will likely include long-term care as well as acute care. The transformation will require a move toward standardization of eligibility and benefits, assuming the actual program administration continues at the state level. A common benefit structure will no doubt result in higher program costs because the benchmarks will move up, not down. Because the range of services is wide and the enrollee characteristics are varied (children with disabilities, adults with degenerative diseases, older people with disabilities, children and adults with developmental disabilities), common standards will be a challenge with these systems already in place.

A shift in the Medicaid financing toward greater federal participation and a standardization of benefits and eligibility may, and probably should, lead to a fundamental reexamination of the structure for delivering long-term care services. The normal model that has developed basically offers two choices: institutionalization in a nursing home and home services delivered by an agency.

The modern nursing home evolved from county poorhouses to boarding homes to the nursing home as a mini-hospital. The Medicaid ICF/MR funding enables many people with developmental disabilities to live in group homes rather than large state institutions, yet receive the intense level of services needed. The Robert Wood Johnson Foundation is spending $15 million over five years to assist in the development of "Green Houses," which is a movement to offer a small-scale alternative to the traditional nursing home. These group homes house ten or twelve residents rather than the ten or twenty times that number who live in a traditional nursing home.[40] This group home feels more like a residence and is run less as a hospital; concerns remain about the financial viability of this approach. Whether Medicaid funding would support this approach, even at somewhat higher costs, may be critical to the long-term viability of this alternative.

For those receiving home services from an agency, a similar alternative approach has developed. Some long-term care insurance policies that cover home care directly send the beneficiary a monthly check rather than pay the agencies. This allows individuals to make their own arrangements for service provision. This payment type is especially appreciated for personal care services in which professional qualifications are not required. Friends and relatives may be better candidates for this assistance than agency employees. Between beneficiary and service provider, there would be better consistency and bonding.

In the late 1990s, Medicaid experimented with a similar model in three states with the Cash and Counseling Demonstration. A provision in the Deficit Reduction Act of 2005 allowed states, with a waiver, to offer this type of individual budget option for a variety of community-based services within the state plan.[41] An initial evaluation of this approach found beneficiaries to be appreciative of the greater control and continuity with consumer-directed budgets. It is not likely that consumer-directed budgets will work for all individuals or types of service,[42] but it would appear to be a mistake to exclusively standardize service delivery in the name of consistency.

Likely Outcomes

The status quo may be sustainable for the decade ahead, but there are so many gaps and inconsistencies in the Medicaid long-term care system that the need for serious overhaul will become more evident with the passage of time. There is no galvanizing number, such as the percentage of uninsured, that symbolizes the need for health reform. Neither is it likely that those most impacted, older people and people with disabilities, will be able to exert the type of political pressure necessary to move the issue to the top of the agenda. Despite the compelling case that can be made for transfer of at least the elderly and those on Social Security Disability to the Medicare system for all of their long-term care needs, in the current political environment it seems unlikely that there will be a coalition to support this type of Medicare benefit expansion.

The private-public insurance option, including CLASS, requires little additional legislative authority. Given the imperfections of this insurance market, it may be feasible to consider expanding the role of the new insurance exchanges to allow them to also serve as a market for long-term care insurance. Unless CLASS is modified, it will not adequately address what is the greatest fear: the need to pay for an extended stay in a nursing home. This is especially daunting when the spouse remaining at home fears a drain of accumulated savings. The public-private mix may be a way to put more resources into long-term care services at a time when there is concern about financing Social Security and Medicare. This system offers a way to have younger, healthier, and probably more economically solid individuals place some additional resources into the system in the form of premium payments rather than push a larger burden on those most in need of care.

The strengths of Medicaid are its flexibility, adaptation to changing circumstances, and innovation in covering individuals who are poor with disabilities. The weaknesses are the mirror image. Flexibility and innovation mean the program may be very different across the country. The fiscal health of state governments reflects the national economy. During economic downturns, states lose revenue and struggle to balance the budget. It is difficult for state officials to cut education or roads without also reducing the Medicaid budget. Over time, the fiscal disparity will likely result in the incremental shift of greater financial responsibility for Medicaid to the federal government. This will both provide greater standardization and reduce the pressure on state Medicaid budgets.

The Changing Landscape of Mental Health

The treatment of people with mental illness usually involves care over an extended period of time. The delivery system and fiscal structure of this care have changed significantly in the past few decades. Mental health spending has grown more slowly than general health spending over the past three decades, but did keep pace with the rise in GDP.[43] Three major trends are evident.

First, the enactment of the Wellstone-Domenici Mental Health Parity and Addiction Act of 2008 was the culmination of a long march toward folding mental health financing into mainstream health insurance. Employment-based private health insurance has been moving steadily to integrate mental health coverage as a basic benefit. The employment of managed behavioral health care has allowed for the application of managed care to this domain. This shift has helped to control growth of costs even as the number of beneficiaries has increased.[44]

Second, the use and effectiveness of a new generation of psychotropic drugs have continued to enable many individuals to remain functioning in the community despite illnesses such as schizophrenia and bipolar disorder. Private insurance plans typically cover these drugs, and their use significantly reduces the need for expensive inpatient hospitalization.

Third, the state hospital continues to decline in total use. These facilities are not eligible for Medicaid funding, but small group home–type facilities may be qualified for reimbursement. State hospitals continue to exist, but the patient population is 5% of its mid-1950s peak.[45] Today, these facilities tend to be the place of last resort for those who have been sent by the criminal courts, are difficult to discharge because of continuing problematic behavior, or are sexually predatory. Many more of these institutions are likely to close in the future, with the money spent on them shifted to community-based care.

Since many people with chronic mental illness have trouble maintaining regular employment and have low income, Medicaid continues to be an important source of funding for essential prescription drugs and other forms of care. For those with access to private health insurance, mental health services are typically available through this coverage.

The Major Challenge of Long-term Care

Two generations ago, older people and people with disabilities were cared for in the home, usually by a daughter or daughter-in-law. Smaller and more geographically scattered families, extensive entry of women into the workforce, and extended periods of disability have led first to the development of the nursing home and, subsequently, professional home care. Yet a systematic and comprehensive approach has not been developed for the organization and financing of care for the frail older people and people with disabilities. The fathers of Medicare did not explicitly seek to cover long-term care. Medicaid quickly evolved as an alternative way of financing institutional care. Both programs subsequently developed their own versions of home- and community-based care as an alternative.

In the 1930s, a system of private insurance developed to spread the risk associated with the high cost of an episode of serious illness. But no extensive system of private long-term care insurance has emerged either by design or spontaneously. Perhaps part of the problem with the politics of long-term care is the broad perception that need occurs only near the end of life. This is not completely true, but accurate enough to shape the perceptions of the average voter. The advocacy system for those in need of acute care services is much more extensive and aggressive than for long-term care. The issues associated with long-term care have not been broadly perceived to be serious enough to place it at the top of the national agenda.

It is easy to forget about long-term care until a family member becomes disabled and needs the service. Our system for care is not very systematic. Long-term care services have grown in a haphazard fashion over a century. Acute care is exemplified on TV as heroic ER doctors and majestic hospitals providing miracle cures. Long-term care, however, is about making people comfortable, not repairing what has been damaged. It is more difficult to generate interest and enthusiasm in the policy process for a set of services that are largely invisible. This is the major challenge for those who wish to modify the status quo.

Notes

1. H. S. Kaye, Charlene Harrington, and Mitchell P. LaPlante, "Long-Term Care: Who Gets It, Who Provides It, Who Pays, and How Much?" *Health Affairs* 29, no. 1 (2010): 11–21.

2. Ibid.

3. Robert Stevens and Rosemary Stevens, *Welfare Medicine in America* (New York: Free Press, 1973), p. 6.

4. Bruce C. Vladeck, *Unloving Care: The Nursing Home Tragedy* (New York: Basic Books, 1980), p. 33.

5. Ibid., chap. 3.

6. Wilbur Cohen, "Reflections on the Enactment of Medicare and Medicaid," *Health Care Financing Review,* supplement (1985): 9.

7. US Congress, House of Representatives, *Medical Care for the Aged: Hearing Before the Committee on Ways and Means,* 88th Cong., 1st sess., November 18, 19, 20, 1963.

8. Vladeck, *Unloving Care,* p. 45.

9. David Mechanic, *Mental Health and Social Policy* (Englewood Cliffs, NJ: Prentice Hall, 1969); David A. Rochefort, *American Social Welfare Policy* (Boulder: Westview, 1986).

10. Joint Commission on Mental Illness and Health, *Action for Mental Health: Final Report of the Joint Commission on Mental Illness and Health* (New York: Basic Books, 1961).

11. Hendrik Wagenaar and Dan A. Lewis, "The Social and Economic Context of Mental Hospitalization," *Journal of Health Politics, Policy and Law* 14, no. 3 (1989): 507–521.

12. Richard G. Frank, Howard H. Goldman, and Thomas G. McGuire, "Trends in Mental Health Cost Growth: An Expanded Role for Management?" *Health Affairs* 28, no. 3 (2009): 649–658.

13. Wagenaar and Lewis, "The Social and Economic Context of Mental Hospitalization."

14. Karen Buhler-Wilkerson, "Care of the Chronically Ill at Home: An Unresolved Dilemma in Health Policy for the United States," *Milbank Quarterly* 85, no. 4 (2007): 611–632.

15. National Alliance for Caregiving and AARP, *2004 Report: Caregiving in the US,* www.caregiving.org/data/04finalreport.pdf (Bethesda, MD: National Alliance for Caregiving, 2004).

16. Buhler-Wilkerson, "Care of the Chronically Ill at Home," p. 614.

17. Ellen O'Brien, "Long-Term Care: Understanding Medicaid's Role for the Elderly and Disabled" (Washington, DC: Kaiser Commission on Medicaid and the Uninsured, November 2005), pp. 13–14.

18. Robyn I. Stone, *Milbank Quarterly Report: Long-Term Care for the Elderly with Disabilities,* August 2000, pp. 15–17, www.milbank.org /0008stone/index.html.

19. O'Brien, "Long-Term Care," p. 5.

20. "Medicaid: A Primer" (Washington, DC: Kaiser Commission on Medicaid and the Uninsured, June 2010), p. 23.

21. Jeffery S. Crowley and Molly O'Malley, "Profiles of Medicaid's High Cost Populations" (Washington, DC: Kaiser Commission on Medicaid and the Uninsured, December 2006), pp. 1–45.

22. "Understanding Medicaid Home and Community Services: A Primer" (Washington, DC: US Department of Health and Human Services, October 2000), pp. 20–25; Gretchen Engquist and Cyndy Johnson, "Medicaid-Funded Long-Term Care: Toward More Home-and-Community-Based Options" (Hamilton, NJ: Center for Health Care Strategies, May 2010), pp. 1–11.

23. "Medicaid Home and Community-Based Service Programs: Data Update" (Washington, DC: Kaiser Commission on Medicaid and the Uninsured, November 2009), pp. 1–14.

24. O'Brien, "Long-Term Care," p. 6.

25. Ibid., p. 9.

26. Terence Ng, Charlene Harrington, and Martin Kitchener, "Medicare and Medicaid in Long-Term Care," *Health Affairs* 29, no. 1 (2010): 22–28.

27. Ng, Harrington, and Kitchener, "Medicare and Medicaid in Long-Term Care," p. 23.

28. Judith Kasper, Barbara Lyons, and Molly O'Malley, "Report: Long-Term Services and Supports: The Future Role and Challenges for Medicaid" (Washington, DC: Kaiser Commission on Medicaid and the Uninsured, September 2007), p. 13.

29. David G. Stevenson and David C. Grabowski, "Sizing Up the Market for Assisted Living," *Health Affairs* 29, no. 1 (2010): 35–43.

30. Anna Sommers and Mindy Cohen, "Report: Medicaid's Long-Term Care Beneficiaries: An Analysis of Spending Patterns" (Washington, DC: Kaiser Commission on Medicaid and the Uninsured, November 2006).

31. Douglas A. Wolf, Kelly Hunt, and James Knickman, "Perspectives on the Recent Decline in Disability at Older Ages," *Milbank Quarterly* 83, no. 3 (2005): 365–395.

32. Clare Ansberry, "Disabled Face Hard Choices as States Slash Medicaid," *Wall Street Journal,* May 20, 2010, p. A1.

33. Joshua M. Wiener, Laurel Hixon Illston, and Raymond J. Hanley, *Sharing the Burden* (Washington, DC: Brookings Institution, 1994).

34. Stevenson and Grabowski, "Sizing Up the Market for Assisted Living."

35. Richard W. Johnson and Cori E. Uccello, "Is Private Long-Term Care Insurance the Answer?" Issue Brief No. 29 (Center for Retirement Research at Boston College, March 2005), pp. 1–8.

36. Anne Tumlinson, Christine Aguiar, and Molly O'Mally, "Report: Closing the Long-Term Care Funding Gap" (Washington, DC: Kaiser Commission on Medicaid and the Uninsured, June 2009).

37. "Health Care Reform and the Class Act" (Washington, DC: Kaiser Commission on Medicaid and the Uninsured, April 2010), pp. 1–4.

38. Ron Lieber, "The Changes to Save a Big Idea," *New York Times,* April 29, 2011, p. B1.

39. "Medicaid Long-Term Services and Supports" (Washington, DC: Kaiser Commission on Medicaid and the Uninsured, June 2010), pp. 1–4.

40. Lucette Lagnado, "Rising Challenger Takes on Elder-Care System," *Wall Street Journal,* June 24, 2008, p. A1.

41. Brenda C. Spillman, Kirsten J. Black, and Barbara A. Ormond, "Report: Beyond Cash and Counseling" (Washington, DC: Kaiser Commission on Medicaid and the Uninsured, January 2007).

42. Adrianne Dulio et al., "Report: Consumer Direction of Personal Assistance Services Programs in Medicaid" (Washington, DC: Kaiser Commission on Medicaid and the Uninsured, March 2008).

43. Richard Frank, Howard Goldman, and Thomas McGuire, "Trends in Mental Health Cost Growth: An Expanded Role for Management?" *Health Affairs* 28, no. 3 (2009): 649–659.

44. Ibid., pp. 650–651.

45. William Fisher, Jeffrey Geller, and John Pandiani, "The Changing Role of the State Psychiatric Hospital," *Health Affairs* 28, no. 3 (2009): 678.

7

Health Care Reform:
The Dream Deferred

President Barack Obama stated that the Patient Protection and Affordable Care Act of 2010 (ACA) enshrines "the core principle that everybody should have some basic security when it comes to their health care" and proceeded to sign the bill with twenty ceremonial pens.[1] The pens were distributed to Democratic congressional leaders who, in a tumultuous year, guided through legislative hurdles the most significant health bill since the passage of Medicare in 1965. In this chapter, I relate the story of the long journey to health reform legislation and conclude by speculating why this will not be the last health reform bill that a president will sign.

Background

Health care bills begin their path through Congress when problems seem serious enough to warrant public action. By 2009 the pressure had been building to take steps to reduce the number of uninsured, which stood at 17% of the non-elderly population. Most of the 45 million uninsured are from families with one or more full-time workers, and two in three are poor or near poor. Adults aged thirty years and younger have a 30% uninsured rate. The uninsured do not have private health insurance, usually because it is too expensive, but they are ineligible for public programs. Most work in blue-collar jobs, in part-time jobs, or for a small business.[2] Those who work for an organization with more than 100 employees are likely to have employment-based insurance. Others are covered by Medicaid, Medicare, or the military system.

Two decades ago, a good employer-sponsored plan paid most of the individual premium with little cost sharing. Today, employers have tried to offset rising costs by requiring employees to pay a larger share of the premium and a greater share of the total bill. An average person with a good employer-sponsored policy still feels the pinch of rising health costs.

Past Policy Efforts

Health care costs are not a new issue on the political agenda. Table 7.1 shows how episodically for a century there have been calls for a public policy solution to the cost of health care. The Blue Cross system emerged almost accidentally in 1929 as a response to middle-class concerns about the cost of hospitalization. Within the Franklin D. Roosevelt administration, policy advisers favored including health insurance as part of the Social Security legislative proposal, but the president feared that opposition from the American Medical Association (AMA) would kill the whole plan. In 1948, President Harry S. Truman proposed the same universal public insurance plan that Roosevelt had rejected, but Congress failed to act.

By the mid-1950s, both unionized and white-collar workers in large firms were typically offered group health insurance through the workplace. This relieved the pressure to pursue a national health insurance program. Liberal reformers narrowed their goals, and began to promote the concept of universal public hospitalization insurance through Social Security for those aged sixty-five years and older. Ultimately, Congress enacted Medicare and Medicaid in 1965. This did not solve the problem of the near poor, those in marginal jobs, and small businesses.

In the late 1960s and early 1970s, the number of uninsured came to be perceived as a problem and health reform appeared on the legislative agenda. Democrats in Congress led by Senator Ted Kennedy proposed public universal coverage similar to what Truman had endorsed. President Richard M. Nixon, a Republican, responded by proposing reform legislation featuring both expansion of employment-based insurance and public programs. The window of opportunity appeared open for compromise legislation, but the Watergate scandal consumed Washington. Nixon left office with health reform languishing in committee. Four years later in 1978, President Jimmy

Table 7.1   Health Care Reform on the Political Agenda

Time Period	Key Factor	Outcome
Pre–World War I	Rising costs	State efforts fail
Mid-1930s	Rising costs and service use	President Franklin D. Roosevelt does not include health insurance in Social Security
1948	Access problems despite growing work-based insurance	President Harry S. Truman proposes national health insurance, but lacks support in Congress
1960s	Older people and the poor not part of work-based insurance system	Medicare and Medicaid enacted, 1965
1973–1974	Cost increases; some poor people not eligible for Medicaid	President Richard M. Nixon and Congress have different plans; no legislation passes
1978–1980	President Jimmy Carter proposes plan as promised in campaign	Democrats divided on type of plan; hostage crisis in Iran diverts attention
1993–1994	Cost increases and loss of work-based insurance; President William J. Clinton proposes plan	President Clinton's plan does not garner majority support
2009–	Cost and access problems drive issue to top of agenda; President Barack Obama makes it a legislative priority	Senate bill is passed by House and adjusted by reconciliation

Carter proposed legislation similar to the Nixon plan, but no majority legislative coalition supported the plan.

Another decade would pass before a new Democratic president, William J. Clinton, put health reform at the top of the agenda. Clinton proposed a comprehensive plan that involved both public program expansion and major alterations of the workplace insurance system. The Democrats enjoyed a nominal majority in the House and Senate, but could not develop a majority coalition and the bill died in committee.[3] In the November 1994 elections, the Democrats lost their majority and there would be no coalition likely to support health reform in the political stream for more than a decade. Clinton was reelected in 1996, but the opportunity to again pursue health reform did not return for fifteen years. In 2009, with Democrat Barack Obama as president, health reform returned to the agenda.

Policy ideas about health reform can be categorized according to three main approaches: social insurance, employer-provided insurance, and consumer choice. Each set of ideas grows out of an advocacy coalition within the policy stream.

Social Insurance Reformers

The spread of risk in a large pool is the fundamental principle of insurance. For a century, some have preferred the creation of one health insurance risk pool composed of all citizens. The United Kingdom and other countries have adopted this model. Whether or not the government has legal ownership of facilities, or directly employs providers in a social insurance model, a public agency assumes the responsibility and risk associated with a universal guarantee of access. The social insurance principle has long been the ideal for liberal reformers. Subsequent proposals envisioned a single national system for financing health care with a dedicated tax. The public agency would pay hospitals, physicians, and other providers for the services rendered. This idea was included in the social insurance legislative package presented to President Franklin D. Roosevelt by his advisers and was a central policy idea in every major discussion of health reform in the twentieth century.

Social insurance reformers enjoyed their greatest success with the enactment of Medicare. On the other hand, Medicaid was a clear second best and temporary solution. In the short term, it provided vital help to the poor who needed financial access to mainstream medical care, but its welfare system origins were seen as an inferior model by those in the advocacy coalition. The policy vision was to expand Medicare with its social insurance approach to the whole population. Various organizational options were actively discussed with the social insurance advocacy coalition, but the core idea was a system in which all citizens would be part of a single risk pool, with little or no cost sharing at the point of service, and the tax system used to raise money to pay providers.

The common approach to cost control of public programs is the use of the budget mechanism. Reform advocates argue that cost would be controlled by the use of a national health budget. As cost became a more high-profile issue in the political stream, advocates in the policy network began to emphasize the budget control aspect of the idea. Eventually this led to the use of the term "single-payer system" to identify the social insurance approach. During the 1980s and 1990s, the Canadian system was frequently cited as an example of a single-payer system.[4]

As the political prospects for reform along the lines favored by those in the social insurance advocacy coalition dimmed, Medicaid received renewed interest among scholars and analysts as a possible vehicle for achieving universal coverage. They still presumed a larger federal share of the total cost, expanded eligibility not tied to the welfare system, and something closer to national eligibility standards. The policy vision of a single national social insurance system was never under serious consideration in the 2009–2010 policy debate, but Medicaid expansion along the lines favored by the social insurance advocates became a key part of the reform bill. The idea of a public-sponsored insurance company in competition with and perhaps ultimately replacing private insurance in the individual market was embraced by the social insurance coalition in the 2009–2010 debate, but the public option died due to insurance company opposition.[5]

Incremental Tinkerers

Social insurance was a policy idea fashioned by academic social activists, and the advocacy coalition developed around this concept has survived for nearly a century. Employment-based insurance was an evolutionary idea that developed ad hoc into the Blue Cross system in the 1930s, not the product of a refined conceptual idea. By the 1950s, employment-based insurance for those working for large firms became commonplace. The system was well entrenched when the health reform debate was at a peak in the 1970s. As the discussions unfolded, a second advocacy coalition developed. The incremental tinkerers did not necessarily reject the policy ideas of social insurance reformers, but concluded that the ideas were not politically feasible or had flaws their promoters were unwilling to acknowledge.

Political scientists and social activists had always been leaders among social insurance advocates. Economists who were concerned about the uninsured and found weaknesses in the employment-based system sought a different conceptual path to universal coverage that built on the strengths of the existing system. They explored policy ideas that accepted health insurance based on employment and sought to strengthen and expand it.

Those who work for firms larger than 100 employees usually have group insurance whether the firm purchases a policy or self-insures. In this perspective, the small business and individual insurance market is the major problem. One policy idea promoted by incremental tinkerers has been the employer mandate, which requires all firms to offer health insurance in some form even to part-time employees. Since two of three uninsured are regularly employed or someone in their family works, this would be a path to significantly reducing the number of uninsured. A variation of the employer mandate idea was proposed in the 1980s and called "pay or play." This provides a formal choice for employers between purchasing health insurance coverage for their employees and paying a tax to the government that is the basis for the employees "buying into" Medicaid even when they do not meet the income limits.[6]

Employment-based group insurance is administratively more efficient for the insurance provider and creates a sizable risk pool, especially for a large firm. The government is not directly involved in the insurance arrangements and tax dollars are not spent for the provision of care. Both employers and medical providers often prefer an arm's-length relationship with government. Premiums are negotiated between employers and insurance companies. Negotiations with providers over payments for services are conducted by insurance companies. This tends to be a satisfactory arrangement for firms with a large number of employees since the risk pool is significant and diverse, fixed administrative costs are spread, and a single large claim resulting from major illness is less likely to be disruptive. Small firms often experience higher premiums, more frequent cancellation of policies, and premium costs that are a higher share of total wages. It is no surprise to find that those who work for small firms are much less likely to have been offered a health insurance benefit. Problems with this approach also include the declining permanence of employment with workers shifting jobs much more frequently than in the past, and the growing use of contract or part-time workers who do not receive benefits.[7]

Insurance company underwriters look for risk pools in which the total premium collected exceeds the anticipated cost of claims. This is the essence of the insurance business. A ten-employee firm with even one high-risk individual is likely to be seen by the insurance company as a bad deal. On the other hand, a firm with 1,000 employees can have multiple high risks and still be a good line of business. One hundred firms with ten employees each who band together to purchase health insurance potentially have the same advantage as a single large firm.

For decades, some trade associations (farm equipment dealers) or leagues of similar employers (local governments in California) have developed purchasing pools. One of the ideas in the incremental tinkerers' advocacy coalition has been to formalize and encourage this practice by proposing either a national or statewide insurance purchasing pool for small businesses. This offers a way to address one of the major weak links in the employment-based system.

Existing groups, such as the two cited above, are usually able to form purchasing pools without additional legal authority. Random collections of small businesses often cannot. Even when legally able to negotiate for a single insurance plan, the purchasing pools are hampered by the potential for adverse selection and the departure from the group of those businesses with a low-risk profile who are able to get a better deal on their own.[8]

It is possible to purchase an individual policy, and about 6% of the non-elderly are covered by individual policies. These tend to be more expensive than comparable employment-based insurance because of administrative and marketing costs, and, in the absence of a common risk pool, underwriting assessment is heavily based on the characteristics of the individual. A young and healthy individual may have a relatively low premium, but age, health conditions, and other risk factors substantially drive up premium costs. On average, those in the individual market pay higher premiums and have greater out-of-pocket costs than those with employment-based insurance.[9]

Consumer Choice Champions

Incremental tinkerers seek to preserve the existing employment-based system by filling in the gaps that have existed for decades. Consumer choice champions reject the basic premises of the existing system and seek to develop policy ideas that employ consumer choice in markets to provide a better approach to health insurance. Within this advocacy coalition, a number of policy ideas have emerged that deserve serious attention. Among these are high-deductible policies, insurance market reform, managed competition, tax credits, individual mandate, medical savings accounts, high-risk pools, tax treatment of insurance, and insurance sales across state lines.

High-deductible Policies

While this idea was not a favorite in the policy community during the early 1970s health reform debate, it had a powerful sponsor in Senator Russell Long, then chairman of the Senate Finance Committee. The Catastrophic Health Insurance and Medical Reform Bill (Long-Ribicoff) featured a public catastrophic insurance coverage approach that would have covered the entire population for expenses above a fairly high minimum threshold.[10] More recent versions of this idea would replace existing employment-based insurance with a high-deductible policy and use tax breaks to lessen the burden on families of the pre-deductible expenses.

Insurance Market Reform

The individual insurance market has always been small. Currently about 6% of the non-elderly obtain insurance through individually purchased policies. Young and healthy individuals often can obtain a basic policy at a reasonable price, but those who are older or have an adverse health history cannot. Consumer choice champions believe that a system of individually purchased insurance is viable with insurance market reform. These elements include allowing companies to sell policies nationwide rather than being subject to individual state regulation, no preexisting condition restrictions, automatic renewal to prevent cancellation for those who have developed serious illnesses, and modified community ratings by limiting the range between the lowest and highest premiums that can be offered for the same policy. This idea is often accompanied by the proposal for an individual purchasing pool as an organizational mechanism to bring together insurance company offerings with those who wish to purchase individual policies.

Managed Competition

Alain Enthoven is a prototype policy entrepreneur. As a member of the Stanford faculty committee reviewing the university health insurance plans, he concluded that the entire system was anachronistic and set out to offer an alternative model. Personally familiar with the Kaiser Permanente health maintenance organization (HMO), he was convinced that the twin issues of access and cost could be addressed with the application of market principles and the reorganization of the health care delivery system. His vision was a system in which providers would be organized into HMOs similar to Kaiser Permanente and employees would avail themselves of purchasing pools to select their coverage from among a variety of insurance options. In the Enthoven model employers would contribute a fixed amount toward the cost of insurance, but workers would choose from among the insurance offerings available in the purchasing pool. Individuals might not necessarily choose the least expensive option, but the one that offered the most value for the dollar. Employers would continue to finance part of the cost, but would not select the insurance company for all employees.[11] Enthoven's ideas were the intellectual basis for the 1994 Clinton health reform plan.

Tax Credits

In a market system in which families purchase individual health insurance policies, cost is a major issue. Consumer choice champions address this with a set of premium subsidies based on the tax system. By offering refundable tax credits, some of the cost of an insurance policy could be offset. Tax credits are a widely used device to encourage preferred behavior. The presumption is that individuals who do not have health insurance are deterred by the premium cost. The tax credit as a subsidy for the purchase of insurance makes it more affordable. Since it is refundable, even a person with no tax liability would be eligible for the subsidy. In addition to the subsidy for the purchase of insurance, an additional credit or subsidy might be available to cover part of the cost-sharing feature of the policy.[12] Many in the consumer choice coalition favor the movement away from an employer-sponsored system to one in which everyone purchases individual policies. In this system, tax credit subsidies replace the favorable tax treatment of employment-based insurance.[13]

Individual Mandate

Many states now require all drivers to purchase liability insurance. This individual mandate seeks to make sure that any driver involved in an accident has insurance to cover court-determined damage. The mandated health insurance concept is similar. If everyone is required to have health insurance, then no one will be uninsured. Hospitals, in particular, will have no need to provide charity care to the seriously ill who show up at their door and cannot be denied treatment. Everyone is part of the risk pool and pays a share of the cost for those who need medical services.

If mandated to purchase insurance, consumer choice champions recognize the need for a subsidy for low- to moderate-income individuals. In a comprehensive policy proposal, the individual mandate is usually accompanied by a tax credit, market reform, and purchase pool provisions. Even with these additions, the effectiveness of mandated insurance may depend on the penalty for noncompliance.[14]

Medical Savings Accounts

The medical savings account (MSA) is an example of recombination of policy ideas. The high-deductible policy idea and the tax credit concept were recombined into a proposal to allow individual families to have a high-deductible policy and a shelter from taxes in MSA money that could be spent for medical expenses up to the deductible amount. John Goodman, a conservative health policy entrepreneur, has promoted this idea with health economist Mark Pauley.[15]

High-risk Pools

This idea is a response to the common insurance company practice of either refusing to insure or charging a high premium for individual policies when the insured person has a past history of serious illness. A number of states have responded by creating special high-risk pools. A few years ago, Congress provided funds to assist states in establishing these mechanisms. A similar approach has been used with car insurance to provide liability insurance for those with a past driving history that renders them a bad risk. To date, a relatively small number of individuals are covered in high-risk pools.[16]

Tax Treatment of Insurance

In the early 1950s, the Internal Revenue Service (IRS) looked at the growing practice of employer-sponsored health insurance for workers. The cash equivalent cost of the benefit had not been considered taxable. As the practice grew, the IRS issued new rules determining that the cost of the insurance policy was tantamount to income and, therefore, taxable. In the outcry that ensued, Congress overturned the IRS ruling and exempted this benefit from taxation.[17]

In recent years many in the policy community, especially economists, have criticized this legislation on the grounds that it distorts the compensation system by giving more weight to health insurance benefits than to wages. The result for both union and nonunion workers is more first-dollar coverage of health costs and less consumer vigilance about utilization. Repeal of all or part of the tax exemption has become a strong policy preference of many consumer choice champions. It fits with their desire to break away from the employment-based system and replace it with an approach that emphasizes individual consumer choice from among alternative insurance arrangements. They also advocate fewer insurance policies with first-dollar third-party payments to introduce more consumer awareness of health costs as a method of reducing expenditures.[18]

Insurance Sales Across State Lines

In the US federal system of government, the regulation of all types of insurance has been the responsibility of state governments. Thus, an insurance company wishing to sell individual health insurance policies across the country needs to gain approval from fifty different state regulators. Some consumer choice champions have looked at this regulatory regime and observed the fact that similar health insurance policies vary widely in premium costs across states. They argue greater competition would exist in the market if an insurance company from one state were allowed to sell its policies in another state.[19]

A Comparison of Policy Ideas

As the health reform debate unfolded in 2009, social insurance advocates, incremental tinkerers, and consumer choice champions had been debating policy ideas about how to reform the health system for decades. The legislative process is often chaotic and rarely leaves time to develop brand-new policy ideas. When a problem appears on the decision agenda, there are typically a set of ideas available to be adopted by policymakers seeking a solution.

For decades, social insurance advocates have preferred a different arrangement for financing health services. Their support of a system of universal coverage is not a reaction to the latest numbers of the uninsured, but a long-held idea that they have been waiting to put on the table.

Consumer choice champions would prefer to see the employment-based system disappear in favor of a more market-oriented approach. They see a market-oriented approach as a potential solution to the widely recognized health system financial problems. Incremental tinkerers wish to retain the existing employment-based insurance system and expand coverage to the uninsured.

In the case study that follows, I look at how these policy ideas were examined, debated, and ultimately combined to create ACA. The story that unfolds is the tale of an epic political struggle over different visions of the future of US health care and a battle over what ideas should form the core of health reform legislation.

The Patient Protection and Affordable Care Act of 2010: A Case Study

In a typical legislative year hundreds of bills are introduced, but congressional time and attention are limited. A new president has a brief honeymoon period with the public and, by extension, with members of Congress. The first legislative priorities are easier than those that follow. In Jonathan Alter's book on the first year of the Obama administration, he states that candidate Obama decided when the campaign began in September 2008 that health reform would be a major issue after the election. He took the first step by emphasizing health care more than he had during the primary campaign.[20] By early spring of 2009, major health reform was a critical first-year issue for the Obama administration. White House Chief of Staff Rahm Emanuel opposed a major push for comprehensive health reform. Emanuel preferred a more incremental approach, suggesting that public support was not strong enough and that, with the global financial crisis, the administrative agenda was already too full.[21]

The first health care issue on the agenda was the reauthorization of the State Children's Health Insurance Program (SCHIP), which had failed in the waning days of the George W. Bush administration because of a presidential veto. This was quickly accomplished. White House and congressional leaders turned their attention to orchestrating the move to enact health reform. In the Obama White House, there were a number of veterans of the Clinton era like Emanuel who were determined not to repeat President Clinton's mistakes. They carefully reviewed the post-mortem studies and determined to follow a different path. Clinton had established a task force headed by his wife, Hillary Rodham Clinton, which, after several months, produced a detailed health reform plan and sent a bill to Capitol Hill. The Clinton plan was built around the managed competition ideas of Enthoven, which had been broadly discussed within the market choice advocacy coalition. This did not represent the approach favored among Democrats in Congress who wanted either a social insurance–based government plan or one that tinkered to expand employment-based insurance combined with Medicaid expansion. There were a number of committees of jurisdiction over health reform; their major point in common was a dislike of the Clinton plan.

Emanuel and other White House strategists sought to find a set of ideas around which a majority in Congress could be constructed. Rather than developing a detailed White House plan, the Obama administration suggested a general approach to health reform based on the campaign proposals advocated by the three major Democratic candidates in the primaries. The Democratic congressional leadership sought to coordinate the activities of the two Senate and three House committees with jurisdiction over health reform to produce a more unified approach than the one in 1994.

Two sets of events in the recent past began to shape the starting point for reform in a way unlike that in 1994. First, the state of Massachusetts had in 2006 adopted a comprehensive state reform program. The basic elements of the Massachusetts legislation were:

- an individual mandate
- employers (with eleven or more employees) required to contribute toward it
- provide employee coverage or employer pays annual contribution
- Medicaid expansion
- subsidies for the purchase of health insurance for those with incomes under 300% of poverty
- a state insurance exchange for individuals and small businesses[22]

Jonathan Gruber, an MIT economist and key participant in developing the package of ideas contained in the Massachusetts legislation, also became a health adviser to the campaigns of all three major Democratic candidates. Thus, the core ideas from the Massachusetts reform were first on the table as the committees began deliberation.

A year or so earlier, Senator Kennedy, who by early 2009 was ill with terminal cancer, had been one of the leaders in organizing various meetings among congressional leaders and major health care interest groups. The message to the groups was that a Democrat was going to be elected president, health reform legislation was to be a priority, and major groups should be part of the solution rather than just naysayers. Implicit in the argument was the notion that cooperating groups would be in a better position to have their key concerns addressed. The hope was to avoid the bitter public conflicts between provider groups and the White House that marked the Clinton effort.[23]

Even after Senator Kennedy was no longer a participant, the discussions continued with White House and congressional staff to negotiate key deals with various interest groups.[24] One of the first interest groups to seek an accommodation with the administration was the Pharmaceutical Research and Manufacturers of America (PhRMA). It as well as other groups sought to limit the amount of money they would lose as a result of cost-saving provisions. Ultimately, it was agreed that $80 billion of the more than $100 billion that would flow to PhRMA companies as a result of health reform would be "given back" through legislative tax provisions. As a result of the negotiations, PhRMA continued to support the bill during the legislative process rather than publicly oppose the plan as it had with the Clinton plan.[25] Other interest groups, such as the AMA and the American Hospital Association (AHA), joined in the discussions and supported rather than opposed health reform.

The Committee Stage

One of the opening moves in the long dance toward reform legislation was a White House summit held March 5, 2009. It was televised on C-SPAN and the more than 100 participants positioned themselves for the coming legislative debates. Participants included major health care–related interest groups as well as legislative leaders.[26] President Obama attempted to set an ambitious schedule where the committee work would be finished by midsummer, followed by quick action in both houses. With a conference committee to resolve differences, a bill could be on his desk by October.

The work of legislation takes place in the key committees. There were five committees, two in the Senate and three in the House, with jurisdiction over health reform legislation.[27] Senator Max Baucus, Finance Committee chairman, had taken a leadership role in initiating the discussion in the Senate by issuing a white paper on reform in November 2008, two weeks after the presidential election.[28] In the House, the leaders of the three committees with jurisdiction developed a unified draft bill. In late June House committees held brief hearings on the bill, and with relatively minor changes each reported out a version of the bill. By the end of the summer, the House leadership had melded the bills into a single House version. Since there were no major differences in the House committees' version, this was not a difficult task. The amalgamated process was a contrast to the 1994 approach when each committee guarded its own prerogatives.

Meanwhile in the Senate, the Committee on Health, Education, Labor and Pensions (HELP) held hearings in June and adopted a bill in July. Senator Kennedy was the nominal chairman of HELP, but his declining health meant that the baton had passed to Senator Christopher Dodd.

The Senate Finance Committee became bogged down as Chairman Baucus tried to fashion a bipartisan compromise. He and two other committee Democrats met throughout the summer with three Republican members of the committee. Eventually, the bill produced by the informal subcommittee was adopted with some modifications by the full Finance Committee. Senator Olympia Snowe was the lone Republican vote for the bill on the committee, and she warned that her vote for the final bill on the floor was not certain. The schedule had fallen far behind. After the Finance Committee approved its bill, Senate Majority Leader Harry Reid attempted to merge the HELP and Finance Committee bills into a single bill that could be brought to the floor of the Senate.

What was remarkable compared to 1994 was not just the passage of a health reform bill by all five committees, but the degree to which each bill was consistent with a core set of common ideas. Still, there was considerable haggling and negotiation at each stage. Most of this took place among Democrats because Republicans in both the House and Senate were unified in their opposition to the bills. They did not attempt to modify parts of them in exchange for their support, which historically has often been the strategy of the minority party.

The Senate and House Take Action

As the bills worked through the committees toward a final floor vote, the division among Democrats in both the chambers reflected the fragile nature of the Democratic electoral coalition. The party's majority and major leaders were from the liberal wing of the party with strength in the cities of big East and West Coast states. Congresspeople and senators from more rural and midwestern states reflected the greater skepticism of their constituents toward the health reform effort. The differences among Democrats were not about the basic philosophical approach to reform, but about legislative details, the cost, and how to pay for it. These were not insignificant disagreements, but paled in comparison to the 1994 basic differences in ideas.

By a five-vote margin, the House passed its bill in early November 2009. Majority Leader Reid then had to be perfect in his accumulation of Senate votes because of the likelihood of a Republican filibuster. A filibuster could only be stopped with all of the sixty Democratic votes. There was no margin for error and this increased the bargaining power of the "last vote." Reid was vulnerable to criticism as a result of various special deals for the home states of some senators. Finally on Christmas Eve, the Senate passed its version of health reform. There were some important differences between the Senate and House versions, but both bills reflected a common approach.

The Final Push

As senators headed home on Christmas Eve 2009, they had passed a historic health reform bill. Still, there was much work to be done. The House and Senate versions were similar. Both bills provided for a significant Medicaid expansion financed mostly by the federal government for several years. The individual and small business insurance market was recognized as a key problem. The bills established both an individual and employer mandate, but exempted very small employers. They included subsidies for individuals purchasing insurance and tax credits for small businesses. Insurance purchasing pools called exchanges were to serve as regulated marketplaces for the purchase of insurance for individuals and small groups. The House version included a public insurance option to compete in the individual market; this option was omitted in the Senate bill. The cost estimate for both bill revisions was a little short of $900 billion over ten years; this was the Obama administration's target.

Given the scope of the health reform bills, abortion coverage was an insignificant part of the whole, but was an enormous political issue. Both bills continued the long-standing policy of prohibiting use of federal funds for abortion, but many perceived the House version to have more restrictive language. On financing issues, the House bill had a tax surcharge on the wealthy. The Senate placed a tax on high-cost employer-sponsored health plans and increased the Medicare payroll tax for the wealthy. There were also small differences in income eligibility for the premium subsidies.

Negotiations between Democratic leaders of the House and Senate proceeded, with everyone expressing a cautious optimism about the ability to bridge the differences. Because of the need to retain sixty votes in the Senate, the Senate appeared to have the upper hand in negotiating several critical issues. Then, a Massachusetts surprise occurred. Senator Kennedy had succumbed to brain cancer the previous August and a former Kennedy aide was temporarily appointed to his seat with a special election to occur in mid-January. Republican state senator Scott Brown unexpectedly won that election, reducing the Democratic votes to one short of the necessary sixty to break a filibuster.

This not only made the legislative process more complicated, but the loss of this traditional Democratic seat worried many House Democrats from more marginal districts. Many doubted that Speaker Nancy Pelosi could assemble the necessary 218 votes to prevail in the House, even if a way was found to circumvent the Republican filibuster in the Senate. Emanuel and others counseled scaling back the broad program to achieve a possible quick success with an incremental expansion of coverage for children.[29]

President Obama and Speaker Pelosi both resisted the call to surrender and settle for one-quarter of a loaf. Slowly, during February, a new momentum began to build. The president and his staff made this the number one priority in time and effort. A lucky break came when the Anthem Blue Cross–Blue Shield insurance company in California announced a 40% rate increase for those in the individual insurance market. This allowed the administration to focus the discussion on why health reform was important for those with insurance, not just the uninsured.

In an early February meeting with Senate Democrats, the level of distrust between the two legislative bodies was evident. Each had complaints and expressed a lack of faith in the ability of Democratic leaders in the other body to produce the votes necessary to pass health reform. In an effort to change the tone of the debate, make one last try to win over a few Republicans, and seize the initiative with the public, President Obama proposed a televised White House meeting with the congressional leadership of both parties. The seven-hour meeting did not produce any converts, but seemed to help the president regain the initiative among some wavering Democrats.

The legislative strategy for the final push was fashioned by Obama aides Rahm Emanuel and Jim Messina, both congressional veterans. Before the Massachusetts surprise election, House and Senate negotiators had, with White House mediation, begun to resolve some of the key differences between the two bill versions. But now the standard process would no longer work. With no Republican support and only fifty-nine Democratic votes, a new compromise bill could not be passed in the Senate. Since the Senate had already passed a bill, the House could simply pass the Senate bill and send it to President Obama for signature. Speaker Pelosi had repeatedly stressed to Majority Leader Reid and President Obama that she could not assemble the necessary 218 votes for passage of the Senate bill.[30] There were too many Senate provisions that remained unacceptable to critical members of the House for this to be achieved.

The strategy of Emanuel and Messina involved a two-step process with a leap of faith on the part of House Democrats. First, the House would pass the Senate bill and immediately pass a second bill under the budget reconciliation process that reflected a compromise on some of the key issues dividing the two bodies. Then, the Senate would take up and pass the reconciliation bill, which, under its rules, was not subject to a filibuster and required only a simple majority to pass.

Once this strategy was in place, President Obama and Speaker Pelosi began the arduous task of lobbying House Democrats who were on the fence to acquire the last few votes for passage. Perhaps the most symbolic and difficult was Cleveland congressman Dennis Kucinich. He had also been a presidential candidate and, unlike many other doubtful votes, was from the very liberal wing of the party. For him, the bill was not liberal enough. Finally, after joining the president on Air Force One for a trip back to Cleveland, Kucinich announced he would vote for the bill.

Most of the House Democrats who were undecided in the final days before the vote were from conservative-leaning districts. In the last days before the vote, the abortion language in the Senate bill rose as an issue for a key group of House Democrats. Led by Representative

Bart Stupak, these pro-life Democrats represented districts with heavy Catholic populations. Many of these districts had voted for President Obama. Stupak's district did so by an almost 2–1 margin. In December before the vote on the House bill, Stupak's group convinced Speaker Pelosi to support an amendment explicitly forbidding any federal funds to be used for abortion, including the tax credit subsidies. The Senate version was slightly less restrictive. Pelosi convinced other liberal legislators to accept the Stupak Amendment as an acceptable trade-off for the last critical votes.

Later, Stupak's group signaled an unwillingness to vote for the Senate bill because of its weaker abortion provision. As the House vote on the Senate version approached, the Stupak group became the critical last holdouts.

The reconciliation bill rules did not allow for nonfinancial issues, such as abortion language, to be included. This was the only path to changing the Senate bill without sixty votes. At the last minute, Congressman Stupak accepted an administration-offered compromise of an executive order clarifying that no federal funds would be spent for abortions. This produced the final few votes needed for passage in the House.

On Sunday, March 21, 2010, the House votes were in place, and by 220–207, it passed the Senate bill and the reconciliation measure. In a few days, the Senate followed with a 56–43 vote. ACA became law with the president's signature on March 30, 2010.

* * *

ACA was a historic achievement for the Obama administration and the Democratic congressional leadership. In the following section, I highlight the political forces, key issues, and special interests at play as well as the impact of public opinion on enactment of the legislation.

Political Forces at Play

Leadership

The term "leadership" is overused and often ill defined. In this instance, it is hard to look at the long and difficult year of twists and turns in the legislative process without concluding that the most critical element in the success was leadership. In the slow and sometimes meandering process of democracy in action, there are usually multiple roadblocks. Failure to navigate around any one of them is often a permanent defeat. It is similar to a close baseball or football game. In retrospect, a win might have been a loss, except for a small but key play or two along the way.

President Obama and Chief of Staff Emanuel demonstrated both strategic leadership vision and a tactical touch at the critical stages of legislative coalition building. Despite the array of other problems facing the administration, the president kept insisting that health reform was a top priority and worth the effort and risk of failure. Emanuel reportedly had doubts from the beginning about the wisdom of pursuing comprehensive reform in 2009, but he was a skillful and tactical leader in the process from the onset and a key player in building the final legislative coalition.

In the process, some of the legislative players felt that the president was not engaged enough and had not clearly articulated his preference on some of the key issues. In retrospect some of those very issues, like the public option or abortion coverage, needed to be part of last-minute compromises. These compromises would have been less feasible if there had been an earlier public presidential position. Sometimes the essence of political leadership is an understanding of timing. The exercise of presidential leadership in the lawmaking process often demands patience above all else. The ability to wait for exactly the right moment to intervene or state a presidential preference is not easy. There is a natural tendency to push forward when the issue is important. Effective leaders understand that bold statements work only at the right time.

Speaker Pelosi and Majority Leader Reid have different leadership styles and tend to reflect the culture of their legislative body. But at critical stages in the process, each was able to gather the last few essential votes necessary for the majority. In the last hours before the House floor vote in December, Pelosi recognized that without the support of the handful of members for whom the Stupak Amendment was vital, the bill would fail. She convinced the abortion rights advocates, especially women members, that without the Stupak Amendment health reform would fail in the House and be dead for perhaps years to come.

Reid, who faced a tough reelection campaign in 2010, had to risk alienation of key liberal support at home in order to build a coalition of sixty votes in the Senate. With no margin for error he had to deftly make deals, one at a time, with the last holdout senators who represented conservative constituents and had doubts about health reform. Without the skillful political leadership of these and other key players in the drama, the Patient Protection and Affordable Care Act of 2010 would not have become law.

Partisanship

Another significant political force was partisanship. President Obama, like Presidents George W. Bush and Clinton before him, entered office with the public hope that the country could be governed with a bipartisan approach. Even before the health reform issue moved to center stage five months into the Obama presidency, earlier bills served notice that bipartisanship was elusive. There is a tendency to recall an earlier era with selective memory about legislative bipartisanship. Medicare succeeded because the landslide 1964 victory of Lyndon B. Johnson created a much larger Democratic coalition. That, and not bipartisan compromise, produced the last great health legislation a generation ago. The tone was more civil in the past, but major philosophical differences have always divided the two parties' leaders as well as the rank and file on health care issues. ACA passed because the Democrats had in two elections, 2006 and 2008, succeeded in building a larger caucus in both the House and Senate. By 2009–2010 there were enough votes in the Senate to barely defeat a filibuster, and in the House to allow for defections of some Democrats who represented what were normally Republican districts. The changing nature of the national media has intensified the partisan tone and many states and congressional districts have become more solidly entrenched for one party or the other. The two parties are deeply divided on the philosophical issues surrounding health policy. The ACA provisions and legislative process reflected this division.

Johnson, perhaps the most accomplished Senate majority leader in history, is reported to have once said the most important skill needed for a legislative leader was the ability to divide by two and add one. Bills pass when successive majorities can be built at each stage of the legislative process. An understanding of the success and the difficulty of ACA passage begins and ends with a sense of the critical legislative coalitions. The 111th Congress (2009–2010) may represent the high-water mark of a Democratic majority for some time to come. Democrats held 255 seats in the 111th Congress, which was a 21-seat gain over the 110th Congress. Half of those new seats were from districts that President Obama did not win.[31]

In 2008 President Obama was victorious in 242 House districts, and 208 of those had Democratic House members; 49 districts voted for John McCain and a Democrat for the House. Democrats in the districts that Obama carried voted 199–8 for health reform. The defections or difficult votes came from the 49 districts carried by McCain with a Democrat in Congress. In the Senate, 33 Democrats were from states whose voters have supported the Democratic presidential nominee in the past five elections. These are the reliable core and mostly liberal base of the party in the Senate. It is from among the other 27 Democratic senators that Harry Reid had to carefully construct the 60 votes to break a filibuster. There was little doubt about a 51-vote majority for health reform legislation. It was the last 9 votes that proved difficult.[32]

Without the solid and perhaps temporary size of Democratic majorities, health reform would have been impossible. But skillful legislative leadership within their own caucuses by Pelosi and Reid, with their key colleagues and staff, represented the difference between a narrow victory and a legislative defeat.

Key Issues

ACA was a large and complex piece of legislation. Some apparently small provisions of the law may in time prove to be much more significant than anyone now anticipates. Some elements, such as Medicaid expansion, were not a subject of major public discussion in the legislative process. Three issues tended to be at the center of the coalition assembly process: cost, the public option, and abortion restrictions.

Cost

The admonition to "follow the money" is always good advice in assessing the legislative process. "Cost" here means both the projected new spending under the law and the policies designed to raise money or shift funds to pay for the new obligations. Since the new legislation would be phased in over a ten-year period, cost could be an elusive concept. One of the lessons learned from the policy failure of the 1988 Medicare

Catastrophic Coverage Act was that collecting revenue in the form of new taxes at the front end and following it later with benefits were a prescription for political disaster. As the summer of 2009 came and went, there was a general and growing apprehension about the long-term federal deficit fueled by legislation addressing economic recovery and the financial crisis. The key moderate Democrats feared they would be hammered during the next election for supporting unsustainable deficits. The measuring point for the cost issue was the accumulated impact of ACA in 2019 and its contribution to the federal deficit after 2019. The net total spending for the decade became a focal point for the discussion. The other key number was the projected new revenue and savings to offset the anticipated new expenditures.

The Congressional Budget Office (CBO) is the agency of Congress responsible for providing official estimates of the costs of legislation under consideration. The CBO director is appointed by the leadership of the Congress and supervises a professional staff. The work of the CBO is nonpartisan and widely respected. It has established rules for how certain types of proposed policies will be consistently treated. These "scoring rules" enable it to be neutral in its assessment of legislative provisions, even those sponsored by powerful figures such as the Speaker. Veteran legislators and staff responsible for constructing the details of bills understand the rules and try to fashion the legislative provisions to receive a favorable score. In the various iterations of the health reform bills in the House and Senate, elements were fashioned to get the best CBO score. A recent analysis of previous CBO scoring of major health legislation found that, in each case, the savings were substantially underestimated because the rule-based methodology did not adjust well to situations in which there was interaction among major program elements and the absence of historical precedent.[33]

The money path was shifting and convoluted. The overall target was set early in the discussion by President Obama, who wished to keep the aggregate costs for the decade under $1 trillion and paid for with a combination of new revenues and cost savings.[34]

As the debate over reform developed, several key points of choice emerged. The cost was going to be about $900 billion over a decade, with greater expenses coming later. Indeed, one of the reasons for the phased implementation schedule was to enhance the possibility of an acceptable CBO score by delaying some of the major costs until later in the decade. The two major expenses under the legislation are the Medicaid expansion, which is almost entirely paid for by the federal government, and the subsidies or tax credits to participants purchasing private insurance in the exchanges. These two items will cost nearly the same and represent about 95% of the total costs. The other 5% will be the tax credits for small employers.[35]

Projected program savings and revenue will be about $1 trillion, with 45% coming from program savings and 55% from additional revenues. There is a small net deficit reduction because savings and revenues exceed costs. Major program savings are derived from the reduction of Medicare Advantage payments and adjustments in provider payments. Together, these account for 75% of the savings. Major new revenue comes from a Medicare tax on high-income families and new fees imposed on the health care industry, which are together 55% of the new revenue.[36] The industry fees were agreed on in the negotiations between industry groups and the White House and Senate Finance Committee. The House was less involved in the negotiations with the groups and its leaders believing that too much had been conceded to them.

The original House bill contained an income tax surcharge on the wealthiest individuals, but the ultimate alternative was an increased Medicare tax on those with high incomes. An original sharp point of conflict between House and Senate was over the so-called Cadillac tax, which was an excise tax on high-cost health insurance plans. The argument is that, because of their extensive coverage benefits, these plans drive up health care spending. Many House members believed some union and public employee group insurance would be subject to the tax and objected.

The House bill cost more because the insurance subsidies were higher, providing more financial protection to those receiving them. The Senate revenue and savings offsets were not as high; therefore, the major spending item had to be held down. The final version was closer to the Senate approach.

The total cost of the bill was the major issue. The approach taken in both the House and Senate was similar on major items; for example, both included subsidies for those purchasing policies in the insurance exchanges. The difference between the bills was in the total cost. The higher total cost of the House proposal was ultimately offset by new higher taxes on the wealthy and higher fees for providers. All of this was done within the context of the CBO scoring system. The CBO system provides an accepted set of rules for everyone, but is not necessarily an accurate reflection of what will happen over a decade with a complex new law. There may be greater savings from the law than scored by CBO. Or, Medicaid costs and insurance subsidies may be much higher if general medical inflation rises sharply. A ten-year projection is nothing more than an educated guess; all the players understood this.

The Public Option

Most of the policy ideas encompassed in either the final legislation or the discussion leading up to it have been circulating in the health policy community for many years. The new idea, or recombination of old ideas, that emerged was the public option. Between the demise of the Clinton plan and the victory of Obama, the health reform approaches of scholars and policy analysts continued to be refined in papers and at conferences. To many, it was clear that major reform was not likely to end employer-sponsored insurance, but it would plug the gaps and weaknesses in the individual insurance market. The individual mandate entered the discussion to help insurance plans serving this group guard against adverse selection in which individuals did not purchase insurance until they were sick. The preexisting condition rules of the companies attempted to guard against adverse selection, but resulted in horror stories when companies denied coverage or would not accept those who had previously been ill.

As it became clear that the Massachusetts model was likely to be the approach taken in the health reform legislation, the concept of subsidies of private insurance within an exchange led some to question whether existing companies would be willing to offer policies at an affordable price, even with subsidies. In response to the concerns about subsidies, the idea that began to circulate was one of creating a public insurance company, similar to Medicare, that could compete with private companies within the exchanges. With national bargaining power and use of Medicare reimbursement rates, this public option would serve as a marker against private company rate increases, help drive down costs by lower reimbursement, and be less likely to engage in what were seen as predatory practices to maximize profit.[37]

During the 2008 presidential campaign, first John Edwards and then the other candidates began to talk about a public option as part of their reform model. This had special appeal for liberal activists who preferred a social insurance universal public approach, but knew this was probably not politically feasible. They believed that the public option might eventually be transformed into something resembling a single universal public insurance plan.

The House bill included a public option, which was strongly supported by many of the Democrats. Senator Baucus originally included a public option in his November 2008 white paper, but opposition among some Democrats on the Finance Committee caused him to remove it from the bill. In response to Senator Kent Conrad, the Finance Committee draft instead included a provision for co-ops to provide insurance.

Since the public option was part of the Senate HELP Committee bill, Senator Reid put a public option provision into the merged Senate bill. But the strident opposition of Senator Joseph Lieberman and the necessity to keep every one of the sixty votes caused the provision for a public option to be removed. The final legislation included a provision that allowed the federal Office of Personnel Management to put in place a new public plan to be set up by nonprofit entities and available to those in the insurance exchanges.[38]

Abortion Coverage

Since the late 1970s, the Hyde Amendment has been part of federal law. It prohibits use of any federal funds for abortions. As the health reform debate began, both pro-life and pro-choice forces agreed not to push their issue onto the table. There was the presumption that the Hyde Amendment would continue to be the policy statement. As the bills began to take shape, the question arose as to whether or not abortion coverage would be provided by policies sold in the insurance exchange with part of the premium cost subsidized by tax funds. If such tax money paid part of the premium cost for a policy that covered abortion, then that was seen by some as breaching the principle of the Hyde Amendment. A compromise of sorts was arranged in which those policies that covered abortion would have a separate premium to be paid in which there would be no public subsidy. As the House floor vote neared in November, Representative Stupak of Michigan planned to introduce an amendment with more restrictive language. At first Speaker Pelosi and the other pro-choice liberal Democrats were unwilling to support this amendment, but as the vote approached it became clear that Stupak had enough support for his amendment that the House could not pass the health reform bill without the votes of his allies on this issue. Pelosi convinced liberals to accept this amendment as the price of health reform.

The abortion issue was likely to be on the agenda as a major item for the conference discussion with the Senate because the Senate bill retained the broader language; supporters argued that both effectively prohibited the use of federal funds. As the time neared for a House vote on the Senate bill and reconciliation, the Catholic Conference of Bishops expressed opposition to any bill that did not include the language of the Stupak Amendment. Once again, some of the Democrats who supported the Stupak Amendment also opposed the reform bill on other grounds. But Stupak and several others signaled they would support the health reform bill as long as the amendment was included.

With the reconciliation strategy the only viable path to passage, a procedural constraint was evident. Under reconciliation rules, a nonfinancial item such as the Stupak Amendment was not allowed. As the final vote on the Senate bill approached in the House, some in Stupak's group signaled they would support health reform even without the amendment. But Stupak held out until the last minute and, on the morning of the vote, announced that he had reached an accommodation with President Obama in which an executive order would be issued to achieve the goal of the Stupak Amendment. This cleared the way for Stupak and his allies to become the critical final votes for reform.

This issue illustrated how a secondary issue can emerge as central when the necessary last votes elevate it. It also demonstrates an ability to compromise to achieve the larger goal. Pelosi and other pro-choice Democrats were originally willing to compromise to accept the Stupak Amendment. In the end Stupak himself, despite vilification from some supporters, was willing to accept something less in order to achieve health reform.

Special Interests

Health care represents close to 20% of the US economy. For health care industry groups, the reform stakes were huge. These groups included hospitals, physicians, insurance companies, drug manufacturers, and a host of other specialized interests. In 1994, most of these groups lined up against the Clinton health reform plan. Well before the 2008 election, there was general anticipation of a Democratic victory and a push for health reform legislation. First Senator Kennedy and then the White House sought a dialogue with major health care interest groups to seek their cooperation in the legislative process. For their part, the various groups concluded that health reform was likely to happen and was going to emphasize an insurance subsidy approach. Each group could envision a scenario in which their members were better off financially with, rather than without, reform. With his public meeting in early March 2009, President Obama signaled a willingness to negotiate on key items with major groups in advance of the actual legislative process. This meeting was followed by dialogue between the groups and high-level staff in the Obama administration.

The Obama approach changed the dynamics of the role of interests in the shaping of legislation. Initially, House members tended to feel omitted from the dialogue and were more willing to go it alone without the agreement of groups. Over the years, many of these groups had been more aligned with Republicans than with Democrats; they now recognized the new power reality in Washington, DC.

Group leaders such as Karen Ignagni (representing health insurers) and Billy Tauzin (head of Pharmaceutical Research and Manufacturers of America) were longtime veterans of Washington with personal ties to those on both sides of the aisle. Unlike the partisan and ideological differences separating legislators, the group leaders sought a deal to benefit their organizations. Other groups representing the public interest were also active. Families USA and its longtime leader, Ron Pollack, as well as Andy Stern of the Service Employees International Union, not only were not lobbying for health reform but were willing to compromise to achieve it.[39]

The Impact of Public Opinion

During the health reform debate, both sides argued that public opinion favored their position. The reformers cited poll results over a long period of time to prove that the public was dissatisfied with the health care system and insurance companies and favored some type of legislative action, especially to protect people against the financial hardship of serious illness. Opponents cited polls showing public concern about cost and too much government involvement in health care decisions. In August 2009, some groups opposed to reform claimed the legislation would create "death panels" that would deny care to the terminally ill.[40]

As with many attempts to interpret public opinion, both sides were right. For a long time, opinion polls had shown majority support for system change that would shelter families from serious health care–related financial hardship. As premiums and cost sharing have increased, the cost of care has increased as a concern. On the other hand, most people are reasonably satisfied with their own care, but still complain that they pay too much. There is growing distrust of government and fear of too much governmental intrusiveness into health decisions in order to save money.

As might be expected with complex legislation, there is also a general lack of accurate information about the legislative details. Throughout the reform discussion, public opinion polls generally found the public about evenly divided on the question of whether or not health reform is a good idea. Among partisans, the division is predictable. Democrats tend to favor reform and Republicans oppose it. When specific provisions of the health reform legislation, such as prohibiting the denial of insurance based on preexisting conditions, are the subject of polls, support is strong.[41]

The interpretation of these public opinion polls led the Obama administration to shift the emphasis and begin stressing health insurance reform rather than health reform. The administration publicly criticized large rate hikes and emphasized that most existing employment-based insurance would not change. The administration hopes that, once the provisions of the law begin to take effect, opposing opinion will move away from the partisan interpretations and support the essential features of the law.

Key Coverage Provisions of ACA

ACA is a complex piece of legislation. What follows is a brief summary of the major provisions. For a more complete summary, the Kaiser Commission on Medicaid and the Uninsured website is an excellent source (www.kff.org).[42]

Medicaid Expansion

- Medicaid expanded to cover all individuals aged sixty-four years and younger with incomes up to 133% of the federal poverty level, thus creating uniform national minimum eligibility requirements.
- The federal government will fund 100% of newly eligible recipients from 2014 to 2016, with a gradually increasing state share

until 2020, when the federal government will fund 90% of all costs for this group.
- Medicaid primary care physician fees will be 100% of Medicare fees with the federal government funding 100% of new spending.

Insurance Market Reform

- By 2014, states will create insurance exchanges, which are purchasing pools for small employers and individuals purchasing insurance.
- The Office of Personnel Management will contract with private insurers to offer at least two multistate plans in each insurance exchange, including one by a nonprofit entity.
- All plans offered in the insurance exchanges must meet minimum standards and offer four levels of coverage.

Premium and Cost-sharing Tax Credits

- Premium credits will be available to individuals and families with incomes between 133% and 400% of the federal poverty level to purchase coverage in the insurance exchanges.
- Premium credits will be refundable tax credits delivered in advance.
- People with income less than 250% of the poverty level will receive additional cost-sharing credits.

New Insurance Market Regulations

- Children will be allowed to remain on parents' health insurance up to the age of twenty-six years.
- Waiting periods for coverage will be limited to ninety days.
- Annual and lifetime limits on policy coverage are prohibited.
- Rescissions of insurance coverage are prohibited.
- Waiting limits for coverage are prohibited.
- Lifetime limits on coverage will be prohibited and rescission of coverage will be prohibited except in cases of fraud.
- All new health insurance plans must provide comprehensive coverage with a minimum set of services, cap annual out-of-pocket spending, not impose cost sharing for preventive services, and not impose annual lifetime limits on coverage.

- Health insurance premiums can vary based on age, only by a maximum 3–1 ratio, geographic area, tobacco use, and number of family members.
- Increases in health insurance premiums will be subject to review.

Employer Requirements

- Employers with more than fifty employees must offer health insurance or pay a fee for each full-time employee if they do not offer coverage.

Individual Mandate

- In 2014, all US citizens will be required to have qualifying health insurance coverage or pay a penalty of $695 per year.

The CBO has estimated a reduction of 32 million uninsured by 2019 as a result of ACA. Of these, 16 million will be newly covered by Medicaid and the Children's Health Insurance Program (CHIP). By 2019, it is estimated that 24 million people will obtain coverage through the insurance exchange.

Prognosis

The Patient Protection and Affordable Care Act of 2010 was a legislative response to a problem that has been recognized for decades and hailed as landmark social legislation. While not as significant as Medicare, it will define health care policy in the years ahead. The legislative provisions reflected the dominant ideas about health reform found in the health policy community. Many policy analysts believe the provisions of this law can be effectively put in place to address the fundamental problems within the health care system. It is possible the immediate features will prove popular and support will grow to the point that opponents will lose interest or see little to be gained by repeal; Medicare prospered with a new administration just four years after enactment. However, external events may prove the optimism and confidence in ACA are misplaced. A further shift in congressional majority fundamentally unrelated to health reform may increase the difficulties of its implementation and thus doom it to failure. There are several prominent questions surrounding what will happen to ACA in the years ahead. One year after passage of the law, the answers to the questions below are as yet undetermined.

Can the Law Be Implemented Effectively?

Implementation is always a critical phase in the life of a piece of legislation. No matter how carefully a statute was drafted, many critical elements remain to be addressed in the regulation writing process. It is during implementation that legislative language is ultimately tested in the real world of daily living. With ACA, both states and the federal government have a complicated set of administrative tasks to perform during the implementation period. These include setting up the insurance exchanges, organizing the subsidy program, writing rules for insurance market reform, and enrolling new Medicaid beneficiaries. These are not trivial challenges, and if state officials are either philosophically opposed or functioning within an environment in which opposition is deeply embedded, even the most basic tasks become exponentially more difficult. Republican control of more governorships and state legislatures after the 2010 election will undoubtedly make the road to implementation more difficult.

If implementation falters, then public support for the law will decline. It is hard to overestimate the difficulties of implementation, especially with a complex program that requires extensive coordination between the federal government and the states.[43] The legislative process was arduous, but implementation may be an even greater challenge.

Will ACA Be Repealed?

The ink of President Obama's signature was barely dry when opponents began to call for repeal. Republican opponents made this a rallying cry in the 2010 midterm elections. This was probably not the major reason that Democrats lost control of the House of Representatives, but the new Republican majority perceives it has a mandate to attempt repeal. In early 2011, House Republicans were able to pass a largely symbolic repeal bill. At least until the 2012 general election, Democrats retain control of the Senate and White House, thus rendering repeal impossible. However, this is likely to be a campaign issue in the 2012 election, which will keep the possibility of repeal at the forefront of health policy discussions.

As ACA is implemented, various elements of it are likely to be popular and thus immune to repeal. These include such provisions as gradual elimination of the Medicare doughnut hole, restrictions on insurance companies, and eliminating cost sharing for preventive services under Medicare and Medicaid. Despite the rhetoric, selective repeal of provisions of the law may be more likely than a complete repeal if Republicans are successful in building a majority coalition in Congress by 2013.

Opponents are pursuing three strategies to fight full implementation of ACA. Repeal is the most drastic and least likely to be effective in the next few years. The second is a legal strategy. A constitutional challenge has been initiated by various state officials who have filed lawsuits trying to have parts of the law declared unconstitutional. At the time of this writing, there have been mixed decisions at the federal district court level, with some upholding the law and others overturning part or all of it. One of the cases will ultimately be taken up by the Supreme Court.[44] The legal argument against the individual mandate in ACA offers the most promising legal grounds to contest the law.[45]

The complex implementation process offers a third approach. It creates an opportunity for opponents to hamper, delay, and obstruct various elements of the law. Republican opponents have both the House majority and control of state governments to render implementation of features such as the insurance exchanges and Medicaid expansion difficult. The appropriation process can also be used to slow down the implementation process. Attempts may be made to deny appropriations for such critical features as IRS personnel for enforcement, and legislative language may be inserted in appropriations bills to restrict the spending of money related to specific sections of the law.[46] Such provisions are subject to House and Senate negotiations, and could trigger a veto by President Obama, thus setting up a government shutdown confrontation similar to what occurred during the Clinton administration.

Two key elements of the new law, Medicaid expansion and the new subsidies for private health insurance, are entitlements that are not subject to annual appropriations. Some additional elements have already been appropriated, but others will need future legislative action.[47]

At the time of this writing in early 2011, it seems fair to state that repeal or dismantling of ACA will remain a major policy priority for conservative opponents. Opposition may lead to implementation difficulties over the next two years, but will not halt the basic trajectory of the law's application. However, the election of 2012 is likely to determine the future of ACA beyond 2013. If Republicans gain control of both houses of Congress and the White House in the election, ACA will surely not survive in its current form.

Will Public Support Grow and Immunize the Law from Repeal?

Medicare was fully implemented in one year. ACA will not be fully implemented until midway into a possible second Obama term. There are many complex pieces in this legislation, but Medicare was also broad in scope. The prolonged implementation probably has more to do with spreading new expenses over a longer time period than its supporters have been willing to admit. This helped the legislation achieve an acceptable score from the CBO, which facilitated passage. After all the fanfare, if in several years there remains a high rate of uninsured, then it may be difficult to sustain public support in the face of political opposition. However, the advantage of passing the legislation with health care interest group support is the stake of those groups in the outcome. The major health provider groups perceived in 2009 that they had an interest in the passage of this law. By 2012 and beyond, will these groups continue to support the ongoing implementation because they still have an interest in the outcome? Repeal without the support of major interest groups may be just as difficult as enactment.

The Kaiser Health Tracking Poll has found public opinion stable and evenly divided. About 40% of the population hold a favorable view of ACA, 40% an unfavorable view, and 20% no opinion. About 25% of the population favor complete repeal, 40% prefer leaving it in place or expanding ACA, and 25% wish to see only parts of the law repealed. The individual mandate is the most unpopular provision. Other provisions remain popular, such as the closing of the Medicare doughnut hole, which is favored by over 70% of the population, including 40% of those who favor complete repeal.[48]

Will the Law Seriously Increase the National Deficit?

At the time of enactment, the CBO predicted that ACA would reduce the deficit by $143 billion by 2019.[49] Despite the CBO analysis, this is probably an open question. If the economy continues to be stagnant, additional Medicaid costs to be borne entirely by the federal government in the early years may be higher than projected. If the cost of health insurance premiums in the exchanges is significantly higher than anticipated, the cost of the subsidies will rise faster than expected. On the other hand, some of the savings embedded in the legislative provisions may be much higher than scored by the CBO and may more than offset any higher expenses.[50]

* * *

The Patient Protection and Affordable Care Act of 2010 was the most significant health policy legislation passed since Medicare. Medicare was completely in place within a year, and quickly developed a positive bipartisan consensus. Conversely, many key ACA provisions will not be in place for several years; and, a year after passage, partisan positions on the law have hardened, not diminished. At best, implementation will proceed with relative ease, and public support for ACA will grow as all provisions become effective. The worst case scenario for ACA supporters, a loss in the 2012 elections of Democratic majorities in the House and Senate and in the White House, will result in the ACA either completely repealed or major provisions substantially modified. Elections matter. The long-term fate of ACA depends on the next two or three election cycles.

Notes

1. Sheryl Stoleberg and Robert Pear, "Obama Signs Health Care Overhaul Bill, with a Flourish," *New York Times,* March 23, 2010, p. A19.

2. "The Uninsured: A Primer. Key Facts About Americans Without Health Insurance" (Washington, DC: Kaiser Commission on Medicaid and the Uninsured, October 2009).

3. Theda Skocpol, *Boomerang: Health Care Reform and the Turn Against Government* (New York: Norton, 1997).

4. Deborah Stone, "Single Payer: Good Metaphor, Bad Politics," *Journal of Health Politics, Policy and Law* 34, no. 4 (2009): 531–542.

5. Jim Brasfield, "The Public Option: Health Reform and a Controversial Policy Idea," paper presented at the annual meeting of the Midwest Political Science Association, Chicago, IL, April 22–25, 2010.

6. Shelia Zedlewski, G. P. Acs, and C. W. Winterbottom, "Play or Pay Employer Mandates: Potential Effects," *Health Affairs* 11, no. 1 (1992): 62–83.

7. Roland McDevitt et al., "Group Insurance: A Better Deal for Most People Than Individual Plans," *Health Affairs* 29, no. 1 (2010): 156–164.

8. L. Blumberg and K. Pollitz, "Health Insurance Exchanges: Organizing Health Insurance Marketplaces to Promote Health Reform Goals. Timely Analysis of Immediate Health Policy Issues" (Washington, DC: Urban Institute, April 2009).

9. M. Doty, S. Collins, S. Rustgi, and J. Nicholson, "Out of Options: Why So Many Workers in Small Businesses Lack Affordable Health Insurance, and How Health Care Reform Can Help" (New York: Commonwealth Fund, September 2009).

10. Karen Davis, *National Health Insurance: Benefits, Costs, and Consequences* (Washington, DC: Brookings Institution, 1975).

11. Alain Enthoven, "The History and Principles of Managed Competition," *Health Affairs* 12, no. 1 (suppl. 1993): 24–48; Alain Enthoven, "Employment-Based Health Insurance Is Failing: Now What?" *Health Affairs,* Web exclusive, May 28, 2003, http://content.healthaffairs.org /content/early/2003/05/28/hlthaff.w3.237.full.pdf.

12. Mark Pauly and John Goodman, "Tax Credits for Health Insurance and Medical Savings Accounts," *Health Affairs* 14, no. 1 (1995): 125–139.

13. M. V. Pauly, P. Danzon, P. Feldstein, and J. Hoff, "A Plan for 'Responsible National Health Insurance,'" *Health Affairs* 10, no. 1 (1991): 5–25.

14. S. Giled, J. Hartz, and G. Giorgi, "Consider It Done? The Likely Efficacy of Mandates for Health Insurance," *Health Affairs* 26, no. 6 (2007): 1612–1621; J. Lambrew and J. Gruber, "Monday and Mandates: Relative Effects of Key Policy Levers in Expanding Health Insurance Coverage to All Americans," *Inquiry* 43, no. 4 (2006–2007): 333–344.

15. Pauley and Goodman, "Tax Credits."

16. Karyn Schwartz and Tanya Schwartz, "How Will Health Reform Impact Young Adults?" (Washington, DC: Kaiser Commission on Medicaid and the Uninsured, May 2010), pp. 1–9.

17. S. Silow-Carroll, J. Meyer, M. Regenstein, and N. Bagby, *In Sickness and in Health? The Marriage Between Employers and Health Care* (Washington, DC: Economic and Social Research Institute, 1995).

18. Martin Feldstein, "The Welfare Loss of Excess Health Insurance," *Journal of Political Economy* 81, no. 2 (1973): 251–280; Jon Gabel et al., "Taxing Cadillac Health Plans May Produce Chevy Results," *Health Affairs* 29, no. 1 (2010): 1–8.

19. David Herszenhorn, "Let Health Insurance Cross State Lines, Some Say," *New York Times,* February 13, 2010, Prescriptions Blog, http://prescriptions .blogs.nytimes.com/2010/02/13/let-health-insurance-cross-state-lines-some -say/?scp=1&sq=Herszenhorn%20February%2013,%202010&st=cse.

20. Jonathan Alter, *The Promise: President Obama, Year One* (New York: Simon & Schuster, 2010), chap. 3.

21. Dana Milbank, "Why Obama Needs Rahm at the Top," *Washington Post,* February 21, 2010, p. A13.

22. "Massachusetts Health Care Reform: Three Years Later" (Washington, DC: Kaiser Commission on Medicaid and the Uninsured, September 2009).

23. Robert Pear, "Health Care Industry in Talks to Shape Policy," *New York Times,* February 20, 2009, p. A16.

24. Bara Vaida, "Super Bowl Moment," *National Journal,* June 13, 2009, p. 20.

25. Jonathan Cohn, "How They Did It: The Inside Account of Health Care Reform's Triumph," *The New Republic,* June 10, 2010, p. 14.

26. Vaida, "Super Bowl Moment," p. 20.

27. House committees: Energy and Commerce, Education and Labor, and Ways and Means.

28. Senator Max Baucus, *Call to Action: Health Reform 2009,* Senate Finance Committee, 110th Cong., 2nd sess., November 12, 2008, p. 27.

29. Sheryl Stolberg, Jeff Zeleny, and Carl Hulse, "The Long Road Back," *New York Times,* March 21, 2010, p. A17.

30. Because of vacancies, only 216 votes were needed.

31. Jonathan Rauch, "A Fix for Addicts—and for Drug Policy," *National Journal,* April 18, 2009, p. 27.

32. Ronald Brownstein, "The Governing Core," *National Journal,* April 3, 2010, p. 53.

33. Jon Gabel, "Does the Congressional Budget Office Underestimate Savings from Reform? A Review of the Historical Record" (New York: Commonwealth Fund, January 2010).

34. Jonathan Cohn, "How They Did It: The Inside Account of Health Care Reform's Triumph," *The New Republic,* June 10, 2010, p. 21.

35. Paul Van de Water, "How Health Reform Helps Reduce the Deficit" (Washington, DC: Center on Budget and Policy Priorities, May 10, 2010).

36. Ibid.

37. Jacob Hacker, "Healthy Competition: How to Structure Public Health Insurance Plan Choice to Ensure Risk-Sharing, Cost Control, and Quality Improvement," Policy Brief (Washington, DC: Institute for America's Future, April 2009).

38. Jim Brasfield, "The Public Option: Health Reform and a Controversial Policy Idea," paper presented at the annual meeting of the Midwest Political Science Association, Chicago, April 22–25, 2010.

39. Vaida, "Super Bowl Moment," p. 20.

40. Lawrence R. Jacobs and Theda Skocpol, *Health Care Reform and American Politics: What Everyone Needs to Know* (New York: Oxford University Press, 2010), p. 21.

41. M. Brodie, D. Altman, C. Deane, S. Buscho, and E. Hamel, "Liking the Pieces, Not the Package: Contradictions in Public Opinion During Health Reform," *Health Affairs* 29, no. 6 (2010): 1125–1130.

42. "Summary of the New Health Reform Law" (Washington, DC: Kaiser Commission on Medicaid and the Uninsured, April 21, 2010); "Summary of Coverage Provisions in the Patient Protection and Affordable Care Act" (Washington, DC: Kaiser Commission on Medicaid and the Uninsured, April 28, 2010).

43. Jeffery Pressman and Aaron Wildavsky, *Implementation* (Berkeley: University of California Press, 1973).

44. Matthew DoBias, "The Mandate and the Court," *National Journal,* January 8, 2011, p. 47.

45. Len Nichols, "Implementing Insurance Market Reforms Under the Federal Health Reform Law," *Health Affairs* 29, no. 6 (2010): 1152–1157; Timothy Jost, "State Lawsuits Won't Succeed in Overturning the Individual Mandate," *Health Affairs* 29, no. 6 (2010): 1152–1157.

46. Robert Pear, "GOP to Fight Health Law with Purse Strings," *New York Times,* November 6, 2010, p. A1; Major Garrett and Aamer Madhani, "Guerrilla War over Government," *National Journal,* December 18, 2010, pp. 24–30.

47. Melissa Seeley, "Funding for Key Health Reform Provisions: Less Endangered Than You Might Think," Health Affairs Blog, January 4, 2011, http://healthaffairs.org/blog/2011/01/04/funding-for-key-health-reform -provisions-less-endangered-than-you-might-think.

48. "The Public, Health Care Reform, and Views on Repeal," Data Note (Washington, DC: Kaiser Family Foundation, January 2011), www.kff.org /healthreform/8131.cfm.

49. Douglas W. Elmendorf, director of the Congressional Budget Office, "Letter to the Honorable Nancy Pelosi," Congressional Budget Office, March 20, 2010, www.cbo.gov/ftpdocs/113xx/doc11379/AmendReconProp.pdf.

50. Paul Van de Water, *How Health Reform Helps Reduce the Deficit* (Washington, DC: Center on Budget and Policy Priorities, May 10, 2010).

8

How Other Countries Do It

In any policy discussion about the US health care system, there inevitably is a reference to the health care systems of major developed countries. The British system may be criticized or the German system lauded, but a comparative analysis is always present. This cross-national comparison is beneficial. Medical professionals draw on research and accumulated knowledge about best practices from around the world. The practice of medicine is the same, but the financial and administrative systems for organizing health care delivery differ. Lessons from the successful approaches in one country are applicable elsewhere.

In order to focus specifically and limit distractions from a variety of different countries, I examine three health care delivery systems. The United Kingdom (UK), Germany, and Canada each offer a unique and relevant vantage point. For many years, US reformers looked to the UK as a possible model. Germany was the first country to move toward a social insurance system with a health care financing component that traces its system back to the nineteenth century. Our neighbor Canada, which has one-tenth the population of the United States, shares many cultural similarities with us.

For each of these three systems, the origins and the basic organizations are significant. In the descriptive segment, the focus for each system is the organization and payment for hospitals and physicians, the sources of revenue, and the scope of benefits. Because every health care system has struggled with cost containment, this is a particular point of interest in the reviews. Finally, I assess the role of the public and private sectors.

The health care systems of the UK, Germany, and Canada have been specifically chosen for discussion because not only does each system offer a unique and relevant vantage point, but periodically some participants in the US reform debate have looked to one of these three to serve as a model.

The United Kingdom

The origin of the National Health Service (NHS) in the United Kingdom is found in 1911 legislation that provided medical coverage for workers. During the hardships of World War II, the coalition government wishing to offer citizens a positive vision of postwar life began to enact into law major elements of the Report on Social Insurance and Allied Services (Beveridge Plan). This proposed comprehensive social insurance system, including a National Health Service for the country, was enacted by Parliament in 1946 and implemented two years later. There have been periodic reorganizations over the past sixty years, but the fundamentals of the system as established remain in place today.

The NHS is a single health care system covering every citizen. It accounts for 87% of all health expenditures. Most health care workers are directly employed by the NHS. There are ten regional health authorities that report to the Department of Health. Within each region, there are primary care trusts (PCTs), which control 80% of the NHS budget. In addition to paying general practitioners (GPs), the NHS pays for services provided by hospitals for citizens in their region. Hospital trusts own and operate facilities. Some are foundation trusts with greater autonomy.

GPs are independent contractors who receive payments from PCTs in the form of capitation payments, salary, and some fees. There is a national contract that defines the basic components of GP payments. Specialists are employed by the hospitals, but often are permitted to also see some private patients. Everyone in the population is registered with a GP practice, which usually includes four or more physicians. Access to specialists is normally possible only through the GPs who serve as gatekeepers. A typical GP has about 2,000 patients on his or her list.[1]

About 75% of the health care system revenue comes from general taxes, with 20% from health insurance contributions. The total amount of money to be spent for health care is determined by the Treasury. The Department of Health then allocates the health budget among the various categories, including hospital and primary care. The money is distributed to the regional authorities on the basis of a demographically modified population-based formula. Hospitals receive funding from an allocation formula based on a payment by results (PbR) allocation in which payments are a function of case mix and volume.

The NHS offers a full range of benefits, including inpatient and outpatient services, dental care, and mental health care. Other than prescription drugs and dental care, there is no cost sharing by patients. Those with low income are often exempted from even these costs.

Private health insurance is available in the UK and covers about 12% of the population. This results in only 1% of total health spending. Some individuals also pay out-of-pocket for health services from private providers. The existence of private insurance allows for shorter wait times for elective surgery, quicker access to specialists, and greater comfort in hospitals. There is a small but growing set of private health institutions, such as surgicenters that are privately owned and operated. These institutions also serve NHS patients under contract with trusts.

Wait lists for elective surgeries has been a major issue in the National Health Service. The Tony Blair government sought to increase health care resources, and in 2000 made the pledge to increase spending to the European Union average.[2] The major target for the increased resources was the wait lists for elective surgeries. The goal was to reduce wait times to a maximum of eighteen weeks.

The primary method of cost containment is the centralized budget, which enables the Treasury and Department of Health to fix the annual rate of growth for the entire system. The United Kingdom is the often-cited example of a single-payer system that produces comparable health care outcomes, with lower per capita expenditures than the United States.

The British system began in 1948 as a premier example of socialized medicine. Access for all was an achieved goal, but with it came wait lists and other evident manifestations of rationing. Those in the United States who found the NHS an attractive model were criticized for supporting an approach that explicitly rationed elective surgery and some services such as kidney dialysis. A major comparative analysis of the US and UK systems three decades ago found a far more complicated story. With some services, such as hemophilia treatment, the NHS responded quickly and efficiently to categories of disease. In others, such as coronary bypass surgery, the NHS lagged compared to the United States.[3]

Political leaders across the spectrum in the UK support the NHS. There have been frequent reorganizations as successive governments have sought to improve both services and efficiency. Political pressure has repeatedly pushed service improvement onto the political agenda. Various attempts at reorganization and restructuring of the NHS administration do not seem to have significantly changed the system. The cumulative impact of the attempts has been to "shift power to primary care providers, to introduce incentives to enhance responsiveness and to make the activities of the service more transparent and measurable than ever before."[4]

In the summer of 2010, the David Cameron government announced plans for another attempted reorganization of the NHS. This change proposes to eliminate the primary care trusts and, with those, many NHS management positions. The local GPs in each region will decide how the funds are spent. Money from the management savings will be put into additional patient care services.[5]

Canada

Led by Saskatchewan in 1947, one by one the Canadian provinces developed public health insurance hospitalization plans. By the mid-1950s, the national government enacted a cost-sharing plan in which the federal government provided funds to each province to assist in financing its health insurance programs. Additional legislation in 1966 paved the way for each province to have a full public insurance plan, including physician payment. The Canada Health Act of 1984 further defined the national standards required of the provincial plans: public administration, comprehensiveness, universality, portability, and accessibility. Extra charges and user fees were also eliminated. In less than thirty-five years, Canadian Medicare reached the goal of comprehensive health care.

Each of the thirteen provinces and territories operates its own health insurance plan under general national guidelines. The entire population is covered for hospital and physician services, with public and private programs covering other services such as vision and dental care. Two out of three Canadians also have private health insurance to cover prescription drugs, dental care, and other services, but private insurance cannot be used to pay for basic medical services. Patient cost sharing or balance billing for physician and hospital services is not permitted. The provincial systems are portable, thus allowing Canadians access to service in other provinces.

Hospitals are owned by nonprofit corporations or local public entities, and receive a global budget from the provincial government. Most have regional health authorities (RHAs) as intermediaries between the provincial government and hospitals. The RHAs receive a budget allocation from the province. They determine the allocation approach and payment to individual hospitals. Capital expenditures are funded by the provincial government.

Most physicians are in private fee-for-service practice and are reimbursed based on a fee schedule negotiated between the medical association and the provincial government. A growing number of general practitioners are paid by the province with a blended system including fees, salary, and capitation. Patients are free to select their primary care physician, who typically determines the patient's access to a specialist when necessary. Hospital-based specialists are also reimbursed on a fee-for-service basis.

Like the United Kingdom, Canada has a single-payer system, but it is decentralized to the provinces. There are thirteen related but distinct systems. The federal government directs payments to the provinces in the form of a health care block grant, which totals about 20% of the cost and is based on a per capita formula. There are additional tax transfers to the provinces, providing additional federal funds for health care. The global budgets and provincially determined fee schedules are major cost-containment tools.

Private health insurance has been limited to coverage of those services not publicly financed. A recent court decision in Quebec may have future implications. In the case *Chaoulli vs Quebec 2005,* the Supreme Court found a Quebec statute banning private insurance for publicly covered services to be in violation of the Canadian Charter of Rights and Freedoms. A basis for the court's rationale was that Quebec had unacceptably long wait times in its publicly funded services. No specific remedy was proposed, and the solution was left to the provincial government. It is not clear if the ruling will also be applied to other provinces.[6] The decision is a challenge to the basic structure of health care financing in Canada. As in the UK single-payer system, Canada's system has led to episodic rationing by use of wait times for certain individual procedures. The rationing has periodically created public discontent, leading to government action to ameliorate the immediate condition. One study indicates that better management of scheduling practices would impact the wait list, and might reduce the problem without the infusion of significant additional resources.[7] If the wait list problem is not addressed in a permanent fashion, the issue will appear on the national agenda. The basic system is unlikely to be radically changed, but the British model of allowing private insurance as a kind of safety valve would appear to be an option.

For-profit clinics have appeared in various parts of Canada. Some serve private paying patients only, but others have contracted with the local health care authority to provide services. Allowing the use of private for-profit clinics under contract with local authorities may be a cost-effective way to address wait list problems in some service areas.[8]

The Canadian system evolved over decades and is deeply rooted in its federal system. Yet primary responsibility for public decision-making rests with the provincial governments. The dual responsibilities make radical change less likely because change would require the concurrence of thirteen different provincial governments. More private contracting on the margins of the health care systems is the most likely experimental change that will occur in the decade ahead.

Germany

The German social insurance system, including health insurance, is the oldest in the world. In 1871, Chancellor Otto von Bismarck developed the benefit system as a governmental response to the problems associated with the advancing Industrial Revolution. This basic structure has survived wars, domestic upheaval, the Nazi regime, and reunification of Germany at the end of the Cold War in the early 1990s.

The core of the system rests with 180 sickness funds. These social insurance funds are organized as not-for-profit entities. Some are industry based and others are organized geographically. Before 1996, Germans were assigned to a fund and typically remained there for life. Now the citizens may choose their fund as well as move from one fund to another.

Previously, each fund collected the payments associated with its members. This led to significant differences in provider payments affecting the fiscal status of the fund and, therefore, variations in premium contributions. These variations were perceived as a violation of the principles of social equity, which led to the change to central collection with a formula distribution.[9] Now all participants and their employers are required to contribute health insurance payments to a central fund, which then remits money to each sickness fund based on a formula of risk-adjusted capitation. This centralized collection began in 2009.

Coverage for children in sickness funds is now financed separately by the federal government from tax revenues placed in the central fund rather than from the employer and employee contributions. The welfare agency of the national government pays the sickness fund contribution for those without income. Civil servants have a special arrangement; self-employed and high-income individuals may participate in a private insurance arrangement. This private insurance funding accounts for only about 10% of total health care spending.

Hospitals are owned by either nonprofit or local public entities. They are paid by sickness funds based on a diagnosis-related group system. Historically, there was a sharp separation between hospital and outpatient care, although this barrier has eroded with the introduction of outpatient surgery and clinics at hospitals. The number of hospital beds and average length of stay have declined in recent years, but both are high in comparison with other European countries.[10] In the past, capital expenditure funding was provided by the state government. Recently it has been bundled into the basic payments, affording the hospitals more direct responsibility for these investment decisions.[11] Some public hospitals have been sold to for-profit entities, and this new ownership structure accounts for about one-quarter of all facilities.[12]

Physicians are mostly organized as solo practitioners. Primary care physicians typically do not exercise a gatekeeping role. Since 2004, sickness funds have offered members a family physician care model option with some gatekeeper-type functions. While some hospitals employ specialists, other specialists practice solo or in small-group clinic settings. All nonhospital specialists are paid on the basis of a contract negotiated between the physician associations and the sickness funds in a region. The funds transfer money based on a per capita formula to the physician associations, which then divide payments among various types of physicians and make individual payments on the basis of a fee schedule. This system is the equivalent of a global budget for physician payment.

All citizens are covered either by a sickness fund or private insurance. The basic benefit package is identical for all sickness funds and includes physician services, hospital care, prescription drugs, and dental and mental health services. As a cost-containment measure some copayments were introduced in 2004, and out-of-pocket costs represented about 13% of total health care spending in 2007.[13]

Cost-containment efforts have taken a variety of approaches. These include the global budget elements of both hospital and physician payments; greater out-of-pocket cost sharing; and various strategies to slow the growth rate of prescription drug costs, including negotiated agreements with pharmaceutical companies for rebates. Physicians are now financially responsible if they exceed a practice volume limit. Further, patients with chronic conditions are enrolled in a special disease management program; sickness funds are paid an additional administrative fee for each individual with a chronic illness who is enrolled in the program.

The most significant challenge for the German health care system in the past few decades has been the integration of East and West Germany in the 1990s. With the fall of the Berlin Wall and unification of the country, the Soviet-style system in the East was dismantled and integrated into the historic German system in the West. Because the infrastructure in the East had deteriorated, significant new resources were needed to fully integrate the two systems.[14]

The German system has retained its essential social insurance character, reflecting more than a century of history. The reforms of the past fifteen years have both increased social equity by modifying the revenue collection system and introduced systems management changes designed to increase efficiency in payments and treatment integration.

Universal Financial Coverage

Each of the health care systems reviewed above provides universal financial coverage for its population. There have been critical points in history when public policy decisions determined the future path of health care financing and delivery in these countries, such as the 1946 establishment of the NHS in the UK. There has been a path dependency from those points forward. The prior decisions have constrained the future choices.

Every health care system has a mechanism for paying physicians and hospitals. This is one of the most critical design elements. Payments must be adequate to maintain service, but provide appropriate incentives for the individuals and institutions to offer sufficient care. Excessive services and unnecessary care need to be discouraged. Cost-effective care is the ideal. Canada, the United Kingdom, and Germany have all tinkered with their payment systems in recent years in attempts to find the best incentives coupled with adequate payment.

When painting the picture with broad strokes, it is easy to make a public system versus private system distinction. Yet all three of the examined systems demonstrate the evolution of a mixed approach. Each system has a private insurance element and a preponderance of public funding. Nonprofit corporations or public entities typically own hospitals, but each entity has some private for-profit hospitals and clinics. Some of these provide individual treatment on a fee-for-service basis and also contract with larger hospitals to provide other services. This helps to relieve the resource problem of the wait list for medical service, minimizing rationing by providing additional facilities and professionals without new public expenditures for capital and long-term employees. In each system, there is likely to be continued discussion about the appropriate public-private mix, even as public funding predominates.

Each of the systems has struggled in recent years with rising costs and has attempted to find new ways to raise additional revenue and constrain the rate of growth of expenditures. All developed countries have aging populations. By itself this is not a huge year-to-year cost escalator, but over time an older population will require more health care services. One of the consequences of successful cost containment in Canada and the UK has been wait lists for some types of procedures. This has created political pressure on the governments to shorten lists. Germany has not had this problem, but has needed to add copayments and take other steps to slow the growth rate of health care costs. All have discovered that there is no silver bullet solution. Incremental tinkering with episodic bursts of policy change and reorganization has been the standard response.

The United Kingdom began with a national system that has since devolved in some significant ways, including greater autonomy for Wales, Scotland, and Northern Ireland. To create greater equity, the German system has centralized the collection and distribution of tax money earmarked for health care. Each system balances the instinct to nationalize for consistency with the recognition of the need to accommodate regional differences.

No national system can be immediately transplanted into another society. The United States is not going to suddenly adopt the British, German, or Canadian system. Each of these countries has looked to the United States for ideas about hospital payment or use of a public and private mix. The United States can also learn from a careful observation of the ideas and approaches elsewhere. The adoption of new ideas will reflect the US experience and culture and be modified accordingly, but the amalgamation of transported practices can help the United States deal with its problems with benefit to all.

Notes

1. *Health Care Systems in Transition* (Brussels: European Observatory on Health Care Systems, 1999).

2. Martin Gorsky, "The British National Health Service, 1948–2008: A Review of the Historiography," *Social History of Medicine* 21, no. 3 (2008): 437–460.

3. Henry Aaron and William Schwartz, *The Painful Prescription: Rationing Hospital Care* (Washington, DC: Brookings Institution, 1984).

4. Gorsky, "The British National Health Service 1948–2008," p. 453.

5. Jeanne Whalen, "UK Will Revamp Its Health Service," *Wall Street Journal,* July 13, 2010, p. A10.

6. Carolyn Hughes Tuohy, "Canada: Health Care Reform in Comparative Perspective," in *Comparative Studies and the Politics of Modern Medical Care,* ed. Theodore Marmor, Richard Freeman, and Kieke Okma (New Haven: Yale University Press, 2009), pp. 78–79.

7. David Naylor, "A Different View of Queues in Ontario," *Health Affairs* 10, no. 3 (1991): 110–128.

8. Benedict Irvine, Shannon Ferguson, and Ben Cackett, *Background Briefing: The Canadian Health Care System* (London: Civitas, Institute for the Study of Civil Society, 2005), www.civitas.org.uk/pdf/Canada.pdf.

9. Tsung-Mei Cheng and Uwe Reinhardt, "Shepherding Major Health System Reforms: A Conversation with German Health Minister Ulla Schmidt," *Health Affairs* 27, no. 3 (2008): 204–213.

10. "HiT Summary: Germany," in *Health Care Systems in Transition* (Brussels: European Observatory on Health Systems and Politics, 2004), p. 6.

11. Kieke G. H. Okma and Michael Decter, "Hospital Care in the United States, Canada, Germany, the United Kingdom, and the Netherlands," in *Comparative Studies and the Politics of Modern Medical Care,* ed. Theodore Marmor, Richard Freeman, and Kieke Okma (New Haven: Yale University Press, 2009), p. 222.

12. Annika Herr, "Cost and Technical Efficiency of German Hospitals: Does Ownership Matter?" *Health Economics* 17, no. 9 (2008): 1057–1071.

13. Reinhard Busse, "The German Health Care System, 2009," in *International Profiles of Health Care Systems* (New York: Commonwealth Fund, 2010), pp. 28–31.

14. Laurene Graig, Health of Nations: *An International Perspective on US Health Care Reform,* 3rd ed. (Washington, DC: Congressional Quarterly, 1999), pp. 42–43.

9

What Can
We Expect by 2021?

You can never plan the future by the past.
—*Edmund Burke*

In the previous chapters, I have concentrated on topical or programmatic health policy issues by examining the past, present, and future of discrete policy domains. In this conclusion, I take a brief integrative look at what appear to be the central health policy issues of the next decade.

The time from the disputed presidential election of 2000 until the historic victory of Barack Obama in 2008 was a quiet health policy period. The battle over enactment of a Medicare prescription drug plan was the only exception. Even attempts to renew the State Children's Health Insurance Program (SCHIP) in the final year of the George W. Bush administration failed despite its bipartisan origins.

The first two years of the Obama administration marked a rapid swing of the pendulum. Legislation renewing the CHIP program was quickly passed in early 2009, and shortly thereafter the year-long struggle to enact major health reform legislation began. The Patient Protection and Affordable Care Act (ACA) touched on most of the major elements of health policy. It expanded Medicaid; shifted Medicare resources away from Medicare Advantage; put in place various strategies to slow the rate of growth of Medicare spending; established, for those currently uninsured, new subsidies and mechanisms for the purchase of private insurance; and set in motion a new, but limited, program for the financing of long-term care. It seems fair to conclude that there was greater health policy activity in 2009–2010 than in all of the previous decade. As we look to the horizon, will the decade from 2011 to the presidential election of 2020 resemble 2009–2010 or 2000–2009?

In 2007, few policy mavens anticipated the global financial crisis and subsequent recession that were about to occur. As the 2000 election was settled and the George W. Bush administration began, no one foresaw the September 11 attacks or the subsequent wars in Afghanistan and Iraq. Policy fortune-telling is a precarious pursuit. Unexpected events in the next few years might push health policy off the political agenda for years to come. But despite this caution, there are several reasons to expect health policy to remain high on the political agenda for the rest of the second decade of the twenty-first century. These are:

- rising entitlement costs
- slow recovery from the recent recession
- the prospect of significant conflict over ACA

First, there is a concern with the serious federal budget implications of the rising level of entitlement spending. The aging of and movement into retirement age of the first wave of the baby boom generation will put additional fiscal pressure on a financial support system for older people that is already under strain. Across the political spectrum, there is a recognition that policy action will be necessary to respond to this challenge. Some believe that both Medicare and Medicaid must be modified as part of any attempt to manage the growth of entitlement programs. Health care programs, far more than Social Security, represent a threat of uncontrolled growth in the next decade and beyond.

Second, recovery from the recession, especially job growth, has been slow. Some economists have speculated that the United States may face a decade or more of economic stagnation in the wake of the recession, as Japan did in the 1990s. A stagnant economy will not produce new tax revenue fast enough to keep up with rising demand for public expenditures, especially for health care and income support. Thus, federal and state budget officials will face significant demands for new expenditures for education, infrastructure, and defense with little revenue growth. Normally, we might expect that this would constrain the emergence of new health policy issues, but Medicare, Medicaid, and ACA all provide financial support of one kind or another for eligible individuals irrespective of changes in the state of the economy. Contraction, not expansion, may be the prominent feature of many health policy debates in the coming decade.

Third, the passage of ACA in March 2010 was hailed as a historic legislative achievement. It certainly was second only to Medicare and Medicaid as significant health policy. But several exceptional vulnerabilities have become apparent even before the law is fully implemented. The passage of Medicare did not engender the same level of fierce opposition by political opponents and was not followed within months of enactment by a shift in the partisan control of the House of Representatives, with health reform as one of the major election issues. Also, popular support for Medicare was high in the wake of the enactment and implementation of the law. The long period of implementation for ACA extending throughout the coming decade contributes to the vulnerability of the law since many of the future beneficiaries cannot see immediate tangible results flowing from its passage.

A Hypothetical Viewpoint: Looking Back from 2021

Let's assume for a moment that we have climbed into a time machine and been transported to January 2021. The third presidential election since 2008 has just occurred and the victor will be inaugurated soon. The fifth congressional election since the 2010 midterms has taken place. To some extent, the health policy issues taken up and the decisions made during this decade will be predictable, if we have a sense of the outcomes of those elections. When we departed in January 2011 for this journey into the future, the country was evenly divided on many critical issues. There is no reason to think that this will have changed appreciably when we touch down in 2021. Party control of the Congress and White House may have shifted during the decade, but fundamental differences in political philosophy are likely to remain.

If we start this orientation to the third decade of the twenty-first century by reading the last couple of months' worth of the *New York Times* (probably online rather than in print) to see what health policy issues remain on the table, the only surprise may be how little has changed. Even if other events have not pushed health policy issues off the agenda, the issues of 2011 are probably still on the table. No doubt we will discover efforts to deal with the fundamental issues by legislative and administrative action. US politics has always been more characterized by incrementalism rather than comprehensive problem solving.

When we left in 2011, the future of the recently enacted ACA was uncertain, especially after Democrats lost control of the House of Representatives after the 2010 midterm elections. As we scan the *New York Times* in January 2021 for news of the health care issues of the day, a sense of how health policy evolved over the past decade will begin to emerge. To organize this fanciful retrospective on the future, I take a brief look at several key issues found in the earlier chapters and seek to integrate the vision of health policy dynamics over the decade.

ACA

ACA was for the Obama administration a significant legislative achievement that was only diminished by the political losses in the 2010 midterm elections. Some Democrats believed the health reform effort should have been postponed until after economic recovery. However, it is difficult to envision a scenario in which health reform would have been easier in 2011 or 2013 than in 2009.

Could the details of the health reform legislation been modified to blunt opposition? Was there a bipartisan option for reform that was ignored? Some opponents were clear from the beginning that they wished to deny President Obama a major legislative victory. For them, no compromise was likely. Others might have supported a less comprehensive (and expensive) set of proposals, but these likely would not have achieved the major goal of significant reduction of the uninsured. Many of the policy ideas in ACA (tax credits, individual mandate, insurance exchanges) had been part of the Republican policy preferences in past debates, but ACA received no support from Republicans.

The individual mandate became the most controversial part of ACA and the piece most likely to be repealed or declared unconstitutional by the Supreme Court. Perhaps, President Obama's original instincts on this were correct. During the 2008 campaign, his health insurance proposal did not include an individual mandate. This provision was included in the legislation as part of an understanding with the insurance industry that restrictions on common underwriting practices, such as exclusion of preexisting conditions, were only feasible if everyone paid into the system.

In 2021, we might expect to see the original individual mandate provision of ACA either modified or eliminated by court or legislative action. More than other provisions of ACA, there seems to be a popular sense of the individual mandate as too much government intrusion. In 2009, there were other policy options to achieve the same goal of universal coverage. For example, requiring an annual enrollment period to gain the cheapest rate and receive government subsidies would create a powerful incentive to purchase insurance. Some alternatives might have cost more; others might have further expanded the role of government as insurer. These other approaches would have diminished insurance industry support or increased its fervent opposition to ACA.

As of this writing in mid-2011, there are various legal challenges pending in the courts. One or more appeals courts will soon rule on the constitutionality of the individual mandate and on whether or not the law is so intertwined that finding the mandate unconstitutional voids the entire statute. This legal challenge will almost certainly be taken to the Supreme Court to be heard perhaps as early as fall 2011. ACA supporters will mobilize to resist an adverse court decision and a legislative attempt to repeal the law.

In the decade following enactment of ACA, it is likely there will be a major modification of the individual mandate, and health policy debate will focus on viable options.[1] ACA is complex and complicated legislation that not only created new entitlement subsidies for the purchase of private insurance by low- and moderate-income individuals and families, but shifted the public subsidy for Medicare recipients away from private plans, expanded Medicaid, required states to establish mechanisms for the purchase of insurance, established new insurance regulations, and created possible new methods for paying hospitals and physicians based on integration and quality. Some of these provisions may even survive a general repeal. Yet other provisions may be abandoned as unwise or unworkable, even by original supporters. At a minimum, there is likely to be substantial policy action in the decade after adoption of ACA to attempt to modify provisions of the law.

Medicare

The aging of the baby boom generation will place renewed policy focus on Medicare during the coming decade. Medicare's fiftieth birthday occurs in 2015. Its financing structure was based on a premise that has long been obsolete; namely, that each succeeding generation will be considerably larger than the previous one so that each generation of retirees will have a larger cohort of workers to support medical care in retirement.

Some wish to address this issue by radically changing Medicare. Others seek to incrementally modify the financial structure while retaining the essence of Medicare as a social insurance program. Medicare reimbursement practices are broadly seen as needing modification despite the improvements enacted in the 1980s. Any such changes will reverberate beyond Medicare because, to some extent, both Medicaid and private plans use the Medicare methodology for reimbursements. Major changes such as the use of accountable care organizations and bundled payments will impact all payers.

In the past, policy action was often triggered by declines in the expected life of the Medicare Part A Trust Fund. If such a decline is projected by the Medicare trustees as the next decade evolves, we might anticipate this to be a triggering device to put Medicare back on the agenda. If there is a serious effort (as opposed to rhetoric) to address the long-term federal deficit, then Medicare financing is likely to be on the table because it represents such a significant part of the federal budget now and in the projected future.

In early 2011 the new House Republican majority passed a budget bill that included provisions for transforming Medicare into a premium support plan beginning with those who reach eligibility in 2021. Very quickly, Democrats seized on this to criticize Republican representatives in swing districts as the first salvo in the 2012 election.[2] This debate over the future of Medicare is likely to persist into 2012 and beyond.

Medicaid

ACA seemed to resolve the question posed by Colleen Grogan and Eric Patashnik about Medicaid at the crossroads.[3] If the Medicaid provisions of ACA survive the current rhetoric of opposition in many states, significantly more individuals will be covered by Medicaid in 2021 than a decade before. There are ample reasons to conclude that this will happen. Medicaid has survived and grown despite many earlier attempts to constrain the program. It also has modified and adapted with more flexibility than Medicare. The extensive use of managed care is one example of this evolution.

Provisions of the ACA, if fully implemented over the decade, will almost certainly move Medicaid toward greater federalization, with the national government paying a larger share of total cost with a consequent standardization of benefits.

Modification of the historic low rates of reimbursement seems to be an essential element of Medicaid evolution. As Medicaid becomes an expanding mechanism for covering health care expenses for many low- and moderate-income individuals and families, the need for reimbursement parity with Medicare and private plans is essential. If each state independently retains its own payment practices, reimbursement will continue to be inadequate. We should expect major policy discussions about improvement of the level of Medicaid reimbursement, perhaps linking it to Medicare practice and rules.

Medicaid has probably become too large to fail and may, as it reaches the age of fifty, finally become a permanent part of the social safety net and the primary source of health insurance for those with low and moderate incomes.

The size and scope of Medicaid have not constrained the new Republican majority in the House of Representatives from once again pushing the idea of transforming Medicaid into a block grant. The spring 2011 House budget resolution included provisions to end Medicaid as an entitlement and thus limit future federal Medicaid commitment. If this proposal becomes law after the 2012 election, much of the health reform effort to expand Medicaid to reduce the number of uninsured would end. This shift of financial responsibility would also likely diminish Medicaid funding for nursing homes.[4]

Health Care Costs

If current projections are accurate, health costs will exceed 20% of gross domestic product (GDP) before 2021. While there is nothing magical about 20% as opposed to 19% or 21%, it will represent one of those defining moments that sometimes propel policy action. Serious consideration of the federal budget deficit cannot ignore government health care costs or avoid the reality that private plan expenditures set the reimbursement systems and expectations.

For at least forty years, policy analysts have warned of impending doom because of the inexorable rise in health care expenditures. But everyone has learned to live with a level of health care costs considerably greater than that of other industrialized countries.

We should expect the warnings of health policy experts to become more strident as the magic 20% approaches. Both incremental and radical proposals will be offered as solutions. Some policy actions will probably be taken because inaction will seem too timid in the face of a serious problem. Nevertheless, by 2021, the problem will not likely be seen as resolved.

Significant rationing, or a policy solution perceived as rationing, is not likely to be politically acceptable. There are limits to simple tightening of provider reimbursements to control the growth rate of health costs. In a large and diverse country with a variety of organizational arrangements and traditions in local health care systems, it is difficult to find a single mechanism for restraining costs. Organizational realignments offer some hope for changing incentives, but the success of pilot projects is not easy to apply across the country. Other societies, which have been more successful in addressing this problem, have also never reached any final resolution. Incremental fixes slow the trajectory, but never seem to permanently take the issue off the agenda as solved.

Long-term Care

For at least a couple of decades, long-term care has been on the fringes of the policy agenda. Medicaid has been the safety valve. Even with more stringent asset conversion limits, Medicaid has in fact been available to even upper-middle-income individuals as a financing mechanism for those in need of institutional care. Medicare and Medicaid have both significantly increased their coverage of home- and community-based care. But in the end, vast amounts of uncompensated care by family and friends have narrowed the gap between need and available resources.

For long-term care, it is again a question of adequate financial support of existing institutions such as hospitals and physicians. Chronic care for older people and people with disabilities is delivered in a mixture of home and institutional settings. Should nursing homes be mini-hospitals or group homes? Should home care be delivered by agency professionals or family and friends who are arranged and compensated by primary caregivers? Is the private insurance industry interested in developing a viable insurance approach to meeting the long-term care needs of middle-income Americans? Or is a public program the only answer because of the inherent difficulties with private insurance plans for long-term care?

Alternatively, nursing homes may be less necessary if the scourge of Alzheimer's disease is mitigated by new medications and treatments. Under this scenario the existing number of nursing homes may be adequate for the country. When the baby boom generation begins to reach their eighties, a diagnosis of Alzheimer's may not dictate an extended nursing home stay.

Policy agendas are short lists, and competition for fiscal resources is intense. Those who must deal with health system problems on a daily basis see a fragile system that may be overwhelmed as the need increases. For the rest of the population, it only becomes a problem when a parent needs care. The average person does not want to think of himself or herself as needing long-term care decades into the future. People hope that, if and when the time comes, Medicaid or Medicare will provide. Short of an obvious crisis, it is hard to see this issue reaching a higher place on the policy agenda than some of the other policy proposals between 2011 and 2021.

The Role of Government as the Enduring Issue

I have looked at more than fifty years of policy history in these pages. If there is a single theme that cuts across time and category, it is the role of government. In every health policy issue, I have addressed ideas and options for problem solving that can be sorted into two diametrically opposed categories. Some policy analysts propose approaches that involve a greater role for government in organizing and financing services while others seek to reduce the role of government and rely more on market mechanisms.

Few experts envision an extensive direct provision of services by a government bureaucracy such as the US Veterans Administration or the National Health Service in the United Kingdom. Across every health policy issue that I have examined, there is a growing divide between those who want to limit the role of government and those who see government as a critical element to ensuring equitable access to services for all. This division exists among policy experts, elected officials, and the general public. It is probably accurate to conclude that in 2011 this disagreement divides the country in half. There is no reason to assume that we will find any change in this philosophical divide in 2021. In fact, we may find the gulf even greater in 2021 than today. The issue has become more pronounced in the political rhetoric.

Medicare has been labeled as national health insurance for older people. This government-based social insurance won legislative approval in 1965 after many years of debate because Democrats expanded their legislative coalition. This approval of Medicare also occurred in an era in which other government institutions, such as Social Security and the Postal Service, were generally held in high regard. This is no longer the case.

For the three decades after its enactment, there was a consensus around the role of Medicare in society and its appropriate organizational form. In the mid-1990s, that consensus evaporated with the emergence of an alternative view of how Medicare might be organized. ACA was also enacted in the wake of an enlarged liberal majority in Congress, but no consensus seems to be emerging about the proper role for government. On the contrary, the even more limited government role in ACA, compared to Medicare, has been the subject of vociferous criticism and inflammatory rhetoric.

This civic debate over the proper role of government in organizing and financing the delivery of health care services will surely be the defining issue for all health policy discussions in the next decade. It will define what are feasible policy options and divide partisans in ways that will make compromise and consensus difficult. The future of Medicare and Medicaid will be ground zero in this debate. The adoption of ACA in early 2010 represented a broadening of financial access to health care by expanding existing Medicaid and making private insurance more affordable with a set of public subsidies. This was considerably short of the "Medicare for all" social insurance system that some preferred, but even this has led to strong opposition and calls for repeal.

For decades, the language of health policy debates was shaped by those who preferred a social insurance approach and held a favorable view of the role of government. Since the 1990s, conservatives who view a government role with greater skepticism have developed an alternative language to describe their preferred reform. Their policy proposals envision a reduced, but not eliminated, role for government.[5] This alternative view of the proper role of government means that when one side or the other gains a working majority among decision-makers, they will try to enact their vision of the best health policy. It also renders compromise and accommodation more difficult because each side believes the ideas of the other are inherently wrong. The debate becomes less a difference of detail than a philosophic confrontation with a clear winner and loser.

When we land the time machine in 2021, we should expect this debate to have been neither replaced by a popular consensus nor ended by a clear victory for one side or the other. It is a philosophical chasm that will continue to shape what is feasible and likely between today and 2021.

Notes

1. Matthew DoBias, "No Easy Alternative," *National Journal* 42, no. 51 (December 18, 2010): 46.

2. Carl Hulse and Jackie Calmes, "GOP Rethinking Bid to Overhaul Medicare Rules," *New York Times,* May 5, 2011, p. A1.

3. Colleen Grogan and Eric Patashnik, "Between Welfare Medicine and Mainstream Entitlement: Medicaid at the Political Crossroads," *Journal of Health Politics, Policy and Law* 28, no. 5 (2003): 821–858.

4. Jennifer Steinhauer, "Critics Fear GOP's Proposed Medicaid Changes Could Cut Coverage for the Aged," *New York Times,* May 10, 2011, p. A17.

5. James C. Capretta and Tom Miller, "A New 'Definition' for Health Care Reform," *Kaiser Health News,* January 14, 2011, www.kaiserhealthnews.org /Columns/2011/January/011311caprettamiller.aspx.

Bibliography

Aaron, Henry J., and William B. Schwartz. *The Painful Prescription: Rationing Hospital Care*. Washington, DC: Brookings Institution, 1984.

Aaron, Henry J., and William B. Schwartz. *Can We Say No? The Challenge of Rationing Health Care*. Washington, DC: Brookings Institution, 2005.

Alter, Jonathan. *The Promise: President Obama, Year One* (New York: Simon & Schuster, 2010), chap. 3.

Anderson, Gerard F., Peter S. Hussey, Bianca K. Frogner, and Hugh R. Waters. "Health Spending in the United States and the Rest of the World." *Health Affairs* 24, no. 4 (2005): 903–912.

Angeles, January. "Health Reform Is a Good Deal for States." Washington, DC: Center on Budget and Policy Priorities, April 2010.

Ansberry, Clare. "Disabled Face Hard Choices as States Slash Medicaid." *Wall Street Journal,* May 20, 2010.

Barnard, Chester. *The Functions of the Executive*. Cambridge: Harvard University Press, 1938.

Blumberg, L., and K. Pollitz. "Health Insurance Exchanges: Organizing Health Insurance Marketplaces to Promote Health Reform Goals. Timely Analysis of Immediate Health Policy Issues." Washington, DC: Urban Institute, April 2009.

Blumenthal, David, and James Morone. *The Heart of Power: Health and Politics in the Oval Office*. Berkeley: University of California Press, 2009.

Bodenheimer, Thomas. "Low Cost Lessons from Grand Junction, Colorado." *New England Journal of Medicine* 363 (2010): 1391–1393.

Brandow, D., and M. Tanner. "The Wrong and Right Ways to Reform Medicare." Policy Analysis no. 230. Washington, DC: Cato Institute, June 8, 1965.

Brasfield, James M. "Health Planning Reform: A Proposal for the Eighties." *Journal of Health Politics, Policy and Law* 6, no. 4 (1982): 718–738.

Brasfield, James M. "The Public Option: Health Reform and a Controversial Policy Idea." Paper presented at the annual meeting of the Midwest Political Science Association, Chicago, April 22–25, 2010.

Brodie, M., D. Altman, C. Deane, S. Buscho, and E. Hamel. "Liking the Pieces, Not the Package: Contradictions in Public Opinion During Health Reform." *Health Affairs* 29, no. 6 (2010): 1125–1130.

Brownstein, Ronald. "The Governing Core." *National Journal,* April 3, 2010.

Buhler-Wilkerson, Karen. "Care of the Chronically Ill at Home: An Unresolved Dilemma in Health Policy for the United States." *Milbank Quarterly* 85, no. 4 (2007): 611–632.

Bundorf, M. K., Anne Royalty, and Laurence C. Baker. "Health Care Cost Growth Among the Privately Insured." *Health Affairs* 28, no. 5 (2009): 1294–1304.

Busse, Reinhard. "The German Health Care System, 2009." International Profiles of Health Care Systems. New York: Commonwealth Fund, 2010.

Butler, Stuart, and Robert Moffit. "The FEHBP as a Model for a New Medicare Program." *Health Affairs* 14, no. 4 (1995): 47–61.

Campbell, Andrea L., and Kimberly Morgan. "The Medicare Modernization Act and the New Politics of Medicare." Paper prepared for the annual meeting of the American Political Science Association, Philadelphia, August 31–September 3, 2006.

Cannon, Michael F. "Medicaid's Unseen Costs." Policy Analysis no. 548. Washington, DC: Cato Institute, August 18, 2005.

Centers for Medicare and Medicaid Services, Office of the Actuary. "Report on the Financial Outlook for Medicaid" Washington, DC: Centers for Medicare and Medicaid Services, Office of the Actuary, October 17, 2008.

Cheng, Tsung-Mei, and Uwe Reinhardt. "Shepherding Major Health System Reforms: A Conversation with German Health Minister Ulla Schmidt." *Health Affairs* 27, no. 3 (2008): 204–213.

Chernew, Michael E., Richard A. Hirth, and David M. Cutler. "Increased Spending on Health Care: Long-Term Implications for the Nation." *Health Affairs* 28, no. 5 (2009): 1253–1254.

Christensen, Michael C., and Dahlia Remler. "Information and Communications Technology in US Health Care: Why Is Adoption So Slow and Is Slower Better?" *Journal of Health Politics, Policy and Law* 34, no. 6 (2009): 1011–1034.

Cohn, Jonathan. "How They Did It: The Inside Account of Health Care Reform's Triumph." *New Republic,* June 10, 2010.

Congressional Budget Office. *Issues in Designing a Prescription Drug Benefit for Medicare.* Washington, DC: CBO Publications Office, 2002.

Congressional Budget Office. *Medicare High Cost Beneficiaries.* Washington, DC: CBO Publications Office, May 2005.

Congressional Budget Office. *Evidence on the Costs and Benefits of Health Information Technology.* Washington, DC: CBO Publications Office, 2008.

Congressional Budget Office. *Key Issues in Analyzing Major Health Insurance Proposals.* Washington, DC: CBO Publications Office, 2008.

Coughlin, Teresa A., Brian K. Bruen, and Jennifer King. "States' Use of Medicaid UPL and DSH Financing Mechanisms." *Health Affairs* 23, no. 2 (2004): 245–257.

Coughlin, Teresa A., and David Liska. "The Medicaid Disproportionate Share Hospital Payment Program: Background and Issues." Issue Brief

No. 14. Washington, DC: Kaiser Commission on Medicaid and the Uninsured, October 1997.

Coughlin, Teresa A., Stephen Zuckerman, and Joshua McFeeters. "Restoring Fiscal Integrity to Medicaid Financing?" *Health Affairs* 26, no. 5 (2007): 1469–1480.

Crowley, Jeffery S., and Molly O'Malley. "Profiles of Medicaid's High Cost Populations." Washington, DC: Kaiser Commission on Medicaid and the Uninsured, December 2006.

Dale, Stacy, and James Verdier. "Elimination of Medicare's Waiting Period for Seriously Disabled Adults: Impact on Coverage and Costs." New York: Commonwealth Fund, July 2003.

Davis, Karen. *National Health Insurance: Benefits, Costs, and Consequences.* Washington, DC: Brookings Institution, 1975.

Davis, Karen, Cathy Schoen, and Kristof Stremikis. "The Commonwealth Fund Report: How the Performance of the US Health Care System Compares Internationally." New York: Commonwealth Fund, June 2010. www.commonwealthfund.org/~/media/Files/Publications/Fund% 20Report/2010/Jun/1400_Davis_Mirror_Mirror_on_the_wall_2010.pdf.

de Brantes, Francois, et al. "Building a Bridge from Fragmentation to Accountability—The Prometheus Payment Model." *New England Journal of Medicine* 361 (2009): 1033–1036.

Dorn, Stan, Bowen Garrett, John Holahan, and Aimee Williams. "Medicaid, SCHIP, and Economic Downturn: Policy Challenges and Policy Responses." Washington, DC: Kaiser Commission on Medicaid and the Uninsured, April 2008.

Doty, M., S. Collins, S. Rustgi, and J. Nicholson. "Out of Options: Why So Many Workers in Small Businesses Lack Affordable Health Insurance, and How Health Care Reform Can Help." New York: Commonwealth Fund, September 2009.

Dulio, Adrianne, et al. "Report: Consumer Direction of Personal Assistance Services Programs in Medicaid." Washington, DC: Kaiser Commission on Medicaid and the Uninsured, March 2008.

Elazar, Daniel. *The American Partnership: Intergovernmental Cooperation in the Nineteenth-Century United States.* Chicago: University of Chicago Press, 1962.

Engle, Jonathan. *Poor People's Medicine: Medicaid and American Charity Care Since 1965* (Durham, NC: Duke University Press, 2006), chap 8.

Enthoven, Alain. "Managed Competition: An Agenda for Action." *Health Affairs* 7, no. 3 (1988): 25–47.

Enthoven, Alain. "The History and Principles of Managed Competition." *Health Affairs* 12, no. 1 (suppl. 1993): 24–48.

Enthoven, Alain. "Employment-Based Health Insurance Is Failing: Now What?" *Health Affairs* (May 28, 2003). Web exclusive. http://content .healthaffairs.org/content/early/2003/05/28/hlthaff.w3.237.full.pdf.

Farrell, Diana M., Eric S. Jensen, and Bob Kocher. "McKinsey Global Institute Report: "Why Americans Pay More for Health Care." McKinsey Quarterly, McKinsey Global Institute Report, December

2008. www.mckinseyquarterly.com/Why_Americans_pay_more_for
_health_care_2275.

Feder, Judith M. *Medicare: The Politics of Federal Hospital Insurance.*
Lexington, MA: Lexington Books, 1977.

Feldstein, Martin. "The Welfare Loss of Excess Health Insurance." *Journal
of Political Economy* 81, no. 2 (1973): 251–280.

Gabel, Jon. "Does the Congressional Budget Office Underestimate Savings
from Reform? A Review of the Historical Record." New York:
Commonwealth Fund, January 2010.

Gabel, Jon, et al. "Taxing Cadillac Health Plans May Produce Chevy
Results." *Health Affairs* 29, no. 1 (2010): 1–8.

Giled, S., J. Hartz, and G. Giorgi. "Consider It Done? The Likely Efficacy of
Mandates for Health Insurance." *Health Affairs* 26, no. 6 (2007):
1612–1621.

Ginsberg, Paul. "Wide Variation in Hospital and Physician Payment Rates
Evidence of Provider Market Power." Research Brief no. 16.
Washington, DC: Center for Studying Health System Change, November
2010.

Gorsky, Martin. "The British National Health Service 1948–2008: A Review
of the Historiography." *Social History of Medicine* 21, no. 3 (2008):
437–460.

Graig, Laurene. *Health of Nations: An International Perspective on US Health
Care Reform,* 3rd ed. Washington, DC: Congressional Quarterly, 1999.

Grogan, Colleen, and Eric Patashnik. "Between Welfare Medicine and
Mainstream Entitlement: Medicaid at the Political Crossroads." *Journal
of Health Politics, Policy and Law* 28, no. 5 (2003): 821–858.

Hacker, Jacob. "Healthy Competition: How to Structure Public Health
Insurance Plan Choice to Ensure Risk-sharing, Cost Control, and Quality
Improvement." Policy Brief. Washington, DC: Institute for America's
Future, April 2009.

Hartman, M., et al. "Health Spending Growth at a Historic Low in 2008."
Health Affairs 29, no. 1 (2010): 147–155.

"Health Coverage of Children: The Role of Medicaid and CHIP." Washington,
DC: Kaiser Commission on Medicaid and the Uninsured, October 2009.

Hearne, Jean. "Medicaid Disproportionate Share Payments." CRS Report for
Congress, Order Code 97-483 (Washington, DC: Congressional Research
Service, Library of Congress, January 10, 2005).

Holahan, John. "The 2007–09 Recession and Health Insurance Coverage."
Health Affairs 30, no. 1 (2011): 1–8.

Holahan, John F., and Joel W. Cohen. *Medicaid: The Trade-off Between Cost
Containment and Access to Care.* Washington, DC: Urban Institute
Press, 1986.

Houlahan, John, and Alshadye Yemane. "Enrollment Is Driving Medicaid
Costs, but Two Targets Can Yield Savings." *Health Affairs* 28, no. 5
(2009): 1453–1465.

Hussey, Peter S., et al. "How Does the Quality of Care Compare in Five
Countries?" *Health Affairs* 23, no. 3 (2004): 89–97.

Irvine, Benedict, Shannon Ferguson, and Ben Cackett. *Background Briefing: The Canadian Health Care System.* London: Civitas, Institute for the Study of Civil Society, 2005. www.civitas.org.uk/pdf/Canada.pdf.

Johnson, Richard W., and Cori E. Uccello. "Is Private Long-Term Care Insurance the Answer?" Issue Brief No. 29. Center for Retirement Research at Boston College, March 2005.

Jost, Timothy. "State Lawsuits Won't Succeed in Overturning the Individual Mandate." *Health Affairs* 29, no. 6 (2010): 1225–1228.

Kasper, Judith, Barbara Lyons, and Molly O'Malley. "Report: Long-Term Services and Supports: The Future Role and Challenges for Medicaid." Washington, DC: Kaiser Commission on Medicaid and the Uninsured, September 2007.

Kaye, H. S., Charlene Harrington, and Mitchell P. LaPlante. "Long-term Care: Who Gets It, Who Provides It, Who Pays, and How Much?" *Health Affairs* 29, no. 1 (2010): 11–21.

Lagnado, Lucette. "Rising Challenger Takes on Elder-Car System." *Wall Street Journal,* June 24, 2008.

Lambrew, J., and J. Gruber. "Monday and Mandates: Relative Effects of Key Policy Levers in Expanding Health Insurance Coverage to All Americans." *Inquiry* 43, no. 4 (2006–2007): 333–344.

Liberman, Steven M., and John M. Bertko. "Building Regulatory and Operational Flexibility into Accountable Care Organizations and 'Shared Savings.'" *Health Affairs* 30, no. 1 (2011): 23–31.

Marmor, Theodore. *The Politics of Medicare,* 2nd ed. New York: Aldine de Gruyter, 1970.

Marmor, Theodore R., Richard Freeman, and Kieke G. H. Okma, eds. *Comparative Studies and the Politics of Modern Medical Care.* New Haven: Yale University Press, 2009.

Martin, Anne, et al. "Recession Contributes to Slowest Annual Rate of Increase in Health Spending in Five Decades." *Health Affairs* 30, no. 1 (2011): 11–21.

Mayes, Rick, and Robert A. Berenson. *Medicare Prospective Payment and the Shaping of US Health Care.* Baltimore: Johns Hopkins University Press, 2006.

McCarthy, Meghan. "Unsustainable." *National Journal,* December 4, 2010.

McClellan, Mark, et al. "A National Strategy to Put Accountable Care into Practice." *Health Affairs* 29, no. 5 (2010): 982–990.

McDevitt, Roland, et al. "Group Insurance: A Better Deal for Most People Than Individual Plans." *Health Affairs* 29, no. 1 (2010): 1–9.

Mechanic, David. *Mental Health and Social Policy.* Englewood Cliffs, NJ: Prentice Hall, 1969.

"Medicaid: A Primer." Washington, DC: Kaiser Commission on Medicaid and the Uninsured, June 2010.

Merlis, Mark. "Health Care Cost Containment and Coverage Expansion." Washington, DC: National Academy of Social Insurance, January 2009.

Milbank, Dana. "Why Obama Needs Rahm at the Top." *Washington Post,* February 21, 2010.

Milgate, Karen, and Sharon Bee Cheng. "Pay-for-Performance: The MedPac Perspective." *Health Affairs* 25, no. 2 (2006): 415–419.

Miller, Vic, and Andy Schneider. "The Medicaid Matching Formula: Policy Considerations and Options for Modification." Washington, DC: AARP Public Policy Institute, September 2009.

Moon, Marilyn. *Medicare: A Policy Primer.* Washington, DC: Urban Institute Press, 2006.

Murray, Robert. "Setting Hospital Rates to Control Costs and Boost Quality: The Maryland Experience." *Health Affairs* 28, no. 5 (2009): 1395–1404.

Nichols, Len. "Implementing Insurance Market Reforms Under the Federal Health Reform Law." *Health Affairs* 29, no. 6 (2010): 1152–1157.

Oberlander, Jonathan. *The Political Life of Medicare.* Chicago: University of Chicago Press, 2003.

Oberlander, Jonathan. "Through the Looking Glass: The Politics of the Medicare Prescription Drug, Improvement, and Modernization Act." *Journal of Health Politics, Policy and Law* 32, no. 2 (2007): 187–219.

Oberlander, Jonathan B., and Barbara Lyons. "Beyond Incrementalism? SCHIP and the Politics of Health Reform." *Health Affairs* 28, no. 3 (2009): 404–406.

Oberlander, Jonathan, and Joseph White. "Public Attitudes Toward Health Care Spending Aren't the Problem; Prices Are." *Health Affairs* 28, no. 5 (2009): 1285–1286.

O'Brien, Ellen. "Long-Term Care: Understanding Medicaid's Role for the Elderly and Disabled." Washington, DC: Kaiser Commission on Medicaid and the Uninsured, November 2005.

Oliver, Adam. "The Single-Payer Option: A Reconsideration." *Journal of Health Politics, Policy and Law* 34, no. 4 (2009): 509–529.

Patashnik, Eric. "Unfolding Promises: Trust Funds and the Politics of Precommitment." *Political Science Quarterly* 112, no. 3 (1997).

Paulus, Ronald, et al. "Continuous Innovation in Health Care: Implications of the Geisinger Experience." *Health Affairs* 27, no. 5 (2005): 1235–1245.

Pauly, Mark, P. Danzon, P. Feldstein, and J. Hoff. "A Plan for 'Responsible National Health Insurance.'" *Health Affairs* 10, no. 1 (1991): 5–25.

Pauly, Mark, and John Goodman. "Tax Credits for Health Insurance and Medical Savings Accounts." *Health Affairs* 14, no. 1 (1995): 125–139.

Pear, Robert. "GOP to Fight Health Law with Purse Strings." *New York Times,* November 6, 2010.

Potetz, Lisa, and Juliette Cubanski. "A Primer on Medicare Financing." Washington, DC: Henry J. Kaiser Family Foundation, July 2009.

Pracht, Etienne E. "State Medicaid Managed Care Enrollment: Understanding the Political Calculus That Drives Medicaid Managed Care Reforms." *Journal of Health Politics and Law* 32, no. 4 (2007): 686–701.

Reinhardt, Ewe E. "The Annual Drama of the 'Doc Fix.'" *New York Times,* December 17, 2010.

Rochefort, David A. *American Social Welfare Policy.* Boulder: Westview, 1986.

Rosenbaum, Sara, et al. "The Children's Hour: The State Children's Health Insurance Program." *Health Affairs* 17, no. 1 (1998): 75–89.

Rosenburg, Charles. *The Care of Strangers: The Rise of America's Hospital System.* New York: Basic Books, 1987.

Rousseau, David, and Andy Schneider. "Current Issues in Medicaid Financing: An Overview of IGTs, UPLs, and DSH." Washington, DC: Kaiser Commission on Medicaid and the Uninsured, April 2004.

Rowland, Diane, and Kristina Hanson. "Medicaid: Moving to Managed Care." *Health Affairs* 15, no. 3 (2003): 150–152.

Russel, Louise B. *Medicare's New Hospital Payment System.* Washington, DC: Brookings Institution, 1989.

Schultze, Charles L., Edward K. Hamilton, and Allen Shick. *Setting National Priorities: The 1971 Budget.* Washington, DC: Brookings Institution, 1970.

Shatto, J., and M. Clemens. *Projected Medicare Expenditures Under an Illustrative Scenario with Alternative Payment Updates to Medicare Providers.* Baltimore, MD: Center for Medicare and Medicaid Services, 2010.

Silow-Carroll, S., J. Meyer, M. Regenstein, and N. Bagby. *In Sickness and in Health? The Marriage Between Employers and Health Care.* Washington, DC: Economic and Social Research Institute, 1995.

Skocpol, Theda. *Boomerang: Health Care Reform and the Turn Against Government.* New York: Norton, 1997.

Smith, David G. *Paying for Medicare: The Politics of Reform.* New York: Aldine de Gruyter, 1992.

Smith, David G. *Entitlement Politics: Medicare and Medicaid 1995–2001.* New York: Aldine de Gruyter, 2002.

Smith, David G., and Judith D. Moore. *Medicaid Politics and Policy.* New Brunswick: Transaction, 2008.

Somers, Herman M., and Anne R. Somers. *Medicare and the Hospitals: Issues and Prospects.* Washington, DC: Brookings Institution, 1967.

Sommers, Anna, and Mindy Cohen. "Medicaid's High Cost Enrollees: How Much Do They Drive Program Spending?" Washington, DC: Kaiser Commission on Medicaid and the Uninsured, March 2006.

Sommers, Anna, and Mindy Cohen. "Report: Medicaid's Long Term–Care Beneficiaries: An Analysis of Spending Patterns." Washington, DC: Kaiser Commission on Medicaid and the Uninsured, November 2006.

Spillman, Brenda C., Kirsten J. Black, and Barbara A. Ormond. "Report: Beyond Cash and Counseling." Washington, DC: Kaiser Commission on Medicaid and the Uninsured, January 2007.

Stensland, Jeffrey, Zachary R. Gaumer, and Mark E. Miller. "Private-Payer Profits Can Induce Negative Medicare Margins." *Health Affairs* 29, no. 5 (2010): 1–7.

Stevens, Robert, and Rosemary Stevens. *Welfare Medicine in America.* New York: Free Press, 1973.

Stevens, Rosemary. *American Medicine and the Public Interest.* New Haven: Yale University Press, 1971.

Stolberg, S., J. Zeleny, and C. Hulse. "The Long Road Back." *New York Times,* March 21, 2010.

Stone, Deborah. "Single Payer: Good Metaphor, Bad Politics." *Journal of Health Politics, Policy and Law* 34, no. 4 (2009).

Stone, Robyn I. "Milbank Quarterly Report: Long-Term Care for the Elderly with Disabilities." New York: Milbank Memorial Fund, 2000. www.milbank.org/0008stone/index.html.

Tanenbaum, Sandra J. "Pay for Performance in Medicare: Evidentiary Irony and the Politics of Value." *Journal of Health Politics, Policy and Law* 34, no. 5 (2009): 717–743.

Thompson, Frank J., and Courtney Burke. "Executive Federalism and Medicaid Demonstration Waivers: Implications for Policy and Democratic Process." *Journal of Health Politics, Policy and Law* 32, no. 6 (2007): 971–1004.

Truffer, Christopher J. "Health Spending Projections Through 2019: The Recession's Impact Continues." *Health Affairs* 29, no. 3 (2010): 522–529.

Tuohy, Carolyn H. "Single Payers, Multiple Systems: The Scope and Limits of Subnational Variation Under a Federal Health Policy Framework." *Journal of Health Politics, Policy and Law* 34, no. 4 (2009): 453–492.

Vaida, Bara. "Super Bowl Moment." *National Journal,* June 13, 2009.

Van de Water, Paul. "How Health Reform Helps Reduce the Deficit." Washington, DC: Center on Budget and Policy Priorities, May 10, 2010.

Vladeck, Bruce C. *Unloving Care: The Nursing Home Tragedy.* New York: Basic Books, 1980.

Vladeck, Bruce C. "Where the Action Really Is: Medicaid and the Disabled." *Health Affairs* 22, no. 1 (2003): 90–100.

Wagenaar, Hendrik, and Dan A. Lewis. "The Social and Economic Context of Mental Hospitalization." *Journal of Health Politics, Policy and Law* 14, no. 3 (1989): 507–521.

Weil, Alan. "The New Child Health Insurance Program: A Carefully Crafted Compromise." Washington, DC: Urban Institute, October 1999.

Wennberg, John E. "Tracking the Care of Patients with Severe Chronic Illness." Lebanon, NH: Dartmouth Institute for Health Policy, April 2008. www.dartmouthatlas.org/keyissues/issue.aspx?con=2944.

White, Joseph. "Uses and Abuses of Long-term Medicare Cost Estimates." *Health Affairs* 18, no. 1 (1999): 63–79.

Wiener, Joshua M., Laurel Hixon Illston, and Raymond J. Hanley. *Sharing the Burden.* Washington, DC: Brookings Institution, 1994.

Wilensky, Gail. "The Challenge of Medicare." In *Restoring Fiscal Sanity 2007: The Health Spending Challenge,* ed. Alice Rivlin and Joseph Antos (Washington, DC: Brookings Institution, 2007), pp. 81–103.

Wolf, Douglas A., Kelly Hunt, and James Knickman. "Perspectives on the Recent Decline in Disability at Older Ages." *Milbank Quarterly* 83, no. 3 (2005): 365–395.

Index

About the Book

This timely and engaging text explores the full gamut of health policy issues confronting the United States—ranging from Medicare and Medicaid, to the heated controversies surrounding health care reform, to the "sleeping giant" of long-term care.

Notable features of the text include balanced and user-friendly discussions of:

- how the real-world policy process works
- competing proposals for Medicare and Medicaid reform
- the details of—and the debates surrounding—the 2010 Affordable Care Act
- the challenges posed by an aging population
- the experiences of other countries grappling with similar problems

For close to a century, health policy issues have never been far from the center of the political agenda. James Brasfield traces the ideas behind the debates, examines the politics of health care, and offers possible scenarios for the decades ahead.

James M. Brasfield is professor of management and director of the Master of Health Administration program at Webster University.